Mukhtasar Minhaj Al Qasidin
(*Towards the Hereafter*)

Ibn Qudamah Al Maqdisi

Translated by
Wa'il A. Shihab

Dar Ul Thaqafah

Dar Ul Thaqafah

www.darulthaqafah.com
www.twitter.com/darulthaqafah

2023 CE – 1444 H

Translation of the Qur'ān

It should be perfectly clear that the Qur'ān is only authentic in its original language, Arabic. Since the perfect translation of the Qur'ān is impossible, we have used the translation of the meaning of the Qur'ān throughout the book, as the result is only a crude meaning of the Arabic text.

Qur'ānic verses appear in speech marks proceeded by a reference to the Surah and verse number. Sayings (*Hadith*) of Prophet Muhammad ρ appear in inverted commas along with reference to the Hadith Book and its Reporter.

Contents

Translator's Note v
Preface vi
Introduction 1
Chapter One: ACTS OF WORSHIP 3
   I.   Knowledge 4
   II. Purification and *Salah* 15
  III. *Zakah* 24
  IV. *Siyam* 31
   V. *Hajj* 35
  VI. The Glorious Qur'an 40
 VII. *Dhikr* and *Du`a'* 46

Chapter Two: CUSTOMS 72
   I.   Serving Food, Sharing It, and Hospitality 73
   II. Marriage 79
  III. Earning Livelihood and Subsistence 56
  IV. The Lawful and the Prohibited 62
   V. Friendship and Brotherhood 103
  VI. Morals of Traveling 126
 VII. Commanding the Right and Forbidding the Wrong 128
VIII. Customary Evils, and Commanding Rulers to Do Good and Forbid Wrong ....
  IX. Manners of the Prophet ....

Chapter Three: DESTRUCTIVE FLAWS 160
   I. Within the Heart 161
   II. Spiritual Exercise for the Soul, Gaining Good
       Morality, and Remedying the Heart Diseases 167
   III. The Appetite of Eating and Drinking and the
        Sexual Appetite 179
   IV. The Flaws Pertaining to the Tongue 182
   V. Anger, Malevolence, and Envy 196
   VI. *Jah* (Prominence and Prestige) and *Riya'*
       (Ostentation and Loving to Be Seen by People):
       Analysis and Remedy 219
   VII. Pride, Arrogance, and Self-admiration 231
   VIII. *Ghurur* 249

Chapter Four: MEANS OF SALVATION 245
   I. Repentance 246
   II. Patience and Gratitude 273
   III. Hope and Fear 306
   IV. Asceticism and Poverty 331
   V. Oneness of Allah and Trust in Him 349
   VI. Love and Pleasure with Allah 357
   VII. Intention, Sincerity, and Truthfulness 383
   VIII. Self-scrutiny 397
   IX. Contemplation 407
   X. Remembering Death and Life after It 413

Glossary of Arabic Terms 454

Tanslator's Note

Praise be to Allah. We thank Him, seek His Help and forgiveness. We seek refuge in Allah from the evils within ourselves and that of our bad deeds. He whom Allah guides, is truly guided, and whom he Allah leaves to stray, none can guide him. I bear witness that there is no god but Allah and that Muhammad is His final Prophet (peace and blessings of Allah be upon him).

In fact, the task of translation is not an easy one. Rather, it is a tremendous one, particularly when it is related to religion. So, I ask Allah to forgive my sins and dedicate this work for His Sake.

However, I would like to draw the attention of the readers to the following points:

1. This translation is not literal one. Rather, it is an abridged translation.

2. The translation of the Qur'anic verses are quoted from Yusuf `Ali's translation of *The Holy Qur'an*.

3. When I see it necessary to clarify or comment on something, I put it between sequare brackets: [t.].

4. The book in hand, *Mukhtasar Minhaj Al-Qasidin*, is an abridged version of ibn Al-Jawzi's summery of Imam Abu Hamid Al-Ghazali's well-known book, *Ihya' `Ulum Ad-Din*.

Finally, all praise and thanks are due to Allah, without Whose help and guidance nothing can be accomplished.

Translator

Wa'il `A. Shihab

Preface

All praise is due to Allah and may peace and blessings be upon the Messenger of Allah, his family, his Companions, his followers and those who disseminate his call until the Day of Judgment.

Today, Muslims are required to reflect on the early righteous Muslims' works so as to improve the modern world by means of authentic and sound theories.

Therefore, **Dar Al-Manarah** works hard to translate the well-reputed works of the early righteous Muslim scholars and thinkers. *Mukhtasar Minhaj Al-Qasidin* is one of these important works. So, we hope that this book would promote a better understanding of Islam all over the world.

Also, we ask our beloved readers to read this valuable book with attentive minds so as to get the benefit therefrom.

Dar Al-Manarah Director

M. `Uthman

Introduction

Praise be to Allah, Who showers His mercy on all His servants, and guides His obedient servants to the straight path. I testify that there is no god but Allah, the One Who has no partner, and that Muhammad is His Messenger and servant. O Allah! Bless our Prophet Muhammad and his honorable family.

When I read ibn Al-Jawziyy's *Minhaj Al-Qasidin,* I found it very beneficial for people. So, I decided to read it once more in order to absorb its deep meanings. Yet, when reading it for the second time, my admiration for it greatly increased. I found it so elaborate that I liked to outline it focusing on the important points and objectives. In doing so, I left out some topics, which are dealt with in other famous books. Also, I did not follow the order of the original book, and included some additional notes that are necessary: Prophetic *Ahadith* and comments.

However, the author of *Minhaj Al-Qasidin,* ibn Al-Jawziyy, says: Imam Al-Ghazali's *Ihya' `Ulum Ad Din* (The Revitalization of the Sciences of Religion) has some defects that only scholars can realise, such as the narrations which have been traced back (to the Prophet) while they are fabricated or inauthentic. Therefore, I have compiled a book free of those defects, and retaining the benefits of the orig inal book (*Ihya'*). I this book, I have relied only on authentic and famous narrations, and I deleted from or added to the original book what seems necessary.

This book is divided into four chapters as follows:

Chapter One: Acts of Worship

Chapter Two: Customs

Chapter Three: Destructive Flaws

Chapter Four: Means of Salvation

Each one of these four chapters consists of numerous titles and sub-titles.

Chapter One

ACTS OF WORSHIP

1. Knowledge

Merits of Knowledge

Allah, Most High, highlights the merits of knowledge, saying,

> ❴*Say: are those equal, those who know and those who do not know? It is those who are endued with understanding that receive admonition.*❵
>
> (Az-Zumar: 9)

> ❴*Allah will raise up, to (suitable) ranks (and degrees), those of you who believe and who have been granted (mystic) knowledge.*❵
>
> (Al-Mujadalah: 11)

Commenting on the above Qur'anic verse, ibn (son of) `Abbas (may Allah be pleased with them both) said, "Scholars will have higher degrees seven hundred times than the other believers; the distance between each degree and the other is five hundred years of marching."

Moreover, Allah, Most High, says,

> ❴*Those truly fear Allah, among His servants, who have knowledge.*❵
>
> (Fatir: 28)

In this context, Abu Umamah (may Allah be pleased with him) said that the Messenger of Allah (peace and blessings of Allah be upon him) was informed about two men: a scholar and a devout worshiper. Thereupon, the Messenger of Allah (peace and blessings of Allah be upon him) said,

> "The scholar is more superior to the devout worshiper by the same amount that I am superior to the lowest amongst you."

Then, the Messenger of Allah (peace and blessings of Allah be upon him) added,

> "Surely, Allah, His Angels, the inhabitants of heavens and earth, and even the ant in its nest, and the whale in the sea pray for him who teaches people virtue."
>
> (Reported by At-Tirmidhi)

In another version,

> "The scholar is more superior to the devout worshiper by the same amount as the full moon is superior to other planets. Scholars have not left behind Dinar or Dirham. Rather, they left behind knowledge. Thus, whoever seeks it, will have an abundant gain."
>
> (Reported by At-Tirmidhi)

Mu`awiyyah ibn Abi Sufyan (may Allah be pleased with them both) reports that he heard the Messenger of Allah of Allah (peace and blessings of Allah be upon him) say,

> "If Allah wishes someone good, he helps him to comprehend the religion (Islam)."
>
> (Reported by Al-Bukhari and Muslim)

Safwan ibn `Assal (may Allah be pleased with him) reports that the Prophet (peace and blessings of Allah be upon him) said,

> "Surely, Angels spread their wings for joy and

pleasure with the knowledge seeker."
(Reported by Ahmad)

Abu Hurayrah (may Allah be pleased with him) narrates that the Messenger of Allah (peace and blessings of Allah be upon him) said,

> *"If one treads a path in order to seek knowledge, Allah will make easy for him the (way) to enter Paradise."*
(Reported by Muslim)

Moreover, the Prophet (peace and blessings of Allah be upon him) said,

> *"Whoever dies while seeking knowledge in order to revive Islam, will be in Paradise and nothing would be between him and the Prophets except one degree."*
(Reported by Ad-Darami)

Amongst the virtues of teaching is what is reported on the authority of Sahl ibn Sa`d (may Allah be pleased with him) that the Messenger of Allah (peace and blessings of Allah be upon him) said to `Ali (may Allah be pleased with him),

> *"It is better for you that Allah guides one man (to the path of Islam) through you than for you to have red (expensive) cattle."*
(Reported by Al-Bukhari and Muslim)

On the authority of Abu Musa (may Allah be pleased with him) who said that the Messenger of Allah (peace and blessings of Allah be upon him) said,

> *"The example of guidance and knowledge with*

which Allah has sent me is like abundant rain falling on the earth, some of which was fertile soil that absorbed rain water and brought forth vegetation and grass in abundance. (And) another portion of it was hard and held the rain water and Allah benefited the people with it, and they utilized it for drinking, making their animals drink from it and for irrigating the land for cultivation. (And) a portion of it was barren which could neither hold the water nor bring forth vegetation (then that land gave no benefits). The first is the example of the person who comprehends Allah's religion and gets benefit (from the knowledge) which Allah has revealed through me (the Prophets and learns and then teaches others. The last example is that of a person who does not care for it and does not take Allah's guidance revealed through me (He is like that barren land.)

(Reported by Al-Bukhari and Muslim)

Al-Hasan (may Allah have mercy on him) is reported to have said, "If there had been no scholars, people would have been like animals."

Mu`adh ibn Jabal (may Allah be pleased with him) said, "Seek knowledge for seeking it for the sake of Allah is a sign of consciousness of Allah; acquiring it is an act of worship; studying it is a glorification (of Allah); and searching for it is (a kind of) *Jihad* (striving in Allah's cause)..."

Seeking Knowledge Is a Duty

Anas (may Allah be pleased with him) said that the Prophet (peace and blessings of Allah be upon him) said,

> *"Seeking knowledge is an obligation upon every Muslim."*
>
> (Reported by Ahmad)

Muslim scholars, however, differ over the meaning of "knowledge" in the previous *Hadith*. Scholars of *Fiqh* (Islamic jurisprudence) hold the opinion that "knowledge" in this *Hadith* refers to Islamic Jurisprudence, which is the means of knowing what is lawful and what is prohibited. Scholars of *Hadith* and *Tafsir* (exegetes of the Qur'an), however, are of the view that "knowledge" in the *Hadith* stands for understanding the Book of Allah and the *Sunnah,* for they are the key to other sciences. Sufism maintains that knowledge is meant for knowing how to attain sincerity and to realize the diseases of the soul. Nevertheless, the view believed to be the most correct is that "knowledge" in the *Hadith* refers to the knowledge of the relation between man and his Lord, Most High.

Praiseworthy Knowledge

You should know, dear reader, that praiseworthy knowledge is divided into two categories:

1- Extremely appraised knowledge: The more one acquires of this field of knowledge, the more virtues he gets. This field of knowledge is what is related to Allah, His Attributes, and His Acts.

2- Knowledge which is recommended to be sought in certain amounts: This kind of knowledge comprises those communal duties Muslims are required to observe; if sufficient number of people seek this knowledge, the remainder will be excused. However, if none of them seek it, all people will be sinful. Examples of this knowledge are medicine and mathematics.

Useless Knowledge

Argumentation with the sole intention of boasting and defeating others is the source of evil manners. It leads to pride and showing-off, which will be of no avail in the Hereafter.

The Prophet (peace and blessings of Allah be upon him) is reported to have said:

> *"On the Day of Judgment, the most grievous torment will be inflicted upon a scholar whose knowledge was of no avail."*
> (Reported by At-Tabarani)

Ethics of the Teacher and the Student

The student should start with purifying his own soul, and steer clear of evil manners, for knowledge is the worship of the heart. He should dedicate his life for seeking knowledge. The early Muslims used to give precedence to knowledge over anything else. For example, Imam Ahmad (may Allah have mercy upon him) did not marry except after the age of fourteen.

To the student the teacher should be like a physician to a patient. The student should serve his teacher. In his *Jami` Bayan Al-`Ilm wa Fadlih*, Ibn `Abdel-Barr states that Ibn `Abbas (may Allah be pleased with them both) used to hold the rein of Zayd ibn Thabit's mount and derive it, saying, "This is what we are required to do with scholars."

The student should be on his guard against feeling pride, for it is the flaw of the ignorant. He, further, should evaluate things and give preference to his teacher's opinion over his own. In *Al-Jami` li Akhlaq Al-Rawi wa Adab As-Sam`*, Al-Khatib Al-Bughdadi reported that `Ali (may Allah be pleased with him) said: "It is the right of the scholar to greet the public in general and to be greeted in particular. You should sit before him and avoid overburdening him with questions. You should not divulge his secrets, nor backbite people in his presence, nor find his faults..."

The student, at the beginning of seeking knowledge, is recommended not to occupy his mind with the differences of scholars in order not to perturb his mind.

As to the teacher, he should be patient and forbearing. He should dedicate his efforts in teaching knowledge for the Sake of Allah, and not to seek not rewards or gratitude from people. Early Muslim scholars used to refuse gifts from students. The teacher should offer advice to his students and follow the best manners in this regard.

The teacher, furthermore, should teach his student what the latter can understand and comprehend. More importantly, the scholar should behave according to his knowledge. Allah, Most High, says:

{Do ye enjoin right conduct on the people, and forget (to practise it) yourselves, and yet ye study the Scripture? Will ye not understand?}
(Al-Baqarah: 44)

Categories of Scholars

Scholars may be classified into two classes, namely, evil scholars and righteous scholars. Each class has its own characteristics, which may be outlined as follows:

Righteous scholars are distinguished by the following characteristics:

a) Avoiding praising and intermingling with rulers and people in charge. Sa`id ibn Al-Musayyab said: "If you see a scholar knocks the doors of rulers, you should beware of him for he is a thief."

Some early scholars said, "Scholars do not gain a worldly gift from rulers except by instructing the latter lessons on religion."

b) Refraining from issuing legal verdicts except with knowledge. Early Muslim scholars used to refer people to one another for the sake of issuing Islamic rulings regarding issues. `Abdur-Rahman ibn Abi Layla (may Allah have mercy on him) criticized scholars who were hasty in issuing Islamic ruling, saying: "I have been contemporary with one hundred and twenty Companions of the Prophet (peace and blessings of Allah be upon him), and it was their custom to wish that no one asked them about a given question but another brother in Islam answered him. However, after they passed away, people claimed to be knowledgeable and hastily answered questions. If they had been presented to `Umar, he would have consulted all those who participated in the Battle of Badr regarding the answer of these questions.

c) Following the way of the Companions and Righteous Successors (*Tabi`un*).

d) Steering clear of (*Bid`ah*) heresy and innovation in religion.

e) Searching for the objectives of the legal rulings as possible.

f) Giving precedence to the Hereafter over this world, and preferring the useful knowledge to other sciences that of scarce benefits.

In this context, Shaqiq Al-Bukhari (may Allah have mercy

on him) said to Hatim, "You have accompanied me for some time, what have you learnt from me?" The latter replied, "I have learnt the following eight:

1- I have noticed that people used to keep every valuable thing they possess. Then I reflected upon the Qur'anic verse:

> ❴What is with you must vanish: what is with Allah will endure.❵

(An-Nahl: 96)

So I decided to keep my valuable things with Allah, Most High.

2- I have observed that everybody has a beloved one, but no beloved one could accompany the lover to the grave. Therefore, I have decided to love good deeds, which would accompany me to my grave.

3- I have reflected upon the Glorious Qur'anic verse that reads:

> ❴And for such as had entertained the fear of standing before their Lord's (tribunal) and has restrained (their) soul from lower desires.❵

(An-Nazi`at: 40)

Accordingly, I have exerted myself to steer clear of whims until my self has accustomed to obeying Allah, Most High.

4- I have looked at people's concern of property and authority. Then I pondered on Allah's saying in the Glorious Qur'an:

> ❴Verily the most honoured of you in the sight of Allah is (He Who is) the most righteous of you.❵

(Al-Hujurat: 13)

Consequently, I concerned myself with consciousness and fear of Allah, Most High, so as to attain honor in this world and the Hereafter.

5- I have noticed the spread of envy amongst people, and reflected on the Qur'anic verse:

❲*It is We Who portion out between them their livelihood in the life of this world.*❳
(Az-Zukhruf: 32)

Therefore, I kept away from envy.

6- I have observed the promulgation of enmity amongst people, and then recited the Qur'anic verse:

❲*Verily Satan is an enemy to you: so treat him as an enemy.*❳
(Fatir: 6)

So I refrained from their enmity and insisted on maintaining enmity to Satan.

7- I have looked at people's humiliation in earning livelihood, and then pondered on the Qur'anic verse:

❲*There is no moving creature on earth but its sustenance dependeth on Allah.*❳
(Hud: 6)

Therefore, I concerned myself with carrying out Allah's Duties and put my trust on Him in earning livelihood.

8- I have observed that people depend on their trade, manufacture, and health. Yet, I decided to rely only on Allah, Most High.

Evil scholars, on the contrary, are those who seek the benefits and interests of this world while disregarding the

Hereafter. In this regard, Abu Hurayrah (may Allah be pleased with him) reported that the Prophet (peace and blessings of Allah be upon him) said:

> *"Whoever seeks knowledge that should be dedicated to Allah with the intention of attaining a worldly gain, will be denied the fragrance of Paradise on the Day of Judgment."*
>
> (Reported by Abu Dawud)

Another *Hadith* states,

> *"Whoever seeks knowledge with the intention of boasting in front of scholars, disputing with naive people, or gaining people's admiration, will be condemned to the Hell-fire (on the Day of Judgment)."*
>
> (Reported by At-Tirmidhi)

Some early Muslims said that the most regretful of people at the time of death are unreasonable scholars.

We should keep in mind, however, that scholars are supposed to abide by the commands and prohibitions of *Shari`ah*, not to refrain from the lawful or and show indifference to this world. Yet, they are recommended not to be extravagant in enjoying worldly pleasures. Sufyan Ath-Thawri, for instance, used to eat delicious foods while Imam Ahmad ibn Hanbal (may Allah have mercy on him) insisted on leading an austere living.

II. Purification and *Salah*

Purification, in fact, can be classified to the following four degrees:

1- Purification of the body from dirt and impurity.
2- Purification of the organs from sins.
3- Purification of the heart from immorality.
4- Purification of the unseen from others than Allah.

The last degree is the most superior one, which can only be attained people of deep insight. Narrow-minded people, in contrast, confine themselves to the first degree, ignoring the other important degrees, and so they waste most of their time in the superficial purification.

The Virtue of *Salah*

Prayer is the pillar of Islam, the pinnacle of good deeds, and the peak of obedience.

`Uthman ibn `Afan (may Allah be pleased with him) reports that the Prophet (peace and blessings of Allah be upon him) said:

> *"If the time for a prescribed Salah comes, and a Muslim performs ablution properly (and then offers his Salah) with humility and bowing (to Allah), it will be an expiation for his past sins, so long as he has not committed a major sin; and this is applicable to all times."*
>
> (Reported by Muslim)

Humran said that he saw `Uthman performing ablution; he washed his hands thrice, rinsed his mouth and then washed his nose, by putting water in it and then blowing it out, and washed his face thrice, and then washed his right forearm up to the elbow thrice, and then the left forearm up to the elbow thrice, then wiped his head with water, washed his right foot thrice, and then his left foot thrice and said, "I saw Allah's Messenger performing ablution similar to my present ablution, and then he said,

> *'Whoever performs ablution (like my present ablution) and then offers two Rak`at (Prayer units) in which he does not think of worldly things, all his previous sins will be forgiven.'"*
> (Reported by Al-Bukhari and Muslim)

You should know that *Salah* consists of pillars, duties, and *Sunnan*. The spirit of Prayer is intention, devotion, and contemplation of heart. Without contemplation, invocation is of no avail since this will be futile utterance. By the same token, all other acts of Prayer will not bring forth its avowed fruits, i.e., the act of *Qiyam* (standing) connotes service and the act of *Sujud* (prostration) implies humility and glorification, which will never be attained through inattention. Allah, Most High, says,

> ❴*It is not their meat or their blood that reaches Allah: it is your piety that reaches Him.*❵
> (Al-Hajj: 37)

It is now clear that what reaches Allah, Most High, is the state of the heart, which compels it to submit to the commands of Allah. In this way alertness and mindfulness are required in *Salah* even if a lapse of negligence is pardoned by the Law-Giver as long as consciousness dominates it.

Salah, nevertheless, consists in the following three:

1- **_Consciousness_**: It means to show indifference for all worldly interests and have absolute consciousness of Allah, Most High. The cause of such consciousness is decisive intention since the man who has decisive intention to do something, necessarily puts his heart to it. Thus, consciousness has no place in *Salah* but through man's mindfulness. Consciousness, in fact, differs according to the strength of belief in the Hereafter and scorn of this world. Therefore, if you miss consciousness in *Salah*, you should know that the root-cause of this is weakness of faith, and so you should exert yourself to strengthen and bolster it.

2- **_Reflection on the words_**, which is the second step after consciousness: Consciousness may be present without grasping the meaning, and so attention should be directed to grasping the meaning by refraining from thinking of other matters.

3- **_Glorification and fear of Allah_**, Most High, which emanate from two facts: realizing the Majesty and Magnificence of Allah, and looking down upon one's self, which would result in humility and consciousness. Hope is also an important factor in *Salah*. The one who offers *Salah* should hope for the reward of Allah, and fear the punishment due to his imperfection.

The worshiper should contemplate on every act of *Salah*. When he hears the *Adhan* he should remember the call on the Day of Judgment, and prepare himself to the answer, thinking how to reply. When the worshiper covers his private parts, he should remember his concealed vices which no one knows except Allah, Most High, and which require repentance.

When the worshiper faces the *Qiblah*, he turns his face towards the House of Allah and turns his back to all other directions. No doubt, directing his heart towards Allah is worthwhile.

When you say: "Allah is the Greatest", your heart should not belie your tongue. If you believe that there is something greater than Allah, you will be a liar. Be cautious.

When you say: "I seek refuge in Allah from the accursed Satan", you should take into account that you resort to Allah, Most High. In this case, if your heart is not in tune with your tongue, what you say will be nonsense and irrational. Try to grasp the meaning of what you say.

When you say: ❴Praise be to Allah, the Cherisher and Sustainer of the Worlds,❵ you should ponder over the meaning of these words. Also, you reflect on Allah's mercy when you read: ❴Most Gracious, Most Merciful❵. Think about Allah's power when you read: ❴Master of the Day of Judgment❵. In this way, one should reflect on what he reads or say in *Salah*.

It is reported that Zararah ibn Abi Awfa (may Allah be pleased with him) fell dead when he recited the Qur'anic verse,

❴Finally, when the trumpet is sounded.❵
(Al-Muddathir: 8)

This is, no doubt, is due to his imagination of this horrible scene.

When bowing, try to show humility to your Lord. Likewise, you should be more humble when prostrating since you place yourself in its proper and original position, namely, the earth from which you have been created. In this case, try to reflect on what you say.

Finally, you should know that performing *Salah* in such a manner purifies and enlightens the heart, which, in turn, could behold the Glory of Allah. In fact, no one but the devout scholars can grasp these meanings.

In contrast, whoever performs *Salah* without observing its requirements would in no way grasp its significance. Such a man, furthermore, may exceed the limit and deny its existence.

Morals Pertaining to Friday and Its Prayer

On Friday, one is required to observe the following:

1- To prepare himself for Friday Prayer since Thursday and Friday night by cleaning his body and washing clothes.

2- To perform *Ghusl* before going to the mosque to offer Friday Prayer as it is recommended in more than one authentic *Hadith*.

3- To beautify himself by using the *Miswak* (tooth-stick) and wearing perfume, shaving the pubic hairs, clipping the nails, and trimming the moustache.

4- To go early to the mosque where he will offer Friday Prayer, to walk, and to intend to observe `*Itikaf* (spiritual retreat).

5- To avoid stepping over others' necks in the mosque.

6- To avoid walking in front of the worshipers.

7- To pray in the first row.

8- To repeat the *Adhan* (Call to Prayer) behind the muezzin, and to listen attentively to Friday *Khutabah* (Friday sermon).

9- To offer supererogatory Prayer: two, four, or six *Rak`at* (units) after the obligatory Friday Prayer.

10- To stay in the mosque until the *`Asr* (Afternoon) Prayer.

11- To seize the Honorable Hour, in which Allah, Most High, answers the call of His devout servants. Muslim scholars have held different views regarding deciding the exact time of this Hour. Some scholars have maintained that it is between the time the Imam sits down and the end of the Prayer. Abu Burda ibn Abu Musa Ash-Ash`ari reported, "`Abdullah ibn `Umar said to me, 'Did you hear anything from your father narrating something from the Messenger of Allah (peace and blessings of Allah be upon him) about the Honorable Hour on Friday?' I said, 'Yes, I heard him say reported the Messenger of Allah (peace and blessings of Allah be upon him) to have said

'It is between the time the Imam sits down and the end of the Prayer.'"
(Reported by Muslim)

Other scholars have held the opinion that it is the last hour after the *`Asr* Prayer, based on a *Hadith* narrated in the *Sunnan* of At-Tirmidhi. Moreover, Anas (may Allah be pleased with him) reported that the Messenger (peace and blessings of Allah be upon him) said,

"Seek it between `Asr Prayer till sunset."
(Reported by An-Nsa'i)

Abu Bakr Al-Athram (may Allah have mercy on him) disclosed the fact that this hour may move between the above-mentioned times.

12- To invoke Allah to send blessings upon His Prophet Muhammad (peace and blessings of Allah be upon him) and to forgive His servants' sins. [T. Aus ibn Aus reported that the Prophet (peace and blessings of Allah be upon him) said, "The most virtuous of your days is *Jum`ah* (Friday). On that day, Adam was created and on that day he died; (on that day) the horn will be blown and the people will be dumbfounded! Increase your prayers upon me as your prayers upon me will be presented to me." The people said, "O Messenger of Allah, how will our prayers be presented to you when you have passed away?" He said, "Allah has prohibited the earth from "eating" the bodies of the Prophets." (This *Hadith* is reported Al-Bukhari and Muslim) Ibn Al-Qayyim says: "It is preferred to pray to Allah to send blessings on the Prophet during the day and night of *Jum`ah*, as the Prophet said, 'Invoke many prayers upon me during the day and night of Friday.' The Messenger of Allah is the leader of mankind, and *Jum`ah* is the best of the days of the week. Prayers upon him during that day are a privilege (he deserves), which belongs to no one other than him. This act also has another wisdom, and that is that all of the good that has passed onto this *Ummah*, in this life and the Hereafter, has passed through him. Allah has gathered the good of this life and the next life for this *Ummah*, and the greatest honor and success will be granted to them on Friday. On that day, they will be granted their houses and palaces in Paradise and that is the day they will be given more when they enter Paradise. It is a day of celebration for them in this life. It is also a day in which Allah fulfills their needs and answers their prayers and requests in this world. They are aware of all of that and are able to attain it because of the Prophet and it is through him (that they received these teachings); therefore, in gratitude and appreciation for the great blessings we received through him, we should send many prayers upon him during the day and night of *Jum`ah*." (Sayd Sabiq, *Fiqh As-Sunnah*).]

13- To recite *Surat* Al-Kahf in the night or in the day of Friday. Ibn `Umar (may Allah be pleased with them both) reports that the Prophet (peace and blessings be upon him) said,

> *"Whoever recites Surat Al-Kahf on Jum`ah will be blessed with a light that will rise from underneath his feet to the peak of the sky. This will be a light for him on the Day of Judgment, and he will be forgiven for what is between the Jum`ah (and the next) Jum`ah."*
> (Reported by ibn Mardwwiyah)

[T. Abu Sa`id Al-Khudri reported that the Prophet (peace and blessings of Allah be upon him) said, "Whoever recites *Surat* Al-Kahf on *Jum`ah* will have illumination from the light from one *Jum`ah* to the next." (Reported by An Nasa'i)]

Supererogatory Prayers

Supererogatory Prayers are divided into the following three kinds:

1- *Sunan*: These are the supererogatory Prayers, which the Prophet (peace and blessings of Allah be upon him) persisted in offering.

2- *Mustahbat*: These are the supererogatory Prayers about which there is a Prophetic Hadith that recommends offering it but there is no indication that the Prophet (peace and blessings of Allah be upon him) persisted in offering them.

3- *Tataw`at*: These are the optional Prayers, which a Muslim offers, although there is no *Hadith* that recommends them.

Supererogatory Prayers, in fact, are the most virtuous acts that a servant of Allah can do to draw himself closer to Allah. These Prayers are dealt with in detail in the books of *Fiqh* (Islamic Jurisprudence).

III. *Zakah* (Obligatory Charity)

Zakah (obligatory charity) is one of the pillars of Islam. Allah, Most High, has usually mentioned it immediately after Prayer. He, for example, says,

> ❴And be steadfast in Prayer; practise regular Charity.❵
>
> (Al-Baqarah: 43)

Kinds, divisions, and causes of *Zakah* have been dealt with in detail in the books of *Fiqh*.

Ethics of *Zakah*

Certain inward attitudes and duties are incumbent on those who seek, through paying *Zakah*, the way that leads to the Hereafter as follows:

1- Understanding the significance and objectives of *Zakah*: Objectives of *Zakah* test the degree of love for Allah, elimination of miserliness, and showing gratitude.

2- Giving *Zakah* in secret: Secrecy in paying *Zakah* is farthest removed from hypocritical display and reputation seeking. Giving *Zakah* openly may harm the poor when he feels humility.

3- Avoiding taunting and hurting peoples' feelings: One should not invalidate his *Zakah* by taunting and hurting peoples' feelings. Whatever that may be, there is no problem between the donor and the poor recipient until the former comes to see himself as a benefactor. One should, moreover, realize that giving *Zakah* is actually paying Allah, Most High, what is due, while the poor man is actually receiving his sustenance from Allah, to Whom it has first passed.

4- Showing humbleness: This signifies thinking little of one's donation, for to regard it great is to invite that sanctimonious pride which is one of the deadly sins, rendering good deeds worthless.

5- Paying *Zakah* from what is good and lawful: According to a *Hadith* narrated by Muslim, Allah, Most High, is Good and does not accept but that which is good. *Zakah* should be given from the best of one's wealth. In this context, Allah, Most High, says,

> {*O ye who believe! Give of the good things which ye have (honourably) earned, and of the fruits of the earth which we have produced for you, and do not even aim at getting anything which is bad, in order that out of it ye may give away something.*}
> (Al-Baqarah: 267)

> {*By no means shall ye attain righteousness unless ye give (freely) of that which ye love; and whatever ye give, of a truth Allah knoweth it well.*}
> (Al `Imran: 92)

6- Giving *Zakah* to those who are most worthy and deserving: One should seek out a truly worthy recipient for his *Zakah*, rather than be content with just anybody who happens who fall within the eight categories of legally qualified beneficiaries. For among those generally eligible persons there are some with special qualities. Consideration should be given to the following six qualities:

First, one should seek out those righteous people who have renounced the world and devoted themselves solely to the

Hereafter. The reason for this is that your charity will help the righteous person bolster his piety; by helping him you will have a share in his worship.

Second, the recipient should be chosen from amongst the people of learning, in order to support him in his quest of knowledge.

Third, the recipient should be sincere in his faith and should have profound devotion to Allah alone. This singleness of worship and devotion (*Tawhid*) is apparent when, on accepting a gift, he offers praise and thanks to Allah, Most High, regarding Him as the source of the blessings rather than any intermediary. Such a man is a truly grateful to Allah, Most High, recognizing that all blessings flow from Him.

Fourth, the recipient should be a person who has remained anonymous and kept his need to himself, not being given to fuss and complaint. In this connection, Allah, Most High, says,

> ❴*(Charity is) for those in need who, in Allah's cause are restricted (from travel), and cannot move about in the land, seeking (for trade or work): the ignorant man thinks, because of their modesty, that they are free from want. Thou shalt know them by their (unfailing) mark: they beg not importunately from all and sundry. And whatever of good ye give, be assured Allah knoweth it well.*❵
>
> (Al-Baqarah: 273)

Such men should be sought out by thorough investigation of the religious people in each neighborhood, and by looking deeply into the circumstances of good and decent people, since the reward for addressing charity to them is many times greater than for spending on those who are vociferous in their begging.

Fifth, the recipient should be someone saddled with a large family, or else disabled by illness or some other cause.

Sixth, the recipient should be a close relative, whether paternal or maternal. The offering will then serve the additional purpose of strengthening ties of kinship, the reward for which is incalculable.

Now, we should keep in mind the fact that if any one can be found in whom all these qualities are combined, that is the greatest treasure and the supreme prize. If one fails to find such a man, then the person in whom five qualities are combined is better than the person in whom four qualities are found, and so on.

Qualities of the Recipient

The recipient of *Zakah* should be one of the eight categories of legally qualified beneficiaries. He, moreover, should be characterized with the following four qualities:

1- He should understand that *Zakah* is levied upon the well-to-do Muslims in order to meet his needs, and so he should concern himself with seeking the pleasure of Allah alone.

2- He should thank the giver of *Zakah* and call upon Allah on his behalf. In a *Hadith* narrated by Abu Dawud it is confirmed that one who does not thank people does not thank Allah, Most High. Yet, this form of voicing gratitude should not exceed the limit of thanking an intermediary whom Allah, Most High, decrees to give that charity, while Allah remains the source of all bounties. This quality necessitates that a recipient should not think little of the gift. Furthermore, a recipient of *Zakah* should cover the faults of the gift.

3- He should accept only what is lawful.

4- He should take only what meets his needs.

Virtues and Ethics of Optional Charity (*Sadaqat At-Tataw`*)

Virtues of optional charity are numerous. Below are some of them:

`Abdullah ibn Mas`ud (may Allah be pleased with him) reported that the Messenger of Allah (peace and blessings of Allah be upon him) said:

> *"Who among you considers the wealth of his heirs dearer to him than his own wealth?" They (the Companions of the Prophet) replied, "O Messenger of Allah! There is none among us but loves his own wealth more." The Prophet said, "So his wealth is whatever he spends (in Allah's Cause) during his life (on good deeds) while the wealth of his heirs is whatever he leaves after his death."*

(Reported by Al-Bukhari)

Abu Hurayrah (may Allah be pleased with him) reports that the Messenger of Allah (peace and blessings of Allah be upon him) said:

> *"If somebody gives out in charity something equal to a date from his lawfully gained money - for nothing ascends to Allah except that which is good - then Allah will take it with His Right (Hand) and bring it up for its owner as anyone of you brings up a baby horse, until it becomes like a mountain."*

(Reported by Al-Bukhari)

Another *Hadith* states,

> *"Give out charity for it guarantees your salvation from the Hell-fire."*
> (Reported by At-Tabarani)

Abu Hurayrah (may Allah be pleased with him) narrates that the Prophet (peace and blessings of Allah be upon him) said:

> *"Charity does not in any way decrease one's wealth; the servant who forgives, Allah adds to his respect, and the one who shows humility, Allah elevates him in the estimation (of the people)."*
> (Reported by Muslim)

The Mother of the Believers, `Aishah (may Allah be pleased with her) narrated that once they slaughtered a sheep when the Prophet (peace and blessings of Allah be upon him) asked her, "What is remained of it (after giving charity)?" She replied, "Nothing has remained except its shoulder." Thereupon, the Messenger of Allah (peace and blessings of Allah be upon him) said:

> *"All of it has remained except its shoulder (meaning that what is given in charity will remain for them in the Hereafter)."*
> (Reported by At-Tirmidhi)

As to the ethics of optional charity, they are the same as the ethics of obligatory *Zakah*.

Muslim scholars, however, have differed on deciding which is better for the poor to take from *Zakah* or from optional charity: A group of scholars has preferred the former while others have given precedence to the latter.

As to the best charity, it is explained in the *Hadith* narrated on the authority of Abu Hurayrah (may Allah be pleased with him) that a man asked the Prophet (peace and blessings of Allah be upon him), "O Messenger of Allah! What kind of charity is the best?" He replied:

> *"To give in charity while you are healthy and greedy hoping to be wealthy and afraid of becoming poor. Don't delay giving in charity until that time you will be on the deathbed when you say, 'Give so much to so-and-so and so much to so-and so,' and at that time the property is not yours but it belongs to so-and-so (i.e., your inheritors)."*
> (Reported by Al-Bukhari and Muslim)

IV. *Siyam* (Fasting)

You should know that the worship of Fasting enjoys particular privilege, namely that is a worship which is attributed to Allah, Most High. In the *Hadith* narrated on the authority of Abu Hurayrah (may Allah be pleased with him) the Messenger of Allah (peace and blessings of Allah be upon him) said:

> *"Allah said, 'All the deeds of Adam's sons (human beings) are for them, except fasting which is for Me, and I will give the reward for it.'"*
> (Reported by Al-Bukhari and Muslim)

Fasting, however, enjoys this particular privilege for the following two reasons:

1- It is a hidden act of worship that no one knows except Allah, Most High, and so it is far from hypocritical display and showing off.

2- It overcomes the accursed Satan, the enemy of Allah, Most High.

Sunan of Fasting

Following are some desirable things in Fasting:

1- To take a pre-dawn meal called *Sahur*. It is highly recommended that it is taken as close to *Fajr* time as possible.

2- To break Fasting as soon as one is sure that the sun has set, and it is recommended to break Fasting with dates.

3- To be more generous, especially to the poor.

4- To do much righteous deeds.

5- To give more in charity.

6- To spend time in studying the Qur'an.

7- To observe a spiritual retreat by staying in the mosque (`Itikaf), particularly in the last ten days of Ramadan. `Aishah (may Allah be pleased with her) reported:

> *"With the start of the last ten days of Ramadan, the Prophet used to tighten his waist belt (i.e., work hard) and used to pray all the night, and used to keep his family awake for the Prayers."*
> (Reported by Al-Bukhari and Muslim)

Degrees of Fasting

It should be known that there are three degrees of Fasting:

1- *Ordinary Fasting* means abstaining form food, drink and sexual gratification.

2- *Special Fasting* means keeping one's ears, eyes, tongue, hands, and feet - and all other organs - free from sin.

3- *Extra-special Fasting* means fasting of the heart from unworthy concerns and worldly thoughts, in total disregard of everything but Allah, Most High.

Special Fasting, however, requires the following:

a) Lowering one's gaze and not looking lustfully at the opposite sex.

b) Guarding one's tongue from twaddle, lying, backbiting, obscenity, etc.

c) Closing one's ears to everything reprehensible.

d) Keeping all other limbs and organs away from sin.

e) Avoiding overeating.

Optional Fasting

In addition to the mandatory Fasting of Ramadan, the following kinds of Fasting are recommended by the *Sunnah*:

1- Fasting six days during the month of Shawwal, the month following Ramadan.

2- Fasting the Day of `Arafah (the 9th of Dhul-Hijjah) provided that the person is not perform *Hajj* (pilgrimage) that year.

3- Fasting during the month of Al-Muharram especially the tenth day (the Day of `Ashura'), and if possible the 9th and the 11th of the same month.

4- Fasting Mondays and Thursdays.

5- Fasting the 13th, the 14th, and 15th of all months.

In the *Sunnah*, it is admitted that the best form of Fasting is that of Prophet Dawud (peace and blessings of Allah be upon him). `Abdullah ibn `Amr (may Allah be pleased with them both) narrates that Allah's Messenger (peace and blessing of Allah be upon him) told me:

> "*The most beloved Prayer to Allah is that of Dawud, and the most beloved fast to Allah is that of Dawud. He used to sleep for half of the night and then pray*

for one third of the night and again sleep for its sixth part, and he used to fast on alternate days."

Hajj (Pilgrimage)

One who intends to perform *Hajj* should first make *Tawbah* (repentance to Allah), repay his debts, prepare sufficient provision for his journey and for his family until his return, give back trusts to their rightful owners, and meet his expenses by lawful means. He is recommended to accompany righteous men to help each other in their journey. If there are a group of people going out for *Hajj*, they should choose one of them to be their leader during their journey so as to ser his affairs aright. The pilgrim should stick to the Islamic good manners in all aspects, ask righteous people to make *Du`a'* (supplication to Allah) for him, and say the authentic Prophetic supplications that the Prophet (peace and blessings of Allah be upon him) is reported to have said on his journey and making *Hajj*. These Prophetic supplications are dealt with in detail in the books of *Fiqh*, so one should refer to them for more information in this regard.

Inward Ethics and Significance of *Hajj*

You should get yourself well-acquainted with the fact that there is no way of attaining to Allah, Most High, except by divesting oneself of desires, abstaining form pleasures, confining oneself to necessities and devoting oneself exclusively to Allah, Most High, in every moment and rest. It was for this reason that the ascetics of previous religions used to isolate themselves from the people, retiring to mountain caves and preferring solitude to the company of others, in quest of intimacy with Allah, Most High. Hajj, therefore, is decreed by Allah to be the ascetic act of the Muslim *Ummah*. The pilgrim is recommended to free his minds from all businesses except the obedience of Allah, Most High. He should be shabbily dressed, disheveled, and dusty, not-over adorned nor inclined to things that excite vainglory and rivalry. Also, he should take a simple riding-beast for transport, abstaining from being carried in a litter unless there is a fear that he could not ride the animal. In this context, the Messenger of Allah (peace and blessings of Allah be upon him) is reported to have made *Hajj* on a riding came, with a worn saddle and tattered pad.

Here, we may recall the narration of Jabir (may Allah be pleased with him) that the Prophet (peace and blessings of Allah be upon him) said:

> *"Allah, Most High, boasts the angels about the pilgrim, saying, 'Look at My servants; they came to Me, disheveled and dusty, from every deep ravine. I make you witness that I have forgiven them.'"*
> (Reported by ibn Khayzamah)

Allah, Most High, has honored His House, sanctified it, and made it a visiting-place.

You should, furthermore, know that every action and pillar pertinent to Hajj comprises a lesson or an admonition to people of sound mind as follows:

When the pilgrim feels himself impelled to take a lot, seeking enough to last him the whole journey without spoiling or going bad before he reaches his destination, let him remember that the journey to the Hereafter is a much longer one than this and that the provision for it is true piety. Apart from piety, whatever one supposes to be provision will be left behind one dies, leaving him in the lurch. It will no more keep than the fresh food that goes bad on the first leg of the journey, leaving one dismayed and helpless in the moment of need. Beware, therefore, in case the deeds, which make up your provision for the Hereafter, do not go with you after death, but get spoiled instead by the taint of hypocrisy and showing-off.

When the pilgrim departs his homeland, let him remember the assured departure of this transitory world to the Hereafter.

When the pilgrim puts off his normal clothes and wears the clothes of *Iharm*, he should recall the shroud in which he will be wrapped for burial.

When the pilgrim utters the words of *Talbiyah*, he should bear in mind that this signifies a response to the summons of Allah, Most High, as it is stated in the Qur'anic verse that reads,

> *{And proclaim the pilgrimage among men: they will come to thee on foot and (mounted) on every kind of camel, lean on account of journeys through deep and distant mountain highways.}*
>
> (Al-Hajj; 27)

Hope, therefore, to be accepted and dread being told: 'No favor to fortune for you!' Oscillate between hope and fear; rid yourself of your power and strength, and rely on the Grace and Generosity of Allah, Most High.

When the pilgrims enters the *Haram* (the Sanctuary of Allah), he should hope to be safe from the Punishment of Allah, Most High, and should dread not being worthy to approach Him, for in that case his entry to the Sanctuary would leave him frustrated and fit to be abhorred. At all times, however, his hope should be uppermost, for Allah's Generosity is comprehensive, the Lord is Compassionate, the honor of the House is tremendous, the visitor's right is respected, and protection is secure for all who seek refuge.

On seeing the Ka`bah, the pilgrim should be conscious in

his heart of the majesty of the House, venerating it with such intensity that he seems to anticipate beholding the Lord of the House. He, further, should express his gratitude to Allah, Most High, for bringing him to this high degree, and for including him in the company of those who reach Him.

On touching the Black Stone, the pilgrim should believe that he is pledging allegiance to Allah, Most High, and vowing obedience to Him. He, also, has to make his resolve to be loyal to his oath, for the wrath of Allah is the traitor's due.

On clinging to the coverings of the Ka`bah and pressing one's breast against its wall (at the part called Al-Multazam), the pilgrim intention should be to draw close in love and yearning to the House and the Lord of the House, seeking grace through the contact and hoping for immunity from the Hell-Fire. At the same time, his intention should be earnestly to seek forgiveness and to beg for mercy, just as one who has sinned against another will cling to his clothes while imploring his pardon, demonstrating that he has no refuge or recourse except to his forgiveness.

On running between Al-Safa and Al-Marwah, the pilgrim should recall how he will oscillate between the two scales of the Balance at the site of Resurrection. Also, he demonstrates devotion to duty and hopes to be viewed with compassion, just like who enters the presence of a king and leaves without knowing whether the sovereign has decided to accept or to reject him. He keeps going back across the courtyard time after time, hoping to receive mercy the second time if not the first.

On standing at `Arafah, the pilgrim should - when he beholds the thronging crowds, hears the loud voices speaking in many tongues, and sees the various groups following their Imams through the ritual observances - recall the site of

Resurrection, the gathering of the communities with their Prophets and leaders, each community following its Prophet, aspiring after the intercession, all wavering with equal uncertainty between rejection and acceptance.

As for casting of pebbles (*Rami*), the pilgrim's purpose in this should be obedience to the Divine command, to demonstrate submissiveness and servitude and readiness to comply without any obvious rational of psychological justification.

When the pilgrim's eyes alights on the wall of Madinah, he should remember that this is the town which Allah, Most High, chose for His Prophet (peace and blessings of Allah be upon him), that he made it the goal of his migration, that this was his home. He should further envisage the footprints of the Messenger of Allah (peace and blessings of Allah be upon him) as he went about the city and recall how he used to go about its streets, picturing to yourself his humility and his graceful gait.

On visiting Allah's Messenger, the pilgrim should feel in his heart his tremendous dignity and realize that he is aware of his presence, of his visit, and that he is receiving his greeting. The pilgrim, also, should imagine the noble form of the Prophet (peace and blessings of Allah be upon him).

The Glorious Qur'an

Merits of the Glorious Qur'an

The most important virtue of the Glorious Qur'an is that it is the Word of Allah, Most High. Allah, Most High, describes His Book, saying,

> ﴾And this is a book, which We have sent down.﴿
> (Al-An`am: 92)

> ﴾Verily this Qur'an doth guide to that which is most right.﴿
> (Al-Isra': 9)

> ﴾No falsehood can approach it from before or behind it.﴿
> (Fussilat: 42)

`Uthman ibn `Affan (may Allah be pleased with him) reports the Prophet (peace and blessings of Allah be upon him) to have said,

> "The best amongst you is the one who learns the Qur'an and teaches it."
> (Reported by Al-Bukhari)

Anas (may Allah be pleased with him) said that the Messenger of Allah (peace and blessings of Allah be upon him) said:

> "Surely, Allah, Most High, has chosen some people (to be His favorite servants)." It was said, "Who are those people, O Messenger of Allah?" "The people of the Qur'an," the Prophet said and added,

"they are the (favorite) people of Allah..."
(Reported by An-Nasa'i)

Furthermore, ibn `Amr (may Allah be pleased with them both) narrated that the Prophet (peace and blessings of Allah be upon him) said:

"(On the Day of Judgment,) it will be said to the people of the Qur'an, 'Read (the Qur'an) and occupy your high degrees. Recite (the Qur'an) as you used to recite it in the world for your position will be at the end of the last (Qur'anic) verse you read.'"
(Reported by At-Tirmidhi)

Buraydah (may Allah be pleased with him) reports that the Prophet (peace and blessings of Allah be upon him) said:

"On the Day of Judgment, the crown of dignity will be put on the head of the one who memorizes the Qur'an, and his parents will be dressed in two garments that the world is not equal to, thereupon they will ask, 'What has made us be dressed in these garments?' and it will be said, 'That is because your son's memorization of the Qur'an (in the world).'"
(Reported by Ad-Darami)

Ibn Mas`ud (may Allah be pleased with him) relates, "One who memorizes the Qur'an should be distinguished by his (Prayer) at night while people sleeping, his (Fasting) in the daytime while people not fasting, his sadness while people rejoicing, his weeping while people laughing, his silence while people indulging in nonsense, and his consciousness of Allah while people being conceited. He should not be barefooted, heedless, vociferous, nor hot-tempered."

Al-Fudayl (may Allah have mercy on him) reports, "The one who keeps the Qur'an by heart is the bearer of the banner of Islam. Therefore, he should not indulge in nonsense, play, or amusement - like other people do – due to his reverence to Allah, Most High. Also, he should not be in need of others' favors; rather people should look forward to his favor."

Furthermore, Imam Ahmad ibn Hanbal (may Allah have mercy on him) is reported to have said: "I have seen the Lord of Mighty in a vision, and asked, 'O Lord! What is most virtuous act that devout people should do to bring themselves nearer to You? He (Most High) said, '(Reading) My Words, O Ahmad.' I said, 'O Lord! Should it be with understanding?' 'It may be with or without understanding,' he declared.

One who recites the Glorious Qur'an is recommended to have an ablution and be pure. Reciting the Glorious Qur'an in Prayer, while one is standing, is more virtuous than reciting it in any other situation. Likewise, one is recommended to read the Glorious Qur'an in the mosque.

As to the period in which one should finish reciting the whole Qur'an, early Muslims were of diverse stances on this point. Some of them used to finish reciting the whole Qur'an every day. Others used to finish it in three, seven, or thirty days. This varied according to each one's circumstances. So, one is recommended to read as much as he can of the Qur'an so long as one reflects upon and understands what he recites, and does not ignore his worldly duties.

In this regard, ibn `Abbas (may Allah be pleased with them

both) said, "To me, it is better to correctly recite only *Surat Al-Baqarah* and *Surat* Al `Imran and reflect upon their meanings than to heedlessly recite the whole Qur'an."

Ibn Mas`ud (may Allah be pleased with him) said, "Whoever finishes reciting the whole Qur'an, will have a *Du`a'* (supplication) that will be responded by Allah." On finishing the recitation of the whole Qur'an, Anas (may Allah be pleased with him) used to gather his family and make *Du`a'*.

Reciting the Glorious Qur'an with sweet voice is recommended. However, if one is not able to read the Glorious Qur'an with sweet voice, he has to exert himself to do so.

Likewise, reading the Glorious Qur'an in a low voice is recommended. In this context, a *Hadith* says,

> *"The superiority of reading (the Glorious Qur'an) in a low voice over reading (it) in a loud voice is like the superiority of giving alms in secret over giving it in public."*
> (Reported by An-Nasa'i)

But we should keep in mind the fact that reciting the Glorious Qur'an in a loud voice is recommended in certain situations such as teaching the Qur'an, awakening a sleeping person, etc.

One, also, should read in a mode that permits him to hear his recitation.

As to lowering and raising one's voice in reading the Qur'an in Prayer, this is dealt with thoroughly in the books of *Fiqh*. On the reading the Glorious Qur'an, one should bear in mind the

Glory of the Speaker, Most High, and reflect upon what he reads. Moreover, if one cannot reflect upon what he recites except after repeating the verses he recites, he is recommended to repeat the Qur'anic verses so as to ponder over them. In this connection, ibn Majah reported on the authority of Abu Dharr (may Allah be pleased with him) who reported that the Prophet (peace and blessings of Allah be upon him) performed a Night Prayer reading one verse, repeating it; this verse reads,

> ❴*If Thou dost punish them, they are Thy servants: if Thou dost forgive them, Thou are the Exalted in power, the Wise.*❵
>
> (Al-Ma'idah: 118)

Likewise, Tamim Ad-Dari (may Allah be pleased with him) prayed a Night Prayer repeating the following Qur'anic verse:

> ❴*What! Do those who seek after evil ways think that We shall hold them equal with those who believe and do righteous deeds, that equal will be their life and their death? Ill is the judgment that they make.*❵
>
> (Al-Jathiyah: 21)

On reading the Qur'anic verse that reads, ❴*Praise be to Allah, Who created the heavens and the earth*❵ (Al-An`am: 1), one should ponder on the Mighty and Power of the Creator, Most High.

On reading the Qur'anic verse that says, ❴*Do ye then see? The (human seed) that ye throw out*❵ (Al-Waqi`ah: 58), one should reflect upon the marvelous stages of man's creation from semen until he becomes a powerful man.

Furthermore, a reader of the Glorious Qur'an should steer clear of what hinders the understanding of the Glorious Qur'an such as concerning himself only with the correct pronunciation of sounds, committing sins, and following his vain desires and whims.

Also, a reader of the Glorious Qur'an should consider the Glorious Qur'an as addressing him, and, therefore, act according to its instructions.

VII. *Dhikr* and *Du`a'*

After reading the Glorious Qur'an, there is no act of worship better than *Dhikr* and *Du`a'*.

Merits of *Dhikr*

The merits of remembrance of Allah, Most High, are highlighted in the following Qur'anic verses:

❮*Then do ye remember Me; I will remember you. Be grateful to Me, and reject not Faith.*❯
(Al-Baqarah: 152)

❮*Men who celebrate the praises of Allah, standing, sitting, and lying down on their sides.*❯
(Al `Imran: 190)

❮*... and for men and women who engage much in Allah's praise, for them has Allah prepared forgiveness and great reward.*❯
(Al-Ahzab: 35)

The Prophet (peace and blessings of Allah be upon him) is reported to have said,

"*Surely, Allah, Glorified and Exalted be He, says, 'I will be with My servant as long as he makes mention of Me and moves his lips in making mention of Me.'*"
(Reported by Al-Bukhari)

"*No people assemble to remember Allah but angels surround them, mercy covers them, Sakinah (calmness) descends upon them, and Allah mentions*

them in His assembly."
                                              (Reported by Muslim)

Abu Hurayrah (may Allah be pleased with him) reported the Prophet (peace and blessings of Allah be upon him) as having said,

> *"No people sit in a gathering and then depart each other without making mention of Allah (Glorified and Exalted be He), but they depart from the like of a carcass of a donkey and this gathering will cause them feel regret on the Day of Judgment."*
>   (Reported by Abu Dawud)

Another *Hadith* reads,

> *"No people sit in a gathering without making mention of Allah (Glorified and Exalted be He) or sending blessings upon the Prophet (peace and blessings of Allah be upon him), but they depart from the like of a carcass of a donkey and this gathering will cause them feel regret on the Day of Judgment."*
>   (Reported by At-Tirmidhi)

Merits of *Du`a'*

As to the merits of *Du`a'*, they are highlighted in the following *Ahadith*:

Abu Hurayrah (may Allah be pleased with him) reported the Prophet (peace and blessings of Allah be upon him) as having said,

> *"In the sight of Allah, Glorified and Exalted be He, nothing is more honorable than Du`a'."*
>   (Reported by At-Tirmidhi)

> *"Verily, the most virtuous act of worship is Du`a'."*
> (Reported by Al-Bukhari)

Abu Hurayrah (may Allah be pleased with him) reported the Prophet (peace and blessings of Allah be upon him) as having said,

> *"Whoever does not ask Allah, will incur Allah's wrath upon himself."*
> (Reported by At-Tirmidhi)

Ibn Mas`ud (may Allah be pleased with him) reported the Prophet (peace and blessings of Allah be upon him) as having said,

> *"Beseech Allah to shower His Bounty upon you for Allah loves to be besought."*
> (Reported by At-Tirmidhi)

Ethics of *Du`a'*

Following are some ethics that one who makes *Du`a'* is recommended to strictly adhere to:

1. Choosing the optimum times to make *Du`a'* therein such as the Day of `Arafah (9th day of the month of Dhu-l-Hijjaj), the month of Ramadan, the Fridays, the last time of the night before the Dawn, the time between *Adhan* and *Iqamah*, after the performance of Prayer, during rain, in times of *Jihad*, after finishing the recitation of the whole Qur'an, during *Sujud*, after breaking one's Fast, etc.

2. Facing the *Qiblah*.

3. Lifting one's hand towards the sky.

4. Wiping one's face with his hands after *Du`a'*.

5. Lowering the voice.

6. Commencing *Du`a'* with praising Allah, Most High.

7. Sending blessings upon the Prophet (peace and blessings of Allah be upon him).

8. Steering clear of oppression and sins.

9. Keeping penitent.

10. Implanting consciousness of Allah, Most High, in the heart.

Awrad of the Day and Night

One should get himself well-acquainted with the fact that the way to bringing himself closer to Allah, Most High, lies in constantly worshiping Him by day and night.

In this context, Allah, Most High, says in the Glorious Qur'an,

> ❮And celebrate the Name of thy Lord morning and evening. And part of the night, prostrate thyself to Him: and glorify Him a long night through.❯
> (Al-Insan: 25-26)

The Number of *Awrad* of the Day and the Night

The day is divided into seven *Awrad* and the night is divided into six *Awrad*. Below is the explanation of these *Awrad* and the virtue of each *Wird*:

The first Wird of the day: This *Wird* begins with the advent of the dawn until rise of the sun. This an honorable time, by which Allah, Most High, has made an oath in the following verse:

❨*And the Dawn as it breathes away the darkness.*❩
(At-Takwir: 18)

When a devout worshiper awakes, he is recommended to make *Dhikr* with the following Prophetic sayings:

"Praise be to Allah, Who has caused us to live after He has caused us to die; and to Him is the final issuing."
(Reported by Al-Bukhari)

Ibn Mas`ud (may Allah be pleased with him) said that when it was evening Allah's Messenger (peace and blessings of Allah be upon him) used to supplicate,

"We have entered upon evening and so, too, the whole Kingdom of Allah has entered upon evening. Praise is due to Allah. There is no god but Allah, the One having no partner with Him. His is the Sovereignty and to Him is praise due and He is Potent over everything. My Lord, I beg of You good that lies in this night and good that follows it and I seek refuge in You from the evil that lies in this night and from the evil of that which follows it. My Lord, I seek refuge in You from sloth, from the evil of vanity. My Lord, I seek refuge in You from torment of the Hell-fire and from torment of the grave."

Ibn Mas`ud added that and when it was morning he said like this,

"We entered upon morning and the whole Kingdom

of Allah entered upon morning..."
(Reported by Muslim)

"In the Name of Allah, with Whose Name nothing in the earth nor in the heaven, and He is the All Hearing, the All Knowing."
(Reported by At-Tirmidhi)

"I have satisfied with Allah as my Lord, with Islam as my religion, and with the Messenger as my Prophet (peace and blessings of Allah be upon him) and Messenger."
(Reported by At-Tirmidhi)

On praying the *Fajr* Prayer, one is recommended to say the following Prophetic supplication while still sitting in the position of *Tashahud*:

"There is no god but Allah, the One Who has no partner, His is the Sovereignty and His is the praise, Giver of life and Death, and He has power over everything."
(Reported by At-Tirmidhi)

Then he is to ask Allah's forgiveness by the most superior form of seeking forgiveness of Allah as follows:

"O Allah! You are my Lord. There is no god but You. You have created my and I am Your servant. I do my best to keep my covenant and promise with You. I seek refuge in You from the evil of what I have done. I acknowledge Your favor upon me and I acknowledge my sin. So, forgive me, for no one but You who can forgive sins."
(Reported by Al-Bukhari)

And, he should say,

> "We have begun the day in the way of Islam and with the word of devotion, in the religion or our Prophet Muhammad (peace and blessings of Allah be upon him), in the nation of our father, Ibrahim, the true Unitarian who was never an atheist."
>
> (Reported by Ahmad)

> "O Allah, set right for me my religion which is the safeguard of my affairs. And set right for me the affairs of my world wherein is my living. And set right for me my Hereafter on which depends my after-life. And make the life for me (a source) of abundance for every good and make my death a source of comfort for me protecting me against every evil."
>
> (Reported by Muslim)

> "O Allah! You are my Lord. There is no god but You. I place my trust in You. You are the Lord of the glorious Throne. Surely, what takes place is according to Your Will and what does not take place is according to Your Will. I believe that Allah has power over all things and Whose knowledge encompasses everything. O Lord! I seek refuge in You from the evil within myself and from the evil of every moving creature that You have the grasp of its forelock. Verily, it is my Lord that is on a straight path."
>
> (Reported by At-Tabarani)

Before going out to perform *Fajr* Prayer in the mosque, one is recommended to pray the Supererogatory Prayer in his house. When going out to the mosque, he should say:

> *"O Allah! I ask You with the right of those who ask You and with this going out of me to You. For, I do not seek with my going out (to You) fun, ingratitude, showing-off, or fame."*
>
> (Reported by Ahmad)

When entering the mosque, he is recommended to call upon Allah, Most High, according to the following *Hadith*:

> *"Whoever enters the mosque, should pray for the Messenger of Allah (peace and blessings of Allah be upon him) and say, 'O Allah! Open for me the doors of Your mercy.' And when he gets out he should say, 'O Allah, I beg of You Yours grace.'"*
>
> (Reported by Muslim)

He should try to pray in the first row of the *Jama`ah*, and engage himself in remembering and making *Du`a'* to Allah between the *Adhan* and *Iqamah*. After *Fajr* Prayer, he is recommended to stay in the mosque until sunrise for Anas (may Allah be pleased with him) reported that the Prophet (peace and blessings of Allah be upon) said,

> *"Whoever prays the Fajr Prayer in Jama`ah and then stay (in the mosque) remembering Allah, Most High, until the rise of sun, and then pray two Rak`at, will have (a reward of) Hajj and `Umrah perfectly..."*
>
> (Reported by At-Tirmidhi)

During his stay in the mosque, he is to engage in *Du`a'*, *Dhikr*, reciting the Glorious Qur'an, and reflection upon the creation of Allah, Most High.

The second Wird of the day: This *Wird* starts from the rise of the sun until the end of the *Duha* Prayer. This *Wird* is approximately three hours. In this *Wird*, one is recommended to carry out the following two:

1. To pray *Duha* Prayer.

2. To pay visits to sick people, to attend educational sessions, to meet the need of his fellow Muslims, or to engage himself in reading the Qur'an and *Du`a'*.

The third Wird of the day: This *Wird* starts from the end of the *Duha* Prayer time until midday. Besides the aforementioned four good deeds that one is recommended to do in (No. a in) the second *Wird* of the Day, he is recommended to do the following two:

1. To earn his livelihood.

2. To sleep for a while in order to help himself pray *Qiyam Al-Layl*, and to awake before the *Zuhr* Prayer to prepare himself to offer it.

The fourth Wird of the day: This *Wird* starts from the mid of the day until the end of the *Zuhr* Prayer. In this *Wird*, one is recommended to repeat the *Adhan* after the muezzin when he calls to the *Zuhr* Prayer, to pray four *Rak`at* as a supererogatory Prayer before praying the *Zuhr* Prayer, to pray the *Zuhr* Prayer, and then to pray four *Rak`at* as a supererogatory Prayer.

The fifth Wird of the day: This *Wird* starts from the end of the *Zuhr* Prayer until the time of the *`Asr* Prayer. In this *Wird* one is recommended to engage in *Dhikr*, *Du`a'*, and all forms of good deeds; amongst the best good deeds is waiting Prayer after Prayer.

The sixth Wird of the day: This *Wird* starts from the time of the `Asr` Prayer until yellowness of the sun. In this time, one is advised to pray four supererogatory *Rak`at* before performing the `Asr` Prayer. Afterwards, he is recommended to engage in doing what he is recommended to do in the first *Wird* of the day, particularly reciting the Glorious Qur'an and pondering over its meaning.

The seventh Wird of the day: It starts from the yellowness of the sun until the set of the sun. This is an excellent time about which Al-Hasan Al-Bisri (may Allah have mercy upon him) said, "Righteous men used to glorify the end of the day more than the beginning of it." In particular, glorifying and seeking forgiveness of Allah are recommended in this *Wird*.

By the set of the sun, the *Awrad* of the day come to an end. So, one should reflect on his acts in the bygone day. If he sees that he has done well through the day, he should express his gratitude to Allah, Most High, for His favor and guidance. In contrast, if he sees that he has had some shortcomings, he should make *Tawbah* and intend to do well in the coming night. He should, further, keep in mind that by the end of the day a part of his life has expired. In this context, Al-Hasan said, "O son of Adam! Know that you life consists in days; so when a day passes, a part of lifetime expires." One, likewise, should thank Allah, Most High, for granting him good health and giving him more time to do good deeds. A group of the early Muslims liked to give alms each day.

Awrad of the Night

The first Wird of the night: It starts by the set of the sun until time of the `Isha'` Prayer. After performing the *Maghrib* Prayer, one is recommended to keep on doing virtues until the end of this *Wird*. Commenting on the glorious Qur'anic verse that reads,

❴*Their limbs do forsake their beds of sleep, the while they call on their Lord, in Fear and Hope: and they spend (in Charity) out of the sustenance which We have bestowed on them.*❵

(As-Sajdah: 16)

Anas (may Allah be pleased with him) said, "This Qur'nic verse was revealed to describe the Companions of the Messenger of Allah (peace and blessings of Allah be upon him) who used to pass the time between *Maghrib* and *`Isha'* Prayers in offering Prayers.

In this connection, Abu Hurayrah (may Allah be pleased with him) narrates that the Messenger of Allah (peace and blessings of Allah be upon him) said:

> *"Whoever performs six Raka`at after the Maghrib Prayer, between them he does not engage in evil talk, will have a reward equal to worshiping (Allah) for twelve years."*
>
> (Reported by At-Tirmidhi)

The second Wird of the night: This *Wird* starts from the disappearance of the red twilight until the time of one's sleep. In this time, one is recommended to pray as much as he can offer. Likewise, he is to read *Surat* As-Sajdah and *Surat* Al-Mulk for the Messenger of Allah (peace and blessings of Allah be upon him), according to At-Tirmidhi's narration, used to not sleep before reading them. Here, we recall another narration of `Abdullah ibn Mas`ud (may Allah be pleased with him) who said that the Messenger of Allah (peace and blessings of Allah be upon him) said:

> *"Whoever recites Surat Al-Waqi`ah each night, will never be inflicted with poverty."*
>
> (Reported by ibn As-Sunni)

The third Wird of the night: This *Wird* consists in offering *Witr* Prayer before sleeping, with the exception of the one who used to offer *Qiyam Al-Layl*, since for him it is better to delay offering the *Witr* Prayer. `A'ishah (may Allah be pleased with her) reported,

> *"Allah's Messenger offered Witr Prayer at different nights at various hours extending (from the `Isha' Prayer) up to the last hour of the night."*
> (Agreed upon <u>Hadith</u>)

After offering the *Witr* Prayer, one is recommended to say,

> *"Glory be the Holy King."*
> (Reported by An-Nasa'i)

The fourth Wird of the night: This *Wird* is sleeping itself. We count sleeping as *Wird* for it, if one applies its morals, is an act of worship in itself. In this context, Mu`adh (may Allah be pleased with him) said,

> *"I sleep and then get up. I sleep and hope for Allah's Reward for my sleep as I seek His reward for my Qiyam Al-Layl."*
> (Reported by Al-Bukhari and Muslim)

Amongst the good manners of sleeping is offering *Wudu'* before retiring to one's bed. `A'ishah (may Allah be pleased with her reported,

> *"Whenever the Prophet intended to sleep while he was Junub, he used to wash his private parts and perform ablution like that for the Prayer."*
> (Reported by Al-Bukhari and Muslim)

Before sleeping, one is recommended to make *Tawbah* to

Allah, Most High, in order to purify his inward soul as he has purified his outward body.

Also, he is to intend to persist in steering clear of deceit, oppression, wrongdoing, and all sins.

One is instructed by the Prophet (peace and blessings of Allah be upon him) to write his will. `Abdullah ibn `Umar (may Allah be pleased with them both) reports the Prophet (peace and blessings of Allah be upon him) as having said,

> *"It is not permissible for any Muslim who has something to will to stay for two nights without having his last will and testament written and kept ready with him."*
>
> (Reported by Al-bukhari and Muslim)

Excess preparation of one's bed should be avoided for it may enlarge the time of his sleeping. Once, the Prophet's bed was folded [in order to be more comfortable] when he said,

> *"This hindered me from offering Qiyam Al-Layl."*
>
> (Reported by At-Tirmidhi)

One is recommended to follow in the footsteps of the early righteous Muslims who used to not sleep until they become overwhelmed by sleep.

Moreover, amongst the morals of sleeping is facing the *Qibalah*, making *Du`a'* to Allah with the authentic Prophetic supplications, and lying on one's right side. Bellow, however, are some relevant *Ahadith*:

Abu Hurayrah (may Allah be pleased with him) reports that the Prophet (peace and blessings of Allah be upon him) said:

"When any one of you retires to his bed, he should take hold of the hem of his lower garment and clean (his bed) with the help of that three times for he himself does not know what he left behind him on his bed. When he intends to lie on his bed, he should say, 'In Your Name, my Lord, I have laid myself down, and in Your Name I shall rise. If you take my soul, then have mercy on it; and if You release it, then protect it in the way You protect Your faithful servants.'"

(Reported by Al-Bukhari and Muslim)

`A'ishah (may Allah be pleased with her) reported,

"When the Prophet (peace and blessings of Allah be upon him) retired to his bed he used to hold his two palms together, blow in them, and recite Surat Al-Ikhlas, Surat Al-Falaq, and Surat An-Nas; then he used to wipe with his two palms much of his body, starting by wiping his head, his face, and most of his body. He used to do so three times."

(Reported by Al-Bukhari and Muslim)

Al-Bara' ibn `Azib (may Allah be pleased with him) reported,

"The Prophet (peace and blessings of Allah be upon him) said to me, 'Whenever you go to bed perform ablution like that for the Prayer, lie or your right side and say: O Allah! I surrender to You, entrust all my affairs to You, and depend upon You for Your Blessings, both with hope and fear of You. There is no fleeing from You, and there is no place of protection and safety except with You. I believe in Your Book (the Qur'an) which You have revealed

and in Your Prophet (Muhammad) whom You have sent. Then if you die on that very night, you will die with faith (i.e., or the religion of Islam). Let the aforesaid words be your last utterance (before sleep).'"

(Reported by Al-Bukhari and Muslim)

`Ali (may Allah be pleased with him) reported that Fatimah complained of what she suffered from the hand mill and from grinding, when she got the news that some slave girls of the booty had been brought to Allah's Messenger. She went to him to ask for a maid-servant, but she could not find him, and told `Aishah of her need. When the Prophet came, Aishah informed him of that. The Prophet came to our house when we had gone to our beds. (On seeing the Prophet) we were going to get up, but he said, "Keep at your places," I felt the coolness of the Prophet's feet on my chest. Then he said,

"Shall I tell you a thing which is better than what you asked me for? When you go to your beds, say: 'Allahu Akbar (i.e., Allah is the Greatest)' for forty-three times, and 'Al Hamdu li l-lahi (i.e., all the praises are for Allah)' for thirty-three times, and Subhana Allah (i.e., Glorified be Allah) for thirty-three times. This is better for you than what you have requested."

(Reported by Al-Bukhari and Muslim)

Abu Hurayrah (may Allah be pleased with him) reported, "Allah's Messenger deputized me to keep *Sadaqah (Al-Fitr)* of Ramadan. A comer came and started taking handfuls of the foodstuff (of the *Sadaqah*) (stealthily). I took hold of him and said, 'By Allah, I will take you to Allah's Messenger.' He said, 'I am needy and have many dependents, and I am in great need.' I released him, and in the morning Allah's Messenger asked me, 'What did your prisoner do yesterday?' I said, 'O Allah's Messenger! The person complained of being needy and of having many dependents, so, I pitied him and let him go.' Allah's Messenger said, 'Indeed, he told you a lie and he will be coming again.' I believed that he would show up again as Allah's Messenger had told me that he would return. So, I waited for him watchfully. When he (showed up and) started stealing handfuls of foodstuff, I caught hold of him again and said, 'I will definitely take you to Allah's Messenger. He said, 'Leave me, for I am very needy and have many dependents. I promise I will not come back again.' I pitied him and let him go. In the morning Allah's Messenger asked me, 'What did your prisoner do? I replied, 'O Allah's Messenger! He complained of his great need and of too many dependents, so I took pity on him and set him free.' Allah's Messenger said, 'Verily, he told you a lie and he will return.' I waited for him attentively for the third time, and when he (came and) started stealing handfuls of the foodstuff, I caught hold of him and said, 'I will surely take you to Allah's Messenger as it is the third time you promise not to return, yet you break your promise and come.' He said, '(Forgive me and) I will teach you some words with which Allah will benefit you.' I asked, 'What are they?' He replied, 'Whenever you go to bed, recite *'Ayat-al-Kursi'* - *Allahu la ilaha illa huwa-l-Haiy-ul Qaiyum* - until you finish the whole verse. (If you do so), Allah will appoint a guard for you who will stay with you and no Satan will come near you until morning.' So, I released him. In the morning, Allah's Messenger asked, 'What did your prisoner do yesterday?' I replied, 'He claimed that he would teach me some words by which Allah will benefit me, so I let him go.' Allah's Messenger asked, 'What are they?' I replied, 'He said to me, 'Whenever you go to bed, recite *Ayat-al-Kursi* from the beginning to the end.' He further said to me, '(If you do so), Allah will appoint a guard for you who will stay with you, and no Satan will come near you until morning.' The Prophet said,

> *'He really spoke the truth, although he is an absolute liar. Do you know whom you were talking to, these three nights, O Abu Hurayrah?' Abu Hurayrah said, 'No.' He said, 'It was Satan.'"*
>
> (Reported by Al-Bukhari)

Anas (may Allah be pleased with him) reports that when the Prophet (peace and blessings of Allah be upon him) retired to his bed he used to say:

> *"Praise is due to Allah Who feeds us, provides us drink, suffices us, and provides us with shelter, for many a people there is none to suffice and none to provide shelter."*
>
> (Reported by Muslim)

When one gets up to offer *Tahjjud* Prayer, he is recommended to say the Prophetic *Du'a'* that is reported in this connection. Ibn 'Abbas (may Allah be pleased with them both) reported that when the Prophet (peace and blessings of Allah be upon him) got up at night to offer *Tahajjud* Prayer, he used to say:

> *"O Allah! All the praises are for You, You are the Holder of the Heavens and the Earth, and whatever is in them. All the praises are for You; You have the possession of the Heavens and the Earth and whatever is in them. All the praises are for You; You are the Light of the Heavens and the Earth. And all the praises are for You; You are the King of the Heavens and the Earth. And all the praises are for You; You are the Truth and Your Promise is the truth, and to meet You is true. Your Word is the*

truth. And Paradise is true and Hell is true. And all the Prophets are true, and Muhammad is true. And the Day of Judgment is true. O Allah! I surrender (my will) to You; I believe in You and depend on You. And repent to You, and with Your help I argue (with my opponents, the non-believers). And I take You as a judge (to judge between us). Please forgive me my previous and future sins; and whatever I concealed or revealed. You are the One Who make (some people) forward and (some) backward. There is none to be worshipped but You."

Sufyan said that `Abdul Karim Abu Umayyah added to the above,

"There is neither might nor power except through Allah."
(Reported by Al-Bukhari and Muslim)

One should exert himself to make his first utterance after getting up and his last utterance before sleeping consist in *Dhikr*, for this is a token of one's true faith.

The fifth Wird of the night: This *Wird* starts from the second half of the night until the last one-sixth of the night. This is an honorable time. Abu Zarr (may Allah be pleased with him) reported that he asked the Messenger of Allah (peace and blessings of Allah be upon him) which time of the night in it *Qiyam Al-Layl* is more virtuous; thereupon the latter replied,

"This is (in) the midnight, and few (people) who do (pray in) it."
(Reported by Muhammad ibn Nasr)

When waking up to offer *Qiyam Al-Layl*, one is

recommended to read the last ten verses of Surat Al `Imran as `Abdullah ibn `Abbas (may Allah be pleased with them both) narrates that he passed a night in the house of Maymunah, the Mother of the Believers, who was his aunt. He said, "I slept across the bed, and Allah's Messenger along with his wife slept lengthwise. Allah's Messenger slept until midnight or slightly before or after it. Then Allah's Messenger woke up, sat, and removed the traces of sleep by rubbing his hands over his face. Then he recited the last ten verses of *Surat* Al `Imran..."

He is advised to commence *Qiyam Al-Layl* with two short *Raka`at*. Abu Hurayrah (may Allah be pleased with him) reports Allah's Messenger (peace and blessings be upon him) as saying,

> *"When any one of you gets up at night, he should begin the Prayer with two short Rak`at."*
>
> (Reported by Muslim)

Then, he should pray two *Rak`at* by two. According to Al-Bukhari and Muslim, `Aishah reports that the Prophet (peace and blessings be upon him) used to offer thirteen *Rak`at* of *Qiyam Al-Layl* and that included the *Witr* and two *Rak`at* (*Sunnah*) of the *Fajr* Prayer.

The sixth Wird of the night: This is the sixth part of the night, which is the time of *Sahar*. Highlighting the virtues of this time, Allah, Most High, praises His devout slave-servants, saying,

> ❨And in the hours of early dawn, they (were found) praying for forgiveness.❩
>
> (Adh-Dhariyat: 18)

Jabir (may Allah be pleased with him) reported Allah's Messenger (peace and blessings of Allah be upon him) as saymg,

> *"If anyone is afraid that he may not get up in the latter part of the night, he should observe Witr in the first part of it; and if anyone is eager to get up in the last part of it, he should observe Witr at the end of the night, for Prayer at the end of the night is witnessed (by the angels) and that is preferable."*
>
> (Reported by Muslim)

Awrad and Categories of People

People who walk in the path of the Hereafter are of six categories:

First, the worshiper who dedicates all his time to worshiping Allah, Most High: Such person does what we have mentioned of the *Awarad* of the day and the night.

Second, the scholar: Such knowledgeable person should divide his time between seeking and teaching knowledge, and worshiping Allah.

Third, the student: Like the scholars, the student should divide his time between learning, and worshiping Allah, Most High.

Fourth, the ruler, the judge, and those who mange the people's affairs: In the day, they should concern themselves with the people's interest besides performing the prescribed acts of worship. In the night, they should offer the Awrad of the night.

Fifth, craftsmen: They should earn their livelihood moderately, and then offer what remains of *Awrad*.

Sixth, true lovers of Allah: They should incessantly stick to offering the *Awrad* and consciousness of Allah, for the Messenger of Allah (peace and blessings of Allah be upon him) said,

> "*Do good deeds properly, sincerely and moderately and know that your deeds will not make you enter Paradise, and that the most beloved deed to Allah's is the most regular and constant even though it were little.*"
>
> (Reported by Al-Bukhari and Muslim)

Masruq (may Allah be pleased with him) asked `Aishah (may Allah be pleased with her), "What deed was the most beloved to the Prophet?" She said,

> "*The regular constant one.*"
>
> (Reported by Al-Bukhari and Muslim)

Qiyam Al-Layl

Merits of *Qiyam Al-Layl*

Praising the characters of the devout believers, Allah, Most High, says,

> ❴*Their limbs do forsake their beds of sleep, the while they call on their Lord, in Fear and Hope.*❵
>
> (As-Sajdah: 16)

Likewise, the Messenger of Allah (peace and blessings of Allah be upon him) is reported to have said:

> "*It is highly recommended for you to observe Qiyam Al-Layl, for it was the practice of your righteous predecessors. Qiyam Al-Layl brings us close to*

Your Lord, atones for our sins, drives disease from the body, and puts a stop to transgression."
(Reported by Al-Bukhari and Muslim)

Jabir (may Allah be pleased with him) reported that he heard the Messenger of Allah (peace and blessings of Allah be upon him) say,

"There is an hour in the night, in which no Muslim individual will ask Allah for good in this world and the next without giving it to Him, and that applies to every night."
(Reported by Muslim)

Al-Hasan Al-Bisri (may Allah have mercy on him) said, "We know of no harder act of worship than enduring through the night and offering up our money." He was asked, "How is it that those who observe *Qiyam Al-Layl* are among the people with the most beautiful faces?" To this he replied, "Because they commune with the Most Merciful and He clothes them in light from His light."

Measures that Help in Observing *Qiyam Al-Layl*

Dear reader, the following measures will help you to observe *Qiyam Al-Layl*: Good intention and devotion to Allah, determination, continual repentance, keeping way from sins, going to bed early, taking a nap if possible, avoiding overeating, depending on Allah, and realizing the merits of observing *Qiyam Al-Layl*.

Degrees of *Qiyam Al-Layl*

Observing *Qiyam Al-Layl* is of various degrees as follows:

First, praying the whole night as some of our early

righteous Muslims were accustomed to.

Second, praying for half of the night. Here, one is recommended to sleep the first third and the last sixth of the night.

Third, praying for one-third of the night. Here, one is recommended to sleep the first half and the last sixth of the night. Prophet Dawud (peace and blessings of Allah be upon him) used to observe *Qiyam Al-Layl* in this way. `Abdullah ibn `Amr ibn Al-`As (may Allah be pleased with him) reports that Allah's Messenger (peace and blessings of Allah be upon him) told me,

> *"The most beloved Prayer to Allah is that of Dawud and the most beloved fasts to Allah are those of Dawud. He used to sleep for half of the night and then pray for one-third of the night and again sleep for its sixth part and used to fast on alternate days."*
> (Reported by Al-Bukhari and Muslim)

Fourth, praying for one-sixth or one-fifth of the night. It is better to pray in the second half or the last sixth of the night.

Fifth, praying with no estimation of time. There are two ways of observing *Qiyam Al-Layl* in this way as follows:

1. Praying from the beginning of the night until sleep overcomes him; then he gets up to pray until sleep overcomes him, and so on. A group of the early righteous Muslims used to observe *Qiyam Al-Layl* in this way. According to Al-Bukhari and Muslim, Anas ibn Malik (may Allah be pleased with him) reports that sometimes Allah's Messenger (peace and blessings be upon him) would not fast (for so many days) that we thought that he would not fast

that month and he sometimes used to fast (for so many days) that we thought he would not leave fasting throughout that month, and (as regards his Prayer and sleep at night) if you wanted to see him praying at night, you could see him praying and if you wanted to see him sleeping, you could see him sleeping.

2. Sleeping at the beginning of the night, and then getting up to pray for the remaining part of the night. In context, Sufyan Ath-Thawri said, "I sleep at the beginning of the night, and then get up to observe *Qiyam Al-Layl* in the remaining time of the night."

Sixth, praying four or two *Rak`at* in the night. The Prophet (peace and blessings of Allah be upon him) is reported to have said,

> "*Pray in the night: pray four Rak`at; pray two Rak`at.*"

Abu Hurayrah (may Allah be pleased with him) reports the Messenger of Allah (peace and blessings of Allah be upon him) as having said:

> "*Whoever wakes up at night and lets his wife to do so in order to offer two Rak`at, will be recorded amongst those who make much Dhikr of Allah in that night.*"
>
> (Reported by Abu Dawud)

Seventh, offering Prayer in the time between the *Maghrib* and *`Isha'* Prayers, and observing the *Wird* of the time of *Sahr*.

When It Is Difficult to Perform Purification at Night

Whoever finds it difficult to perform purification at night

and to offer Prayer, should sit facing the *Qiblah* and engaging himself in making *Dhikr* of Allah and *Du`a'*. If he, however, is not able to sit, he is recommended to make *Dhikr* of Allah while he is lying on his bed. Whoever is accustomed to observe certain *Wird*, but once sleep overcomes him, should make it up after praying the *Duha* Prayer.

Whoever get himself accustomed to offering *Qiyam Al-Layl*, should beware of leaving it, for the Messenger of Allah (peace and blessings of Allah be upon him) said to `Abdullah ibn `Amr (may Allah be pleased with them both),

> *"O `Abdullah! Do not be like so and so who used to pray at night and then stopped offering Qiyam Al-Layl."*

The Optimum Times for *Qiyam Al-Layl* and Good Deeds

The most virtuous nights, that the devout slave-servant of Allah should observe *Qiaym Al-Layl* therein, are:

- 17th, 21st, 23rd, 25th, 27th, and 29th of Ramadan,
- 1st, and 10th of Muharram,
- 1st, and 15th of Rajab,
- 15th of Sha`ban,
- 9th of Dhul-Hijjah,
  1st of Shawwal, and
- 10th of Dhul-Hijjah.

As for the most virtuous days, they are as follows:

- the day of `Arafah (9th of Dhul-Hijjah),
- the day of `Ashura' (10th of Muharram),

- 27th of Rajab,

  17th of Ramadan,
- 15th of Sah`ban,
- Fridays,
- `Idul-Fitr* (1st of Shawwal),

  `Idul-Adha* (10th of Dhul-Hijjah),
- the first ten days of Dhul-Hijjah,
- the days of Tashriq (11th, 12th, and 13th of Dhul-Hijjah)
- Mondays,
- Thursdays, and
- 11th, 12th, and 13th of every month.

Chapter Two

CUSTOMS

I. Serving Food, Sharing It, and Hospitality

We have several kinds of manners while serving food to guests, either before eating, during it, or after finishing it.

Before Eating

We should wash our hands before starting to eat so as to secure its cleanliness. Food should also be served on a modest table fixed to the ground rather than a high one as has been done by the Prophet (peace and blessings of Allah be upon him). One should sit on his left sole while erecting the right knee, intending to strengthen oneself thereby rather than merely relishing food. Such an intention is marked by satisfaction rather than satiation. The Prophet (peace and blessings of Allah be upon him) said,

> *"A human being has not filled any vessel which is worse than a belly. Enough for the son of Adam are some mouthfuls which can keep his back straight; but if there is no escape he should fill it a third with food, a third with drink, and leave a third empty."*
> (Reported by At-Tirmidhi and ibn Majah)

Man should not eat except when he is hungry. In that way, man becomes healthy. He should also be content with whatever food he has and share it with others as far as he can.

During Eating

Man should start eating with mentioning the Name of Allah and finish it up with thanking Him. Man also should eat with his right hand taking small morsels and chewing them very good. Man never takes a second morsel till he swallows the first one. He should not show dislike to any sort of food and eat from what is near to him, unless there is a variety of food such as fruits. Man should eat with three fingers. If a morsel drops, he should pick it. Likewise, he should not breathe into the hot food. He should not also put his refuse with food; as if putting date pits with dates in one plate. He should rather receive it on the back of his hand then put it away.

Man should not drink water while he eats. Likewise, man should receive the drinking pot with his right hand, look into it and then drinks in small sips. Man should also breathe thrice while drinking, i.e., take three intervals in drinking.

> *"Allah's Messenger (peace and blessings of Allah be upon him) has been reported as taking breath three times when drinking."*
> (Reported by Al-Bukhari)

This means that the Prophet (peace and blessings of Allah be upon him) used to remove the pot away from his mouth and breath rather than breathing into the pot.

After Eating

Man should stop eating before reaching satiation. He should also lick his hands rather than wiping them. Further more, he should not leave any food remains in the pot. Thanking the Almighty should be given at the very end. The Prophet (peace and blessings of Allah be upon him) said,

> *"Allah is pleased when a man eats and thanks Him therefore; drinks and thanks Him therefore."*
> (Reported by Muslim)

Finally, man should wash his hands after eating.

Sharing Food with Others

When sharing food with others, one should not proceed with eating before the elders. All participants should chat together in decent terms. Each of them should prefer his brother to himself and start eating freely at the same time. One should not glance at other's eating lest they become discouraged.

One should avoid vile habits such as shaking out his hand in the pot or stretching his head over the pot while eating. If one takes something out of his mouth, he should divert his mouth and take it out with his left hand. In addition, did one eat a little pit of a morsel, he should not sip it into the pot again.

Serving Food to Brothers

Serving food to others is commendable. Imam Ali said,

> *"Collecting brothers around food is better for me than setting a slave free."*

Khaithama used to prepare many tasty foods and invite Ibrahim An-Nakh`i and Al-'A`mash and say,

> *"Would you eat, I have prepared it for you."*

Then he would serve whatever food he had. One, however, should reserve some of the food to his family. A visitor should not suggest a certain kind of food In case he is asked to choose between two kinds, he should opt for the less expensive unless the host is pleased by his choice of the expensive one and hastens to bring it. Once Ash-Shafi`i visited Az-Z`afarani, who used to write a paper of the daily food and give it to the maiden. Ash-Shafi`i took the paper and added another kind of food. Knowing this, Az-Z`afarani became strongly delighted.

Avoiding People When They Eat

Knowing that some people are eating, one should not approach them. However, if he unintentionally comes across them and they invite him to share their food, he should consider it prudently. If they shyly invite him to eat, he should not eat. Otherwise he can share food with them. If it happened that one visited a friend who is out and food are offered at his place one can eat, if he is certain that his friend would be pleased if he eats of his food.

Hospitality

One should invite the righteous people. Some early Muslims said,

> *"You should eat of the righteous' food and vise versa."*

In addition, one should look for the poor rather than the rich and serve them properly. He should also invite his friends and acquaintances. By serving food to others, one should seek adherence to the *Sunnah*, show intimacy and try to pleasing others rather than ostentation. One should also invite those who can hardly respond to the invitation due to one reason or another.

As for responding to an invitation, if it is for a marriage banquet one should accept it, when invited on the first day. One should not accept the rich's invitation only but also that of the poor. If he happens to be fasting, he should also respond to the invitation. If his fast is voluntary, and he knows that his host will be pleased by sharing his food, he should break his fast.

Furthermore, if he knows that his food is forbidden, he should not accept the invitation. The same ruling applies in case of using prohibited gadgets or serving food with music. Likewise, one should not accept the offender's, the sinner's, the oppressor's, or the tyrant's invitation.

Accepting an invitation, food should not be the end, but rather to abide by the Prophet's *Sunnah* (peace and blessings of Allah be upon him), honoring brothers and avoiding misunderstanding due to declination. Declining an invitation, one may be ignorantly presumed as an arrogant. In the same vein, one should behave modestly amongst the fellow guests. One should also sit where his host guides him. One should also avoid glancing at food when served, lest it may be taken as a sign of greed.

Serving Food

Manners of Serving Food to Guest

1- Food should be served promptly as soon as the guest rests.

2- Fruits should be served first, Allah says,

> ﴾*And with fruits any that they may select; And the flesh of fowls any that they may desire.*﴿
> (Al-Waqi`ah: 20-21)

Then meat is served, then any other food. Finally, the dessert is served. At the end one drinks cold water and washes his hands with warm water.

3- All available kinds of food should be served.

4- Guests should be afforded ample time to be satisfied.

5- Food should be quite enough. The host's share of the food should be set aside before it is served to the guests. After eating, if a guest seeks departing, the host should see him out with a cheerful smile and kind terms. The guest, too, should, out of his modesty and good manners, be satisfied and contended even if he finds something wrong. He should not depart unless the host lets him go. The guest should be mindful of the time he stays by the host.

II. Marriage

Its Manners

Scholars unanimously agree on the point that marriage is commendable and has manifold virtues, such as having offspring, pleasing the Almighty by procreation, pleasing the Prophet (peace and blessings of Allah be upon him) by increasing his followers, being blessed by a prayer of a righteous child.

Marriage has also some other virtues such as warding against satanic temptations amusing one's self with his wife. By marriage, man gets all his household activities properly cared for whereby he enjoys ample time for seeking knowledge and working, a good wife will be there to help her husband. In marriage man trains himself on responsibility and guardianship, meeting his household needs and bearing their bad behavior if any, and exerting utmost efforts to reform them. Getting married, man duplicates his efforts to seek his livelihood and care for bringing up his children. The Prophet (peace and blessings of Allah be upon him) said,

> *"Spending a Dinar in the cause of Allah, in setting a slave free, as a charity and another one on your family, the last is the best of all."*
> (Reported by Muslim)

Evils of Marriage

The worst evil of Marriage is man's inability to satisfy his desire with his own wife in a lawful way. This may cause him to resort to unlawful ones. A man may also fail to fulfill his wife's rights, or bear her bad manners. This is a quite dangerous thing since man is responsible for his household. Furthermore, man's household may distract him from divine remembrance; thus becoming totally preoccupied by them and enjoys his doing so. Therefore he may forget all about the Hereafter.

Against this background, each represents a specific case in judging whether marriage is obligatory for him or not. This depends on all the above-mentioned information. In fact, seeking marriage, man should first consider all these factors. Ascertaining that its virtues overcome its evils, marriage becomes obligatory, and *vise versa*.

Good Treatment between Couples

As for the woman, she should possess certain qualities whereby a mutual good treatment with her husband is secured. These are,

1- She should be a religious woman. The Prophet (peace and blessings of Allah be upon him) said,

> *"Try to marry the religious woman."*
> (Reported by Muslim)

If she happens to be irreligious, she will undermine his religion. If being madly jealous, she will spoil his life.

2- She should be well-disposed, otherwise she will be strongly harmful.

3- She should be satisfactorily beautiful in order to fortify her husband. Therefore, we have been commanded to look at the would-be wife. However, some persons have disregarded this point. Imam Ahmad is said to have chosen a one eyed woman rather than a beautiful one. This is quiet scarce.

4- The woman's dower should be reasonable. Sa'id ibn Al-Musaib accepted only two *dirhams* as a dower for his daughter. `Umar ibn Al-Khattab (may Allah be pleased with him) said, "do not excessively raise your daughters' dowers." Likewise, man is required not to covet for his wife's property. Ath-Thawri said, "if a suitor asks what the woman possesses, know that he is a robber."

5- She should be a virgin. A virgin is more intimate with her husband than a non-virgin. People naturally become deeply affected by the first attachment.

6- She should be fertile.

7- She should belong to a righteous family.

8- She should not be of his family.

The same criteria apply to the man. The girl's guardian should ascertain these norms in the would-be husband of his dependant.

Rights and Obligations of the Couples

As for the husband, he is required to justly observe these manners,

1- Preparing a banquet for his wedding.

2- Treating his wife kindly bearing her bad behavior if any. The Prophet (peace and blessings of Allah be upon him) said,

> "*Treat women kindly for they have been created like a curved rib. The most curved part of a rib is its head. Trying to straighten it, you break it. Leaving*

it alone, it remains curved. Therefore, treat women kindly."

(Reported by Muslim)

However, treating one's wife kindly doesn't mean not harming her, but rather to bear hers generously following the example of the Prophet (peace and blessings of Allah be upon him). `Umar (may Allah be pleased with him) said,

"The Prophet's wives used to argue with him and desert him from day to night"

(Reported by Al-Bukhari)

3- He should flirt and banter with her. The Prophet (peace and blessings of Allah be upon him) raced with his wife `A'ishah (may Allah be pleased with her) and used to joke with his wives. Jabir ibn `Abdullah reports that the Prophet (peace and blessings of Allah be upon him) said to him,

"Why didn't you marry a virgin, so that you might play with her and she with you, and you might amuse her and she amuse you."

(Reported by Al-Bukhari)

4- He should banter with his wife in a moderate way so that he should not lose his respect and prestige before her.

5- Being modest in jealousy, that is to say that he should not overlook such matters as leading to harmful results. However, such jealousy should not cause mistrust. The Prophet (peace and blessings of Allah be upon him) has highlighted that,

"A man should not return to his wife from traveling at night."

(Reported by Al-Bukhari)

6- He should moderately expend on his household.

7- He should be well-informed about woman's private matters and her periods, and how to approach her during these times. He is required to teach her the correct articles of faith. He should refute all innovations she might have. He should also teach her how to pray and how to cleanse herself after her periods; informing her that if her period ends before the sunset as much as one performs one *Rak`ah*, she should make up for the *Zuhr* and *`Asr* Prayers. The same applies to *Fajr* Prayer. In fact, women hardly observe such rulings.

8- Having more than wife, he should treat them justly in all aspects rather than love and intercourse due to their being out of one's control. If he travels and wishes to take one of his wives with him, he should draw lots between them.

9- If the wife violates her marital duties, he should admonish her till she fulfills them. His admonition should range from counsel to reprimand and warning. Being futile, he should desert her for not more than three days. If useless, he should lightly beat her avoiding her face and bleeding.

10- Going into his wife, man has to adopt certain manners. First, he should mention the Name of Allah and avoid the direction of the *Qiblah*. He and his wife should be wrapped rather being totally nude. He should begin with some sort of flirting and joking, kissing and hugging. In intercourse, getting satisfied, he should afford her ample time to get satisfied too. In addition, desiring to go into his wife once more, a man should first cleanse his private parts and do ablution. Man should not cut his hair or his nails until he gets washed. As for man's coitus interrupts, it is permissible but not preferable.

11- If gifted with a child, man should not feel happier if the newborn was a male baby rather than a female, since none knows where goodness lies other than Allah. On its delivery, the father should reiterate the normal call of prayers in its ears and choose a good name for it; the Prophet (peace and blessings of Allah be upon him) said,

> "`Abdullah and `Abd Ar-Rahman are the best names in the sight of Allah."
>
> (Reported by Muslim)

12- A father isn't allowed to give his children ominous names. The Prophet (peace and blessings of Allah be upon him) changed similar names of some of his Companions (may Allah be pleased with them all.) Furthermore, a father should offer a banquet. A child should be circumcised.

Divorce

Though permitted by Allah, divorce is the most detestable act to Him. A husband should not divorce his wife suddenly. She should not also enforce him to divorce her. Seeking to divorce a wife, a husband should observe four things,

1- He should divorce her in an interval between her menstruations where no sexual intercourse with his wife has taken place.

2- He should also divorce her one time in order to be able to revoke her.

3- He should make up her injury by giving her a satisfactory payment. Once Al-Hasan divorced his wife and gave her ten thousand *dirhams*, whereupon she commented, "A little pay from a dear deserter."

4- A man should not disclose his wife's secrets. The Prophet (peace and blessings of Allah be upon him) said,

> "The most wicked among the people in the eye of Allah on the Day of Judgment is the man who goes to his wife and she comes to him, and then he divulges her secret."
>
> (Reported by Muslim)

Complementary Manners

A husband commands very great rights over his wife so much that she is required to obey him willingly and happily. Such rights range between two important factors, namely,

1- Chastity and protection of his honor.

2- Contentment.

Early Muslim women abided by these two norms. When a husband left his house to earn living, his wife would say, "Lo! Beware of illegal gains; we can bear hunger rather than torture in the Hellfire." A wife should not squander her man's property. If she spends it by his leave, she shares the reward. Otherwise, she is guilty while he alone receives the reward. Her parents should inculcate such manners in her long before she gets married. A woman should not leave her house especially when her husband is absent. A wife also exerts her utmost to please her husband. She should be faithful to her husband in all aspects of her life. She should not admit any one into her husband's house if he hates him. Her household and its prosperity should be her first priority.

III. Earning Livelihood and Subsistence

Out of His Wisdom, the Almighty Allah has created this world for man to seek subsistence either for his life in this world or that to come. Here, we will deal with manners pertaining to earning living through various crafts.

Merits of Earning Living

Allah says in the Glorious Qur'an,

﴿*We made the Day as means of subsistence.*﴾
(An-Naba': 11)

Here, the Almighty enumerates His favors amongst which is subsistence. Allah also says,

﴿*We have provided you therein –Earth- with means for subsistence; small are the thanks that you give!*﴾
(Al-A`raf: 10)

In this verse the Almighty clearly states that people should thank Him for this favor.

Elsewhere He says,

﴿*It is no crime in you if you seek of the bounty of your Lord.*﴾
(Al-Baqarah: 198)

Likewise, the Prophet (peace and blessings be upon him) said,

"*Allah loves thecraftsman.*"
(Reported by Al-Tabarani)

He (peace and blessings of Allah be upon him) also said,

> "No one has ever eaten something better than what he has earned; verily, prophet Dawud used to eat from what he earned."
> (Reported by Al-Bukhari)

In another report, he (peace and blessings of Allah be upon him) said,

> "Zakariyah (peace and blessings of Allah be upon him) was a carpenter."
> (Reported by Muslim)

Ibn `Abbas said,

> "Adam was a farmer, Nuh a carpenter, Idris a tailor, Ibrahim and Lut farmers, Salih a trader, Dawud a smith, Musa, Shu`ayb and Muhammad (peace and blessings of Allah be upon them) tended the sheep."

It is also reported that Luqman told his son,

"Son! Subsist on lawful means, for in case of poverty, man's religion could be weakened, and his intellect and honor may be undermined. The worst is people's disdain for him."

Imam Ahmad was once asked about a person confining himself at home or in the mosque saying, "I wouldn't do anything till I receive my subsistence [from Allah]?" He replied, "He is ignorant. Hasn't he listened to the Prophet's saying,

> "Verily, Allah has put my subsistence under my spear."
> (Reported by Al-Bukhari)

Also, he (peace and blessings of Allah be upon him) referred to birds as,

"Going hungry in the morning and returning satiated in the afternoon."
(Reported by At-Tirmidhi)

The Prophet's Companions followed all lawful roads seeking subsistence. Abu Sulayman Ad-Darani said, "In my view, worship doesn't mean performing prayers while others support you. One should secure his food then observe acts of worship. If argued, Abu Ad-Darda' said, "I observed both trade and worship but they didn't come together, thus I preferred the latter. In fact, trade is undertaken to achieve self-content, supporting one's family and giving charity. If wealth is solely sought thereby, it is abominable."

A contract should fulfill four conditions, namely,

a) Validity

It should be valid. For example if it is a sale contract, it has to have three aspects; contracting parties, object and wording.

1- **The contracting parties:** A merchandiser should not conclude any contract with an insane person, or a slave unless his master gives permission, a dependant unless his guardian allows him to do so. However Imam Ash-Shafi`i excludes dependants' and the blinds' contracts. But the latter transactions are truly valid. A trader should deal only with pious people who earn their property through lawful means.

2- **The object:** Dogs are forbidden goods due to their impurity. The same rule applies to insects, lutes, woodwind, and statues. A seller should possess the good so much that he is able to deliver to the purchaser. If not, such as birds flying or a fleeing slave, he can't sell it.

3- **Wording of a contract**, i.e., proposal on one side and acceptance on the other: According to some scholars, proposal should come first then acceptance, be it in the past tense or in the present one. Abu Ya`la confines this ruling to limited cases, where the commodity isn't expensive. In fact, both aspects should be affected to avoid the possibility of dispute. Usury has been strongly condemned and prohibited in the Qur'an, therefore; it must be shunned. People should be well-informed about its ruling and its vile outcomes. All ruling pertaining to other transactions should be made known to people.

b. Doing justice and avoiding inequity

The second aspect is doing justice from both parties and avoiding inequity with its two types, general and specific.

1- The former refers to monopoly. It is forbidden since it leads to an increase of prices and tightening the grip of living over people. Monopoly signifies hoarding goods and selling them in time of price increase. However, if a person harvests a certain crop from his own field and stores it, he is not a monopolist. Generally speaking, people's food should not be made a commodity.

2- The latter stands for falsely praising a certain good or rather conceal its defect; thus harming a would-be buyer. The Prophet (peace and blessings of Allah be upon him) said,

"Whoever cheats us doesn't belong to us"
(Reported by Muslim)

Cheating is forbidden in all aspects of human life. Imam Ahmad was once asked about darning ropes whereupon he replied,

"Its seller mustn't hide its defect."

Scale should also be justly fulfilled. Mixing food with dust then weighing it is totally *Haram*. Bargaining over other buyers to increase a good's price is also condemned.

c) Good Treatment

The Almighty has commanded us to be just and treat others in good terms. In selling, a seller should be moderate warding off defraud. A buyer may offer an excessive price for a certain good due to his dire need for it, in that case the seller should not be opportunist. Reaching the payment due, he should ask for his money moderately. He may also alleviate the debt in case of adversity.

d) Trader's concern about his religion

A trader should be well-concerned about his religion and avoid being wholly preoccupied with worldly affairs. This is achieved through fulfilling six criteria,

1- Good Intention. He should seek thereby to achieve self-content, free himself from covetousness and support his family.

2- He should seek thereby fulfilling a communal obligation. If trade is not practiced by any one, people's lives would be undermined. However, some crafts are more important in order to fill a gap in the community. A teacher of the Qur'an should not receive any payment for teaching the Qur'an.

3- He should not be totally distracted by the worldly gaieties; thus leading him to forget all about the Hereafter. He should devote his life to the life to come while undertaking his trade. Early Muslim traders dedicated their whole lives to the Hereafter while observing their works. Therefore, he should keep prayers in their due times.

4- He should continually remember the Almighty in the market.

5- He should not be greed so much that he reaches the market the first and leave it the last one.

6- He should also shun suspicious transactions. He should consult his heart in all cases in order to avoid mischief.

IV. The Lawful and the Prohibited

Everyone should know that Seeking for the *Lawful* is obligatory. However, many ignorant persons assume that there is nothing lawful. They look suspiciously at every thing. This is sheer ignorance. The Prophet (peace and blessings of Allah be upon him) said,

> *"Both legal and illegal things are obvious, and in between them are (suspicious) doubtful matters."*
> (Reported by Al-Bukhari)

Being an insidious innovation, it has been greatly harmful and dangerously undermining people's religion. Hence, it should be refuted clarifying the difference between the lawful, the doubtful and the illegal matters.

Virtues of the Lawful and Evils of the Prohibited

The Almighty Allah says in the Glorious Qur'an,

> ❴*O you Messengers! Enjoy (all) things good and pure and work righteousness for I am well-acquainted with (all) that you do.*❵
> (Al-Mu'minun: 51)

He also says,

> ❴*And do not eat up your property among yourselves for vanities.*❵
> (Al-Baqarah: 188)

The Prophet (peace and blessings of Allah be upon him) said,

> *"O people, Allah is Good and He therefore, accepts only that which is good. And Allah commanded the believers as He commanded the Messengers by saying, ⟨O Messengers, eat of the good things, and do good deeds; verily I am aware of what you do⟩ (As-Sajdah: 51). And He said, ⟨O those who believe, eat of the good things that We gave you⟩ (Al-Baqarah: 172). He then made a mention of a person who travels widely, his hair disheveled and covered with dust. He lifts his hand towards the sky (and thus makes the supplication), "O Lord, O Lord," whereas his diet is unlawful, his drink is unlawful, and his clothes are unlawful and his nourishment is unlawful. How can then his supplication be accepted!"*

(Reported by Muslim)

Sa'd ibn Abi Waqqas (may Allah be pleased with him) once asked the Prophet (peace and blessings of Allah be upon him) how to have his supplications answered by Allah, Most High. The Prophet (peace and blessings of Allah be upon him) said,

> *"To have your supplication answered, your food should be lawful."*

(Reported by At-Tabarani)

Abu Bakr (may Allah be pleased with him) once ate something. Doubting its legality, he forcibly vomited it at once.

Degrees of the Lawful and the Prohibited

All the lawful things are good but some are better than others. The same applies to the prohibited. It ranges from bad to worse and the worst in accordance with the gravity of the sin. For example, taking something through an invalid contract is forbidden whereas extortion is extremely forbidden and entails a sever punishment since it involves harming others and violating basic Islamic rulings. The same applies to appropriating an orphan's property or that of a poor or a righteous person.

Degrees of Piety

Piety has four degrees, namely,

1- Disregarding all prohibited things.

2- Warding off all doubtful matters. The Prophet (peace and blessings of Allah be upon him) said,

> *"Leave dubious matters to certain ones."*
> (Reported by At-Tirmidhi)

3- Giving up some lawful means lest they should lead to unlawful ones.

4- Giving up all worldly-related affairs and sticking to divine ones. This state is entertained by the righteous. Yahya An-Naysaburi once dosed himself with medicine, then his wife asked him to move around so that medicine would penetrate into his body and be effective. He replied, "I don't know such a kind of movement. Actually, I have been considering my actions for thirty years." He declined a single move since he didn't intend thereby to strengthen his faith. In fact, piety has a starting point and an end. In between lie degrees of caution. The degree of caution one follows determines man's movement on the Straight Path on the Day of Judgement.

Levels of Doubtful Matters

The Prophet, peace and blessings of Allah be upon him, said,

> *"Both lawful and prohibited things are obvious, and in between them are (suspicious) doubtful matters. So whoever forsakes those doubtful things lest he may commit a sin, will definitely avoid what is clearly illegal; and whoever indulges in these (suspicious) doubtful things bravely, is likely to commit what is clearly illegal. Sins are Allah's Hima (i.e. private pasture) and whoever pastures (his sheep) near it, is likely to get in it at any moment."*
>
> (Reported by Al-Bukhari)

In this *Hadith*, the Prophet (peace and blessings of Allah be upon him) has classified things into three categories, namely, lawful, prohibited and doubtful matters.

First of all, lawful things as those matters which are clearly premitted as well as their causes, such as water received from rain before stored by anyone. On the other hand, the prohibited is the contrary, such as wine and urine, usury and transgression. A third group is dubious matters. It is a thing which is originally lawful but its lawfulness may became doubtful due to an external reason. Doubtful matters has two famous examples, namely,

First, doubting the cause of legality and prohibition. It has four subdivisions,

1- Doubting the permissibility of a certain thing which is originally permitted; thus turning it forbidden. For example, one may hunt an animal which falls in water. Finding it later on, he becomes unable to determine whether it died due to his shot or drowning. Therefore, it is prohibited

2- Doubting the prohibition of a certain thing which is originally permitted. For example, seeing a bird flying. A man might say, "If it were a raven, my wife would be divorced." Another man might say, "If it weren't, my wife would be divorced." But it is unfeasible to determine whether it is a raven or not. However, forbiddance is precluded; but both wives should rather be divorced.

3- Something may originally be illegal, but it becomes permitted due to a new means leading thereto which is generally lawful. For example, one may hunt an animal which runs out of sight. Searching for it, one finds it injured only with his shot. Therefore, it becomes allowed, otherwise, it is forbidden.

4- On the other hand, something may originally be valid but another lawful means turns it illegal, such as doubting the impurity of water in one of two jars due to a certain trace of impurity. Thus, it is forbidden to use this water.

Second, both the lawful and the prohibited may be confused so much that they become unidentifiable such as,

1- Confusing a dead animal with a *Shar`i* slaughtered one. Doubt here results in forbiddance.

2- Confusing a limited prohibited thing with an unlimited lawful one, as if one being unable to identify his foster mother or sister from amongst various women in a big town. Accordingly, he can marry whose daughter he likes; since it is greatly unfeasible and gravely harmful to turn them all exogamous to him. During the Prophet's (peace and blessings of Allah be upon him) and his Companions' era (may Allah be pleased with them), lawful property was mixed with unlawful ones, but transactions weren't totally abandoned.

3- Confusing an unlimited prohibited thing with similar lawful one. This ruling applies to properties in our modern age. However, if something proves that it is illegal, it must be avoided; as if receiving something from a tyrant ruler. Otherwise, it is allowed. During the Prophet's (peace and blessings of Allah be upon him) and his Companions' lives (may Allah be pleased with them) some illegal property was mixed with lawful ones, but none of them ever prevented people from transactions. Hadn't they been allowed, people's interests would have been hindered. Likewise, `Umar (may Allah be pleased with him) performed ablution from a Christian's pot, though Christians were, and are still, known for drinking wine and eating swine which are prohibited in Islam. Christians also don't cleanse themselves after answering the call of nature.

Third, investigating the lawful and the prohibited. Having food served to us or being given as a gift, we should neither declare our doubt as to its validity nor give it up altogether. In fact, investigating such a thing's status is sometimes obligatory, forbidden, abominable or commendable. In fact, a question reflects doubt because of the thing itself or its owner. As for the owner, his character may be unknown to the receiver, i.e. there is no certain proof that indicates his being a tyrant or a righteous person. In this case, investigation is neither obligatory nor permitted at all; since it harms him. Thus, we should not argue that his personality is suspicious, since suspicion should be grounded; as if adopting manners of tyrants and their customs. As for the property itself, it may be mixed with illegal ones. For example, prohibited food may be displayed in a market for sale. Then traders buy it. Customers are not demanded to investigate the status of this food. However, if most of what traders have is known to be prohibited, investigation becomes obligatory; otherwise it is rightly commendable.

Practically speaking, suspicion initiate investigation. Thus, its absence repudiates its effect.

Fourth, repentance from economic inequity: If some one repents while possessing property: some of which is lawful and the other is illegal. If identifiable, it becomes resolvable. If not, it may have equivalents such as cash, grains and fats whose amounts are ascertained. In this case, it must be singled out. If not ascertained, one has two ways out,

1- Either to follow the most likely view,

2- Or to behave according to certainty as entailed by piety.

Singling the prohibited property out, if it has a certain owner, he must restore it to its rightful owner or his inheritors. Being unable to determine its owner, he has to give it as a charity. If the property happens to be from spoils and the like, it should be spent in the Muslims' interests.

Having lawful property and a doubtful one, the Muslim should suffice himself with the lawful one. If his parents possess illegal property, he should not share their food. If doubtful, he should appease them. If not satisfied, he should only eat a little.

Receiving Gifts from Rulers

Receiving something from a ruler, one should consider the cause behind it as well as his eligibility to receive it. He should also consider the amount received. Early Muslims refrained from taking such things. Others took them but gave them as a charity. However, we should shun such gifts, since their origin is clearly identified. Furthermore, they are received after humiliation, request and approval of mischief. Some early Muslims declined these gifts arguing that other eligible persons didn't receive their dues.

Dealing with Rulers, Officials and Tyrants

Dealing with rulers, officials and tyrants, one has three cases,

1. **Approaching them**: This is the worst of all. The Prophet (peace and blessings of Allah be upon him) said,

   "Approaching rulers lead to temptations."
   (Reported by At-Tirmidhi)

   He also said,

   "The nearer a person becomes to a ruler, the more far he becomes from Allah."
   (Reported by Abu Dawud)

   Hudhayfah (may Allah be pleased with him) said, "Ward off instances of temptation!" Asked about them, he replied, "They are rulers' doors. You may approach a ruler and approve his lies and falsely praise him." Once a ruler addressed a mystic, "Why don't you visit me?" He replied, "I do so lest I become tempted by your company, and deprived by your severance. You don't have what I yearn for, nor do I have what claims your wrath. Those who approach you seek content with you, but I'm content with Him [Allah] Who has provided you." Reaching rulers may incur sins; such as being hosted in an appropriated place or even served by a similar gadget. Even if they happen to be lawful, one may be induced to commit other sinful acts such as prostrating before him, standing in reverence for him, serving him or dealing with him modestly due to his office. Such things are purely forbidden. The ruling also applies to reaching the rich in a modest way because of their richness.

Reaching rulers may drive a man to pray for them, praise them or falsely approve their utterance, gestures or even features of their faces. One may also display his adherence and allegiance to them. It is reported that,

> *"Saying, "Long live" for a tyrant is sign of one's readiness to disobey Allah"*
> (Reported by Al-Shawkany)

If one is obliged to pray for such a kind of rulers, he should rather say, "May Allah guide you" and the like.

Furthermore, approaching rulers may drive man to tacitly approve their wrongdoing, such as using silver pots or silk clothes and sheets. The same rule applies to listening to vile utterances from them, since he should command the good and forbid the evil. Arguing that he may be afraid, in fact we agree with this point. However, he should rather avoid sins and mistakes as far as he can. Hadn't he reached rulers, he would have been exempted from commanding the right and forbidding the wrong. If one ascertains mischief in a certain place and his inability to reform it, he must shun it.

Justification of Reaching Tyrant Rulers

If man is secured against all the above-mentioned harms, though untenable, his heart can be tainted, due to their negligence of Allah's bounties over them. Others visitors can be seduced to follow their abominable example. Sa`id ibn Al-Musayb was asked to pledge his allegiance to Al-Walid and Sulayman sons of Abd-Almalik. He opined, "I will never pledge allegiance to two rulers at one and the same time so long as day and night follow each other." When asked, "You may enter from one door and exit from another." But he strongly declined. Accordingly he was severely hurt and dressed in the harshest clothes.

Against this background, reaching tyrant rulers may have two justifications,

i) Settling a grave dispute that may lead to harmful effects.

ii) To support an oppressed Muslim provided that one should avoid sycophancy and flattery.

2- **Hosting rulers:** Receiving a ruler at one's home, one should respond to his greeting. He should also be served generously due to his being a Muslim whereby he becomes praiseworthy. On the other hand he is blameworthy due to his tyranny. In that way, receiving a ruler in the middle of people, one should receive him properly lest that he would be harmed or the subjects would be disordered. He should also advise the ruler and inform him of the gravity of what he commits in case he ignores it. He should inform them of the penalty prepared by the Almighty to such sin which he knows to be illegal. Likewise, he should guide him to the ways where the people's interests are fulfilled.

3- **Avoiding them completely**: This is the best. However, he should abhor them due to their transgression, declining to meet them, to praise them, to inquire about them, to approach their courtiers and never regret missing their gifts. Someone said, "Dealing with kings lasts only for one day. Yesterday was a good memory. Tomorrow is dreadful for both of us. But, what about today? We both wonder!"

Receiving a certain property from a ruler to distribute it among the poor while it has a rightful owner, one mustn't take it. Otherwise, he can distribute it. Some scholars are known to have declined doing likewise.

V. Friendship and Brotherhood

Intimacy comes from good manners and severance from bad ones. Good manners initiate mutual affection and harmony whereas bad manners entail hatred and dissension. Commending good manners, the Prophet (peace and blessings of Allah be upon him) said,

> *"Nothing is heavier in the believer's scale on the Day of Judgement than his good manners."*
> (Reported by At-Tirmidhi)

In another report, he said,

> *"The most endeared and nearest of you to me on the Day of Judgement are those whose manners are the best. The most abhorrent and farthest of you to me on the Day of Judgement are those who have bad manners."*
> (Reported by At-Tirmidhi)

The Prophet (peace and blessings of Allah be upon him) was once asked about the best things leading to Paradise. He answered,

> *"Fearing Allah and good manners."*
> (Reported by At-Tirmidhi)

As for love for Allah's sake, The Prophet (peace and blessings of Allah be upon him) said,

> *"Allah will give shade, to seven, on the Day when there will be no shade but His... two persons who love each other only for Allah's sake and they meet and part in Allah's cause only."*
>
> (Reported by Al-Bukhari)

The Almighty said in a *Qudsi Hadith*,

> *"My love is due to those love one another in My cause, who spend in My cause and those who visit each other in My cause."*
>
> (Reported by Imam Malik)

In another report the Prophet (peace and blessings of Allah be upon him) said,

> *"The most reliable hold of Iman –faith- is to love in Allah's cause and hate in His cause."*
>
> (Reported by At-Tabarani)

It is self-evident loving in Allah's cause initiates hating in His cause. One may love someone due to his obedience to the Almighty. Thus, if he disobeys Allah, he will give up his love to him and instead hates him. Likewise, if someone possesses commendable qualities and abominable ones, he becomes lovable in one aspect and detestable in another. A Muslim should be loved for his being as such, and detested for his disobedience if any. However, inadvertent mistakes should be overlooked. If he insists on sinning, he should obviously be hated and severed.

Kinds of Disobedients to the Almighty

1- **Disbelievers:** If they stay in the abode of war, they deserve being killed and enslaved. This is the utmost humiliation they can receive. If they are subjects in the Muslim country, they should rather be disregarded. If it happens that a non believer greets a Muslim, we should reply, "The same to you." We should avoid dealing with them or sharing their food. We should not talk at length with them as if they were friends.

2- **Innovators:** They may peddle their innovations, which turn their adherents unbelievers. They are more harmful than non-Muslim subjects since they neither pay *Jizyah* nor are tolerated by an agreement of protection. If they do not lead to disbelief, they hold a milder position. They are more condemned than disbelievers, since their harm is transitive, in the sense that they can mislead others. Accordingly, they should strongly and clearly be disregarded and rebuked. As for other ordinary innovators who cannot propagate their innovations, they pose an easier case. They should be kindly advised. If futile, they should be disdained and scorned. If they insist on their misdeeds, they should decisively be severed in order to annihilate innovations.

3- **Practical disobedience rather than creedal one:** If a man's disobedience harms others such as maltreatment, anger, giving false testimony and backbiting, we should severe him. The same ruling applies to people who commit despicable acts such as mixing of men and women, intoxicating, theft, illicit intercourse or negligence of religious duties. Coming across him while committing any of these vile actions, he must be prevented therefrom.

Attributes of Friends

We should know that friendship is a very serious affair. Therefore, we should choose our friends carefully. In that way, a friend should possess certain qualities. Each one opts for certain qualities according to his/her desired ends deemed from befriending someone. These ends can be worldly such as becoming rich, authoritative or even enjoying intimacy. They can also be religiously motivated such as seeking knowledge. Furthermore, friendship may also incite by achieving self-content, securing support in times of adversity and ease and enjoying intercession in the Hereafter. Some early Muslims said,

> *"You should have as much brothers as you can for a believer enjoys intercession [to one another on the Day of Judgment]."*

In brief, a friend should possess five qualities, i.e., he should be sane and good-natured. He should not also be an innovator or an obscene person nor should he be preoccupied with worldly gaieties. Sanity is the pillar of every thing. A foolish friend is good for nothing, since he harms his friend where he expects to benefit him. Good manners are also necessary, since a sane person may be easily irritable or rather possessed by his desires. Likewise, an obscene person never fears the Almighty; thus he is constantly unreliable. Likewise, befriending an innovator possibly supports his innovation and undermines man's dignity and honor. `Umar ibn Al-Khattab said, "Befriend the truthful and live under their shield. In prosperity, they enhance you and, in adversity, they support you. Discredit not your brother unless it is grounded. Keep away from your enemy. Be on guard against your friend but for the trustworthy who fears the Almighty. Keep away from obscene lest his obscenity disgraces you. Entrust him. Consult the righteous people only." Some friends of Al-Hasan once paid him a visit while he was sleeping. They were invited and served some fruits. They accepted the invitation and ate of the fruits. When informed of this, he remarked, "May Allah bless you, true brothers do like what you have done." Once Fath of Mosul visited his friend `Isa At-Tammar, but he found him out. He asked his maid-servant to bring him his purse of money. She did and he took two *dirhams*. When `Isa returned, she informed him of what had happened. He told her, "If this truly has happened, I will set you free." Thus she was freed.

Rights of Brotherhood

Brotherhood commands various rights, namely,

1- **Fulfilling brother's needs:** Whenever requested to help a brother, one should willingly and happily hasten to do so. In fact, one should be ready to assist his brother without even being asked thereto. In addition, a brother's need should be given priority over one's own needs.

2- **Heedful of your words:** You should be heedful of your words before your brother, in the sense that you should not highlight his defects either in his presence or in his absence. Likewise, you should give up arguing with him and troubling him with irrelevant questions. You should not also reveal your brother's secrets even after severance. You should neither disgrace his kin nor inform him of others' claims against him.

3- **Irritate him not:** You should avoid irritating him as far as you can unless you urge him to do the good and forbid the evil.

We should know that none is perfect. We look for a brother whose good traits overcome his bad ones. Ibn El-Mubarak remarked, "Believers find excuses but hypocrites hunt errors." Al-Fudayl said, "Chivalry necessitates forgiving brothers' errors." You should also avoid suspicion for the Prophet (peace and blessings of Allah be upon him) said,

> *"Beware of suspicion, for suspicion is the worst of false tales."*
>
> (Reported by Al-Bukhari)

Practically speaking, suspicion leads to spying, while overlooking others' deficiencies is obligatory. Furthermore, man's faith becomes full-fledged only when he loves for his brother what he loves for himself. At least you should treat your brother in the same way you require him to treat you. In fact, every one wants his brother to disregard his defects and cover his infirmities. Allah says in the Qur'an,

> ﴿*Those who, when they have to receive by measure from men, exact full measure. But when they have to give by measure or weight to men, give less than due.*﴾
>
> (Al-Mutafifin: 2-3)

You should also perceive that frequent argumentation saws malice and hatred among brothers. It is almost instigated by one's desire for distinction and depreciating of his counterpart. Arguing with a brother leads him to ignorance and foolishness, to inadvertence or heedlessness. Such things harm the brother's feelings and incite enmity.

4- **Pleasing one's brother:** You should also do and say things that please your brother. Only the dead are satisfied with silence. Brotherhood necessitates exchanging benefits. In that way, a brother should talk with his brother about his life, his problems and all other affairs. In addition, you should also inform your brother of your love of him. The Prophet (peace and blessings of Allah be upon him) said,

> *"Loving your brother, you should inform him thereof."*
>
> (Reported by At-Tirmidhi)

You should also call him with the dearest name to him. 'Umar ibn Al-Khattab (may Allah be pleased with him) remarked, "Three things enhance good relations with your brother: greeting him when you behold him, making a room for him to sit with you and calling him with the dearest name to him." Likewise, you should remember your brother in good terms before responsible persons. You should mention in praise your brother's children, righteous deeds, good manners and so on and so forth. You should also inform him of other's praise of him. You should thank him for his favors and defend him in his absence. The Prophet (peace and blessings of Allah be upon him) said,

> *"A Muslim is a brother of another Muslim, so he should not oppress him, nor should he hand him over to an oppressor"*
>
> (Reported by Muslim)

If one did not defend his brother, then he did humiliate him. To measure how far you are a good brother and ready to defend your brother, ponder over the following:

i. Imagine that what was said against him was said about you in his presence; therefore say what you would like him to say about you if he were in your place.

ii. Imagine that he hears your defense; therefore say what you like him to hear. Your praise of him should not differ whether he is present or absent, otherwise one becomes a hypocrite.

You should also exert utmost efforts to impart knowledge to your brother. Man's need for knowledge is not less important than his need for money. Thus, you should advise him secretly. Therefore, whenever you find an error, you should reform both kindly and secretly. If he insists, you should boycott him.

5- You should make *Du`aa'* for your brother in his lifetime and after his demise. The Prophet (peace and blessing of Allah be upon him) said,

> *"There is no believing servant who supplicates for his brother behind his back (in his absence) that the Angels do not say: The same be for you too."*
>
> (Reported by Muslim)

Abu Ad-Dara' (may Allah be pleased with him) used to supplicate for numerous brothers while naming them. Ahmad ibn Hanbal also prayed at the last part of night -Sahar- for six persons. As for supplicating for brothers after their death, `Amr ibn Huraith remarked, "supplicating for a dead brother, an angel would take your supplication to the dead brother and say, "You lonely resident in this tomb, here is a gift from a loving brother."

6- You should be loyal and truthful to your brother. Loyalty signifies constantly loving him till his death and continuing afterwards the same love with his family. The Prophet (peace and blessing of Allah be upon him) treated an old woman kindly and pointed out,

> *"She used to visit us during Khadiyjah's life (may Allah be pleased with her); in fact good commitment is a part of Iman -faith."*
>
> (Reported by Al-Hakim)

Loyalty also entails maintaining modesty whatever rank you may achieve. You should not also tacitly approve of his negligence of some religious duties.

7- You should give up what is called "mannerism" and lead a reasonable life. In that way you should not overburden him at all. Your loving him should be for Allah alone, being blessed by his supplications, seeking support in religion. You should avoid dealing with him in excessive modesty in order not to drive him to feigned demureness. You should deal with your friend as if you were alone as highlighted by Ja`far ibn Muhammad. A wise man said, "Mannerism curtail intimacy."

Complementary Manners

You should show manners without pride, and be modest without humility. You should meet your friend and enemy alike with neither fear nor humbleness. You should avoid interlocking your fingers, spitting and yawning in the middle of people. You should listen carefully to your brother. Do not ask him to repeat his words. Your attire and appearance should be modest. You should also deal kindly with your household, with being neither stiff nor lenient. You should not banter with your servants in order to keep your dignity. Walking down a street, do not look backwards. You should avoid company of rulers, but if you are obliged, you should ward off sinning. You must not reveal rulers' secrets. Being drawn close to him, you should be very careful. When chatting up freely with you, you should be heedful of their unstable modes. Deal with him as gently as a child. You should never interfere between him and his household or courtiers. You should know that "a friend in need is a friend indeed." Your honor commands priority over your property. Joining a group, one should get seated in a modest place. You should avoid sitting on roads. If happened, you should lower your gaze, assist the oppressed and guide the lost. You must not spit in the direction of the *Qiblah*, but rather on your left hand side under your left foot. Beware of joining the grassroots. If any, never get mixed in their vile acts or in their idle talk. Give up excessive jesting, since it invites envy and boldness.

Rights of Muslims, Kinship, Neighborhood and Ownership

You should greet the Muslim whenever you meet him, accept his invitation, visit him when he is ill and follow his funeral. You should fulfill his oath, advise him when he consults you. You should maintain his dignity in his absence. You should not hurt Muslims in any way. You should not backbite them to one another. You should not severe a Muslim brother for over three days. Abu Ayyub Ansiri reported Allah's Messenger (peace and blessings of Allah be upon him) as saying,

> *"It is not permissible for a Muslim to have estranged relations with his brother beyond three nights, the one turning one way and the other turning the other way when they meet; the better of the two is one who is the first to give a greeting."*
>
> (Reported by Muslim)

Such a kind of estrangement applies to worldly affairs. However, estrangement due to violation of religious duties should last unless he repents and reforms himself. You should treat all Muslims hospitably as far as you can. Before entering a Muslim's house, you should seek permission three times. If no permission is given, you should return. You should receive all people according to their psychological needs. An ignorant should not be received with knowledge. You should honor the elderly and have mercy on the young. You should meet all people gently, fulfill their promises and treat them justly. You should avoid troubling them, as you want them not to trouble you. Al-Hasan said, "Allah inspired four words to Adam saying, 'They cover every thing. The first is for you, I reward you for your deeds. The second is for Me, i.e. to worship none but Me Alone. The third is between Me and you, i.e. you are to ask Me and I am to answer your supplication. The fourth is between you and fellow humans, you treat people as you wish them to deal with you."

Contemplating over Allah's screen spread over humans, you should entertain the same kindness. Allah has determined that the crime of illicit intercourse should be established by four upright witnesses, who should have observed the factual act of intercourse. This is quite scarce. You should also ward suspicious situations, in order to avoid distrust. You should also intercede for his fellow Muslims to fulfill their needs. You should greet every Muslim and shake hands with them. Anas ibn Malik reported that Allah's Prophet (peace and blessings of Allah be upon him) said,

> *"When two Muslims meet and shake hands, Allah has pledged Himself to hear their supplications to one another and forgive them before they disperse."*
> (Reported by Ahmad)

It is not harmful to kiss the hand of righteous people. Ibn `Abbas (may Allah be pleased with him) go in front of the camel of Zaid ibn Thabit (may Allah be pleased with him). You should stand when receiving righteous persons. As for bending before them, it is not allowed. You should keep your brother's honor, his life and his property against violation. When inflicted with an adversity, you should give condolence to him. `A'ishah (may Allah be pleased with her) reported,

> "A person sought permission from Allah's Messenger (peace and blessings of Allah be upon him) to see him. He said: Grant him permission. (and also added,) He is a bad son of his tribe or he is a bad person of his tribe. When he came in the Prophet talked with him gently. `A'ishah is reported to have said: 'O, Allah's Messenger, you said about him what you had to say (i.e. that he is a bad person) and then you treated him with kindness.' The Prophet, peace and blessings be upon him, said, 'O, `A'ishah, verily in the eye of Allah, the worst amongst the persons in rank on the Day of Resurrection is one whom the people abandon or desert out of the fear of indecency.'"
>
> (Reported by Muslim)

You should avoid the rich and deal with the poor. You should support the orphans and visit the sick. Visiting a sick person, you should pray for his speed recovery, curtail your stay and lower your gaze. The sick person should follow the Prophet's instructions (peace and blessings of Allah be upon him) as reported by `Uthman ibn Abu Al-`Aas,

> "Put your hand where you feel the pain, then say three times, in the name of Allah. Then repeat seven times, I seek refuge with Allah and His Might from what I feel and fear."
>
> (Reported by Muslim)

A sick person should endure patiently with neither disgust nor complaint. He should constantly ask Allah for speed recovery. You should also follow Muslim funerals. Al-`A`mash said, "Following funerals, we could not ascertain the deceased's relatives due to the prevailing sadness. You should also visit Muslim graveyards, supplicate for the dead and move one's heart. Following a funeral, you should walk reverently, avoid speaking, think of death and getting prepared therefore.

A neighbor commands various rights more than those enjoyed due to Islam. He may have three rights because of his being a Muslim, a kin and a neighbor at the same time. He may also command two due to his being a Muslim and a neighbor. Even an unbeliever enjoys the right of brotherhood.

A Muslim should not only refrain from harming his neighbors but also endure his harm. A neighbor should be treated and greeted gently. You should visit your sick neighbor, condolence him in times of adversity and congratulate him in times of prosperity. You should overlook his errors. You should not peep into a neighbor's house. His honor should be preserved.

Rights of Kinship

`A'isha (may Allah be pleased with her) reported Allah's Messenger (peace and blessings of Allah be upon him) as saying'

> "The tie of kinship is suspended to the Throne and says: He who unites me Allah would unite him and he who severed me Allah would sever him."
> (Reported by Muslim)

Abu Huraira (may Allah be pleased with him) also reported,

> "A person said, Allah's Messenger, I have relatives with whom I try, to have close relationship, but they sever (this relation). I treat them well, but they treat me ill. I am sweet to them but they are harsh towards me. Upon this he (the

Holy Prophet) said: If it is so as you say, then you in fact throw hot ashes (upon their faces) and there would always remain with you on behalf of Allah (an Angel to support you) who would keep you dominant over them so long as you adhere to this (path of righteousness)."
(Reported by Al-Bukhari)

The Prophet (peace and blessings of Allah be upon him) said,

"Al-Wasil is not the one who recompenses the good done to him by his relatives, but Al-Wasil is the one who keeps good relations with those relatives who had severed the bond of kinship with him."
(Reported by Muslim)

As for rights of children, parents are naturally inclined towards them and are ready to care for them. However, they may passively affect them due to excessive tenderness. Therefore, Allah says in the *Qur'an*,

❮*Save yourselves and your families from a Fire whose fuel are men and stones.*❯
(At-Tahrim: 6)

Exegetes of the Qur'an remarked that it means, "educate and discipline you offspring." Parents should choose good names for their children. Becoming seven years old, they command them to perform *Salah* and get them circumcised. Reaching maturity, they get them married. Concerning servants, their masters should feed them, clothe them and entrust them with appropriate works. They should not be disdained. Rather they should be forgiven in case of erring, remembering Allah's Forgiveness.

Seclusion and Solitude

It is frequently asked, whish is better, solitude or companionship? However, each of them has its own virtues and vices. Mystics have opted for the former. It has also been adopted by Sufyan Ath-Thawri, Ibrahim b. Adham, Dawud At-Ta'I, Al-Fudail and Bishr. On the other hand, Sa`id b. Al-Musayib, Shurayh, Ash-Sha`bi and Ibn El-Mubarak have preferred Keeping company.

In fact, each group has sought to support their view. As for the former, they quote Abu Sa`id Khudri saying,

> *"A man came to the Holy Prophet (peace and blessings of Allah be upon him) and said, Who is the best of men? He replied: A man who fights in the way of Allah; spending his wealth and staking his life. The man then asked: Who is next to him (in excellence)? He said: Next to him is a believer who lives in a mountain gorge worshipping hid Lord and sparing men from his mischief."*
> (Reported by Muslim)

The Prophet (peace and blessings of Allah be upon him) also said,

> *"Have full control over your tongue, stay at your home and regret committing sins."*
> (Reported by At-Tirmidhi)

Furthermore, `Umar ibn Al-Khattab (may Allah be pleased with him) said, "You should have some proportion of solitude." Sa`d ibn Abi Waqqas (may Allah be pleased with him) said, "I wish I had a metal door between me and humans, so that neither of us would reach the other till I die." Ibn

Mas'ud (may Allah be pleased with him) remarked, "Be springs of knowledge and moons at night. Remain at your homes. Refresh your hearts [with divine remembrance] and put on worn clothes; thus you become known to the angels and anonymous to humans." Abu Ad-Darda' (may Allah be pleased with him) said, "One's home is the best hermitage where he controls his tongue, his gaze and maintains his chastity. You should abandon sitting in markets, since they cause distraction and engaging in talk." Dawud At-Tai'y said, "Ward off humans as you ward off a lion." Abu Muhalhil remarked, "Once Sufyan Ath-Thawri took me to the graveyard. We secluded ourselves, then he began to cry and said, "If you can isolate yourself totally from dealing with people, you should do so. You should be preoccupied with reforming your affairs."

Likewise, adherents of keeping company with people support their view in the same way. The Prophet (peace and blessing of Allah be upon him) said, "A believer who keeps company with people and endures their harms is better than the one who isolates himself and does not endure their harms." However, their argument is not grounded enough. They quote the *Qu'anic* verse,

> ⟨*Be not like those who are divided amongst themselves and fall into disputation after receiving Clear Signs.*⟩
>
> (Al `Imran: 105)

In fact, this verse denotes different meanings ad cannot be taken as strong evidence.

They also quote the Prophet's saying (peace and blessings of Allah be upon him),

> "*There should be no estranged relations beyond*

three days."

(Reported by Muslim)

But this *Hadith* refers to boycotting, disregarding and common company.

Virtues of Seclusion

Seclusion comprises various virtues, namely,

1- **Dedication to worship:** Being in solitude, man enjoys ample time to worship Allah. A wise man was once asked, "Where has seclusion lead you?" He replied, "to the Almighty." In that way, if solitude renders man fully observant of the Almighty, he should dedicate himself thereto.

2- **Getting away from sins:** Solitude wards man against various sins that is committed when accompanying people. They include:

a. Backbiting: listening to people's unkind remarks about any one's honor and so on and so forth while tacitly approving their views. You should share Allah's wrath upon them. If you keep silent, your share may increase their malice. If you reform them, they dislike you and nurture their offence.

b. Commanding the good and forbidding the evil: Dealing with people, you may encounter sins. If you keep silent, you disobey Allah. Forbidding them to so, you may be harmed. Thus, solitude spares you all these troubles.

c. Hypocrisy: This is the most implacable malady. Dealing with people starts with longing for them. This strongly involves lying. Once an Early Muslim was asked, "How are you today? He replied, I am week and sinful, receiving my subsistence and waiting for my term."

Thus, if your inquiry after your brother is not motivated by intimacy and affection, it is dissemblance and hypocrisy. An inquiry may also hide malice and rancor. In that way solitude frees you from all these anxieties.

d. Being inadvertently imbued by their bad manners. This illness is so insidious that it is not easily detectable. An obscene person is scarcely accompanied for along time. Comparing yourself before sitting with an obscene person and after, you will sense the difference in condemning his viles. Habituation leads to indifference. In that way, seeing others committing grave sins heedlessly, minor sins unfortunately become insignificant. Likewise, considering early Muslims' worship and renunciation of worldly pleasure, one feels his inferiority. Hence, we sound the real meaning of the dictum saying, "Remembrance of righteous persons showers us with mercy." The above-mentioned fact can virtually be supported by giving this example, i.e. seeing someone eating during the day in *Ramadan*, Muslims become strongly irritated and annoyed so much that they may think of his being an unbeliever. However, they do not do the same as the man who postpones performing *Salah*, although neglecting even one time of prayer may turn him an unbeliever. The sole reason behind this attitude is the fact prayers are performed five times a day. The same applies to a jurist wearing silk or gold, and seeing him backbiting others, which is graver than putting on silk cloths and wearing gold rings. Accordingly, you should beware these subtleties. Beware of keeping company with people, since they may enhance your desire for worldly pleasures and negligence of the Hereafter. They may also undermine your inclination towards obedience; thus rendering disobedience more acceptable. In that way, finding a group remembering Allah, stick to them.

3- **Freeing oneself from temptation and dissension:** It also protects man's religion. Describing temptations, the Prophet (peace and blessings of Allah be upon him) said,

> *"Seeing that people's promises become confused and their trust diminished, being like this –then he interlocked his fingers." Whereupon a man asked, What should I do? The Prophet (peace and blessings of Allah be upon him) replied, "Stay at your home, have control over your tongue, do the good and give up the evil, stick to the knowledgeable and shun the common people."*
>
> (Reported by Abu Dawud)

4- **Saving oneself from the evils of humans:** People may harm you through backbiting, distrust and suspicion. Dealing with people, you meet envy, enmity and so on and so forth. `Umar ibn Al-Khattab (may Allah be pleased with him) remarked, "Solitude frees you from evil friends." Ibrahim ibn Adham, "Never approach whatever you do not know." A man asked his friend to company him in *Hajj*, he replied, "Let us rather enjoy Allah's shield, lest we may find in one another what saws hatred amongst us."

5- **To avoid people's greed as well as yours:** As for the former, satisfying all humans is untenable. It is said, "satisfying none, you please." As for yours, meditating over worldly gaieties enhances your longing therefore; thus moving your greed. The Prophet (peace and blessings of Allah be upon him) said,

> "Look at those who stand at a lower level than you but don't look at those who stand at a higher level than you, for this would make the favors (conferred upon you by Allah) insignificant (in your eyes)"
>
> (Reported by Muslim)

The same meaning is highlighted by the Almighty saying,

> ❨Nor strain your eyes in longing for the things we have given for enjoyment to parties Of them, the splendor Of the life of this world❩
>
> (Taha: 131)

6- **Getting rid of unpleasant and foolish persons:** You are not also troubled by persons of bad manners. If harmed by such persons, one becomes ready to backbite them; thus undermining one's religion.

Evils of Solitude and Benefits of Keeping Company

You should perceive that religious objectives are fulfilled through assistance of others. This is solely achieved by company. Therefore, company has its own virtues such as learning and teaching knowledge, exchanging benefits, improving one's manners, enjoying intimacy, receiving rewards due to fulfilling others' rights, getting accustomed to modesty and gaining more experience. We will consider each virtue in details as follows,

1- **Learning and teaching knowledge:** We have already dealt with this subject in "Chapter of Knowledge". However, getting contented with the communal obligations only, one can resort to solitude. If someone can achieve a high status in knowledge, resorting solitude before reaching such an end renders him a loser. Therefore, Ar-Rabi` b. Khaytham remarked, "obtain knowledge, then resort to solitude." Knowledge forms the roots of religion. A scholar was asked, "what about solitude of an ignorant?" He answered that it is insanity and harmful. The man asked, "what about the scholar?" He replied, "What is that to you?! Leave it alone. Like a traveler, knowledge is its provisions till it meets its Lord." Teaching knowledge commands great rewards depending on the scholar's intentions. If he seeks thereby glory, gaining more followers, he undermines his religion. This is quite prevalent in our age. In this case, solitude is better. Coming across a sincere learner seeking Allah's pleasure, he should not be secluded. Knowledge should not be grudged to a seeker.

2- **Exchanging Benefits:** Practically, one needs to deal with people in order to secure their benefits such as gaining subsistence. If one is self-contented, he can resort to solitude. If he seeks by working to spend in charity, it is better than solitude. However, if solitude draws him nearer to the Almighty through knowledge and insight, it is better. As for benefiting others, it can be financial or even physical such as fulfilling their needs. Being able to render these benefits, solitude is not recommended.

3- **Improving one's Manners:** This signifies experiencing people, enduring their harms, admonishing oneself and subduing one's desire. This is better than solitude. Experience is not sought on its own right. It is rather a bridge leading to the Hereafter. A monk was addressed, "O monk..." But he suddenly remarked, "I am not a monk. I am rather voracious, and I have tied myself in order not to hurt people. One should also endeavor to improve others' manners in the same way.

4- **Enjoying intimacy:** It can be commendable such as

establishing intimate relations with the righteous or entertaining oneself; unless the rest of one's time is harmed. Religion should dominate one's conversations in these meetings.

5- **Receiving rewards:** One can gain rewards by following funerals, visiting the sick and attending weddings. One should also afford others the opportunity to be rewarded. Thus, he should receive people's condolence and congratulations and visit him whereby they are rewarded. However, such relations' virtues should be compared to their evils and determine accordingly either to resort to solitude or not. Most early Muslims preferred solitude.

6- **Modesty:** This is not fulfilled in solitude. Pride may lead man to solitude since he prevents him from dealing with people and being generous to them. This is marked by man's preference to be a host rather than a guest. In that case, solitude is a sign of ignorance, for modesty never degrades a prestigious person.

Thus, the status of solitude necessitates detailed consideration according to the person himself and his rank among many other factors. Ash-Shafi`y said, "Deserting people incurs their enmity whereas intimacy with them is harmful. Therefore, keep a balance between the two." In that way, personal experience does not form the norm to judge other cases.

Manners of Solitude

One should seek by solitude to spare the evils of humans and the vice versa. One also wants to avoid inability of fulfilling the rights of fellow Muslims, and being dedicated to worship. In one's solitude, one should stick to obtaining knowledge and righteous deeds, divine remembrance and contemplation. Thus, solitude should yield its fruits. People should scarcely visit him in solitude so that he should enjoy his time properly. He should also give up inquiring about their affairs and disregard idle talk. All such things find their way to his heart so much that they will turn up and tease him while performing prayers. The news to one's ears is like seeds to the land. He should be contented with reasonable living, otherwise; he will be impelled to mix up with humans. He should endure their evils and overlook their praise of him; since this can undermine his resolution to advance towards the Hereafter. He should resort to a righteous friend who can entertain him for a while. In fact, this will assist him to carry on. Enduring solitude comes from giving up all hopes in the life of this world. He should frequently remember death and solitude in one's grave whenever his resolution weakens. Truly, death never abolishes intimacy with the Almighty. Allah says,

❦Think not of those who are slain in Allah's way as dead. Nay, they live, finding their sustenance in the presence of their Lord❧

(Al `Imran: 169)

The same applies to a man combating his whims and dedicating himself to virtues.

VI. Morals of Traveling

By traveling man seeks either to escape from something or achieve a certain end. Traveling has two kinds, namely, physical where one's body only moves from place to another while his heart is still attached to his origin, and spiritual where his heart also travels with him.

Physical traveling has its categories, virtues and evils. Its virtues range from escape to pursuit. As for the former, it maybe worldly such as escaping from plagues, dissention, conflict, increase of prices or a detriment to one's religion due to influence or richness. One may also seek to avoid supporting an innovation or undertaking an illegal post, therefore he travels to ward off them. As for the latter, it can also be worldly such as property or influence, or religious such as pursuing religious knowledge or contemplating over Allah's prodigies spread in the universe. In fact, all famous scholars, since the Companions (may Allah be pleased with all of them) till our present time have obtained knowledge through traveling. Man may also seek thereby to sound the depth of his soul, thus improving his manners. The Arabic word "*Safar*", i.e. traveling, is named as such for it results in good manners. Actually, defects never turn up in one's home, but undergoing the hardships of traveling and new experiences, these defects speak of themselves.

As far as contemplating over Allah's signs is concerned, Allah has spread in the earth diverse though neighboring tracts, fields and deserts, seas and oceans, diverse kinds of animals and plants. All of these profess the Almighty's Oneness and hymn His praise, Behold, verily in these things there are Signs for those who understand! Religion never resides in heart negligent of Allah. Man can manage his worldly affairs, but they should not be his utmost longing, otherwise, it is for his detriment.

Permitted Traveling

Traveling for consideration of signs and excursion is allowed where mere tourism without any purpose is not. Imam Ahmad b. Hanbal said, "there is no tourism in Islam. Neither Prophets (peace and blessings of Allah be upon them) nor the righteous (may Allah be pleased with them) has observed it." Since traveling troubles one's heart, it should be meant to obtain knowledge or meet a famous scholar. Traveling commands a great deal of manners. Man should clear himself from wrong doings, pay his debts, secure subsistence for his dependants and restore trusts to their owners. He should choose an upright companion. He firstly should do the *Istekharah* prayers. He should travel at night along with comrades. He should constantly hymn Allah's praise. He should take along with him all necessary gadgets.

Requirements for Traveler

A traveler should take a provision with him for this world, and the Hereafter. As for the former, it is like food and water. This does not contradict relying on the Almighty. As for provision for the Hereafter, it is having knowledge of all necessary affairs such purification, *Salah*, rituals of worship, curtailing prayer. He should also be well-grounded in all matters affected by traveling such as direction of the *Qiblah* and times of prayers.

VII. Commanding the Right and Forbidding the Wrong

In fact, commanding the right and forbidding the wrong form the cornerstone of Islam. It is the message sent by Allah to His Prophets (peace and blessings of Allah be upon them all). If neglected, corruption would be the order of the day. Allah says in the *Qur'an*,

> ⟪*Let there arise out of you a band of people inviting to all that is good, enjoining what is right, and forbidding what is wrong: they are the ones to attain felicity.*⟫
>
> (Al `Imran: 104)

The Arabic preposition *"Minkum"*, translated here as "out of you", signifies that commanding the right and forbidding the wrong is a communal obligation, in the sense that it can be observed by certain specialized persons. The Glorious *Qur'an* contains numerous reference to this issue. In addition, the Prophet (peace and blessings of Allah be upon him) said,

> "*The example of the person abiding by Allah's order and restrictions in comparison to those who violate them is like the example of those persons who drew lots for their seats in a boat. Some of them got seats in the upper part, and the others in the lower. When the latter needed water, they had to go up to bring water (and that troubled the others), so they said, 'Let us make a hole in our share of the ship (and get water) saving those who are above us from troubling them. So, if the people in the upper part left the others do what they had suggested, all the people of the ship would be*

destroyed, but if they prevented them, both parties would be safe."

(Reported by Al-Bukhari)

Degrees of Forbidding the Wrong

The Prophet (peace and blessings of Allah be upon him) said,

"Whoever of you sees something wrong, let him change it with his hand. If unable to, then let him change it with his tongue. If unable, then with his heart. This is the weakest degree of faith."

(Reported by Muslim)

In another report, the Prophet (peace and blessings of Allah be upon him) said,

"The best Jihad is speaking the truth to an unjust ruler"

(Reported by Ahmad)

Furthermore, he (peace and blessings of Allah be upon him) said,

"When you see my community too intimidated by an oppressor to tell him, "You are a tyrant", then you may as well say goodbye to them."

(Reported by Abu Dawud)

After having praised the Almighty Abu Bakr (may Allah be pleased with him) said,

" O people, you recite the verse which reads,

{O you who believe you are responsible for

yourselves; those who go astray will not harm you if you are guided⟩

(Al-Ma'idah : 105)

"But we have heard the Messenger of Allah (peace and blessings of Allah be upon him) said, "People who do not change something wrong when they see it are on the verge of a sweeping punishment from Allah"

(Reported by ibn Majah)

Integrals of Commanding And Forbidding

It has four integrals as follows:

First, the person who commands and forbids: He should be legally responsible, Muslim and able to do so. Thus, a child under the age of maturity is rewarded for condemning something wrong though it is not obligatory for him to do so. As for the moral rectitude of the person doing so, some scholars have opined that a corrupt person is not entitled to religious censorship. They support their opinion by quoting the verse which reads,

⟨*Do you enjoin Piety to others and forget yourselves*⟩

(Al-Baqarah: 44)

But, in fact, this verse does not enhance their inference.

Furthermore, some scholars stipulate that the person delivering the censure must have permission from the ruler or his official. For them, individuals are not eligible for censorship. This is quiet ungrounded and untrue. The *Qur'an* as well as the *Sunnah* indicate that whosoever sees some thing wrong and does nothing is sinful. It is totally odd to know that the *Rafidah* sect, *Shi`i*, denied religious censorship unless their infallible imam turns up.

Levels of religious Censorship

1- Explaining the offensive nature of the act,

2- Admonishing the person politely,

3- Harshly reprimanding him,

4- Forcibly stopping the wrong, such as breaking musical instruments and pouring out wine.

5- Intimidation and threatening to strike the person or actually hitting him, so that he should give up his offence. This level is confined to the ruler since it may lead to disorder within the community.

The early Muslim invariable practices of reprimanding those in authority decisively prove their consensus that commanding the right and forbidding the wrong requires no authorization. One may argue, is a child entitled to reprove his parent, a wife her husband or subjects their rulers? In fact all are entitled thereto.

We have highlighted five levels for religious, the child should clarify the nature of the wrong done, to admonish and advise his parents politely. However, he may change the wrong according to the fourth level by breaking a lute and pouring out wine. This goes also for the wife. As for subjects and their rulers, it is more serious than these precedents. Hence, they are entitled only to clarify the nature of the wrong committed.

The person who is going to condemn something should be

able to do so. If unable, he is not obliged to condemn anything wrong. If there is a fear of physical harm or injury one should only resort to the degree of condemning the wrong only by heart. In this respect, we have four situations,

1- Ascertaining that the wrong will be corrected through his reprimand, in that case he should condemn it.

2- Knowing that his words will be futile and that he may be harmed, he is not obliged to.

3- Recognizing that his condemnation is ineffective, but he will not be injured, he is not obliged to, but his censure is recommended to highlight Islamic rules and revive religion in people's hearts.

4- Knowing that he will be harmed, but the wrong will be eliminated through his condemnation, such as breaking the lute and pouring out wine, he is not obliged to do so but it is rather recommended for him. The Prophet (peace and blessings of Allah be upon him) said,

> *"The best Jihad is speaking the truth to an unjust ruler"*
>
> (Reported by Ahmad)

Scholars unanimously agree that it is permissible for a single Muslim to attack the army of unbelievers even if he knows that he will be killed. However, if he perceives that he will not hurt them at all, such as being a blind, he should not do so. In addition, seeing a corrupt person alone with a bottle of wine while having a sword, and fearing that he may smite him therewith if tries to correct him, he is not permitted to do so, as it would not entail any religious advantage worth giving one's life for. However, it is recommended when his censure is proven effective.

Knowing that his censure would harm any of his companions, it is not permissible for him to do so, for his being unable to reform a wrong thing without leading to another. His knowledge here means what he believes will probably happen. Thus, if he strongly thinks that he would be harmed if he censures an evil, he is not obliged to do so. Neither cowardice nor foolhardy courage is the norm but rather the common sense with natural disposition.

Problems that may result from condemnation of the wrong range from robbery, beating, killing and defamation among many other things. However, reviling and disdain do not support one to remain silent.

Second, what is censured: It should overtly be blameworthy. It should be prohibited by Islamic Law. The Arabic Word *"Munkar"*, i.e. evil, is wider than mere disobedience, for seeing a child or an insane person drinking wine, one is obliged to pour it out and forbid them; though it is not a sin in their regard.

Condemnation has to do with the wrong committed at present, excluding one who has drunk wine but he has now fmished. It also excludes things that will take place later, as if there is evidence that someone would commit an evil in the future, there is no censorship in these cases.

The wrong should decisively be condemned without any further consideration.

Third, the wrong-doer: It is sufficient that he be a person. It does not matter if he is legally responsible or not; as we have already elaborated in respect to censuring a child and an insane person

Fourth, the act of religious censorship: It commands eight degrees, namely,

1- Knowledge of the wrong act. One should not eavesdrop at another's house to hear the sound of musical instruments or try to catch him at the wine place. He should not hug, touch or search him to find out something hidden under his clothes, nor even ask his neighbors to spy on him. However, if two upright persons witness that someone is drinking wine, one may enter his house and take him to task.

2- The act itself should be clarified. An ignorant person often does things which he does not consider as evil, but he will stop when he finds out. So the nature of the wrong act should be clarified politely, such as saying, "People are not born scholars; we are unfamiliar with many things in Islamic Law till scholars clarify them to us. Perhaps, there are not many of them in your hometown." In that way, he diplomatically comes up to the point one wants to clarify. Avoiding the evil of remaining silent when some wrong is done; replacing it with offending a Muslim when able not to, is like washing blood with urine.

3- The third degree is to prohibit the wrong by admonition, advice and fear from Allah; citing the *Ahadith* of divine punishment for it and highlighting how early Muslims behaved. These things should be done with kindness. However, it is badly serious that explaining the nature of the wrong, the person doing so may be proud of his knowledge and show off thereby. This is like casting your self into fire to save someone else. This signifies extreme ignorance, disgrace and distraction. The criterion is to ask oneself whether one would prefer the censured person would stop at his or another's behest, or whether one would prefer to forbid him oneself. If reproving him is difficult preferring others doing it on his behalf, he should do that seeking Allah's pleasure. Otherwise, censorship becomes a means of pride and caprice. One should rather reform himself. Dawud At-Ta'i was once asked, "What about a man approaching rulers commanding them to do good and forbid evil? He replied, "I fear that he may be flogged." They said, "He can withstand it." He replied, "I fear that he may be killed." They said, "He can endure that." Then he replied, "I fear that he may plagued with the insidious malady, that is self-conceit."

4- Condemning the person doing the wrong with severe and harsh words. One should resort to this only when is unable to reform the person doing the wrong, he insists on his mischief or disdains the advice and admonition. We may give example of these words such as, "You ignorant." "You idiot." and "Do you fear the Almighty" and so on and so forth. Allah says in the *Qura'n*,

⟪*Fie upon you, and upon the things that you worship besides Allah! Have you no sense?*⟫
(Al-Anbiya': 67)

5- This level involves changing the evil with one's hand, such as breaking musical instruments, pouring out wine and turning him out of the appropriated house. This level has two aspects, namely,

   i. When a wrongdoer is ready to reform himself, he should not coerce him to do so.

   ii. He should break musical instruments, for example, so

much that they become useless. On the other hand, pouring out wine, bottles should not be broken. If unable to censure drinking wine but by breaking the bottles through stoning them as if their heads are so narrow that its pouring would take very long time; thus affording the obscene ample time to reach him and prevent him therefrom, he should do so and he is not to make up the damage. One may wonder, is the same applicable to dragging an offender out of the appropriated house as a determent to others? In fact this measure should be done by rulers rather than ordinary subjects due to the obscurity of the decision-making criteria in this situation.

6- Changing the wrong through threatening and intimidation, such saying, "give up this, or I will...." If tenable, it is given priority over hurting him. Furthermore, threats should be applicable such as "I will seize your house." And the like, since stating such things seriously is quite unlawful. If not serious, it is lying.

7- Hitting the wrongdoer. In this measure, no harmful weapon should be employed. If necessary, ordinary individuals can do so but with a limited degree. It should only be confined to reforming the evil. Having the wrong corrected, one should stop doing anything further as the end has been fulfilled.

8- Inability to censure an act by himself and need for armed assistance of others. Being reprimanded, an obscene person may resort to his fellows to defend him. Thus, this virtually necessitates the ruler's authorization, lest it should lead civil disorder.

Attribute of the Religious Censurer

Having elaborated the rules of commanding good and forbidding evil, we may summarize then the three attributes that a Muslim censurer should enjoy to be capable of undertaking the task. They are;

1- Knowledge of the appropriate circumstance where censure is required, their limits and definitions; so as to keep it within the *Shar`i* bounds.

2- Fearing the Almighty, in whose absence one may disregard a certain rule to secure some interests.

3- Good manners. In fact, this is essential. Getting angry, one is calmed down by his good manners along with piety and his knowledge. This clearly stated by some early Muslims, "commanding right should be observed by a kind, gentle and knowledgeable man." He should also reduce the scope of his worldly interests and his dependence on others so that his principles are not compromised. Once an early Muslim had a neighbor who was a butcher. He used to take from him an offal for his cat. One day, he noticed something evil with his neighbor. Before going to reform him, he turned out the cat. Getting reproved, the butcher said, "I will never give any thing for your cat." Whereupon he remarked, "I have turned out my cat before reproving you." In fact, one can not reform others so long as he is worried by two factors, these are things he receives from them and their pleasure with and praise of him

The main difference between commanding the right and forbidding the wrong is clearly stated in the *Qur`an*, where Allah says,

{But speak to him mildly; perchance he may take Warning or fear (Allah)}

(Taha: 44)

It is reported that once Abu Ad-Darda' passed by a sinful person while people were reviling him. He told them, "Finding him fallen in a well, would not you take him out?" They replied in the affirmative. Whereupon he remarked, "Do not revile your brother." They asked him, "Do you not hate him?" He said, "I rather hate his deed. If he gives it up, he will be my brother."

VIII. Customary Evils, and Commanding Rulers to Do Good and Forbid Wrong

Customary Evils

Customary evils are countless, but we will rather highlight some of them in the following lines.

First: people do some evils even in mosques such as performing prayers (*Salah*) improperly. They may just hit their prostration (*Sujud*) and kneeling down (*Ruku`*) without assurance. They may not also clean their dress appropriately. Likewise, they may not be directed to the *Qiblah* due to blindness or darkness.

Even when reciting the *Qur'an* in *Salah*, the *Imam* may commit mistakes. Callers for prayers may also add to the *Adhan* new words and elongate its vowels incorrectly. The orator should not also wear silk clothes or take a golden sword at his hand. Disputes should not be settled in mosques. There should not be mixing between men and women in mosques. If any, it should be censured.

Second: evils found in markets. A trader may lie to secure profits. He may hide the goods' defects. Getting wind of the trader's scheme, one should inform the seller thereof. If he remains silent for the trader's interest, he became as betrayer as the seller. The same norm applies to disparities between different measurements according to their various tools. Illegal conditions as well as usury should be clearly condemned and reproved. This also applies to selling musical instruments.

Third: evils observed down the streets. One may build a shop attached to already built houses, thus narrowing streets.

He may also plant some trees that block the way before the pedestrians. This disapproval does not apply to putting movable things in streets till their removal into houses because people used to do this. Riding beasts should not be fastened down roads in a way that hinders movements. They should not also be overloaded. Waste should not be thrown in streets. Water should not be poured down roads to hurt people.

Fourth: evils found in public baths. Photos should not be hung to doors of baths on inside. If any, they should be deformed. If unable to do so, one should not reach such baths unless he is obliged thereto. Thighs as well as privities should be concealed. Impure hands should not be put in water.

Fifth: evils observed in hospitality. Silk mattresses should not be spread for guests. Incense should not be burned in golden or silver pots, nor should water be served therein. Curtains should not contain pictures. Guests should not be entertained by singers. All these evils should be proscribed. If unable to reprove them, one should leave the place at once. This rule does not apply to pictures on pots and carpets, using gold and silk by women. Young girls' ears should not be pierced to put earrings, for it is extremely painful. If there is an innovator among the guests who propagates his innovation, one should leave them at once. If he keeps silent, one may attend showing his disdain of him. If a certain person entertains the guest through vile and obscene speech, they should be avoided. Otherwise, one can stay with them.

Finally: Common evils. Knowing that there is a certain evil in a market that can be reformed, one should rectify it. Every Muslim should reform himself first, keeping obligations and deserting sins. He should then do the same to his household and relatives, then comes his neighbors, then his fellows of his hometown, then citizens of his country. Finally, come people of the whole world.

Commanding Rulers to Do Good and Forbid Wrong

We have already stated the levels of commanding good and forbidding wrong. However, as far as rulers are concerned, one is entitled only to the first two levels, namely, clarification of the wrong act and admonition. As for addressing them with harsh words such as "Are you tyrant?", "Do you not fear Allah?", if one is not sure that it would not hurt others, he should not do so. If his fear is only confined to himself, according to the majority of scholars, he should do so. However, I think that he should not, since he seeks to reprove the wrong rather leading the ruler to commit a major one.

In this respect, *Imam* Ahmad said, "You should never disparage a ruler, for his sword is unsheathed." We should not think of the examples of the early scholars and their courage to reprimand rulers. In early times rulers used to honour and revere scholars. This is not the case anymore.

Once Sa`id ibn `Amir told `Umar ibn Al-Khattab (may Allah be pleased with both of them), "I advise you with certain recommendable acts of Islam, fear Allah for your subjects not the vice versa. Your words should conform to your deeds, since deeds speak for themselves. Love for all Muslims what you love for yourself. Rush into perils to reach the truth so long as you recognize it. Fear none but Allah Alone." Omar (may Allah be pleased with him wondered, "Who can uphold all this!" He answered, "a man entrusted with your trust [being a ruler]".

Qatadah narrated, "One day `Umar went out of the mosque with Al-Garood. He came across a woman. Greeting her, she responded and said, "I know you since you were a quite young boy called `Umair` (young `Umar) and when you became a strong man called `Umar`. Days have passed and you are now called the Caliph of the Believers. `Umar, fear Allah for your subjects. Be mindful of the fact that fear from death instigates fear from loss." Whereupon `Umar cried. Al-Garood told her, "You have spoken boldly to the Caliph and caused him to cry." `Umar remarked, "Let it be! Do you not know this woman?" She is Khawalah ibn Hakim whose complain the Almighty has heard. Thus, `Umar should also do the same.

A man from the tribe of Azd approached Mu`awyah and told him, "Fear Allah, and know that every day your life becomes shorter and the Hereafter nearer. Death follows you wherever you are, neither of you will escape the other. The life of this world is transient, whereas the Hereafter is everlasting. The former initiates the latter's status, be it good or bad."

Furthermore, Ad-Daramy reports that Sulayman b. Abdul Malik once entered Al-Madinah and stayed there for three days. Wondering if there were still some people who co-lived with the Prophet's companions, he was told that there was only one of them named Abu-Hazem. He summoned him. Reaching him, Sulayman said, "Abu-Hazem, what is this severance?" Abu-Hazem wondered, "What does that have to do with me?" Sulayman said, "All the nobles of Al-Madinah have visited me but you have not." He replied, "I have no relation with you to visit you." Sulayman said, "You have spoken rightly. Abu-Hazem, why do detest death?" he answered, "Because you have prospered this life and ignored the Hereafter. Hence, you prefer prosperity to adversity. Sulayman said, "You have spoken rightly. How shall we return to the Almighty?" he replied, "The good doer returns to Allah like a traveler to his household delighted and pleased. But the wrong doer returns like an eloping slave returning to his master distressed." Sulayman asked, "What share shall we receive from Allah?" He said, "Judge yourself according to the *Qur'an*, then you would know your share." Sulayman asked, "Where can I find this in the *Qur'an*?" He said, "Allah says,

❨*As for the Righteous, they will be in Bliss; And the Wicked they will be in the Fire.*❩

(Al- Inftar: 13-14)

Sulayman wondered, Where is Allah's Mercy?" He replied,

❨*The mercy of Allah is (always) near to those who do good.*❩

(Al- A`raf: 56)

He asked, "Abu Hazem, who is the most sensible of human?" He replied, "Who learns wisdom and teaches it." He said, "Who is the most foolish?" He said, "Who follows whims of a tyrant, thus preferring the tyrant's pleasure to his own Hereafter." He asked, "What is the supplication that is to be answered?" He said, "It is of the humble and sincere." He asked, "What is the best charity?" He replied, "That is spent on the poor."

Then Sulayman asked, "What about my office?" Abu Hazem asked him to pardon him from the answer but Sulayman insisted. Abu Hazem said, "Some people have appropriated this right with neither consultation nor consensus, thus; they have shed innocent blood to enjoy this world, but they have passed away. I wonder, how have they been reckoned! And how have they responded!" Then, a man said, "What an evil reply!" Abu Hazem rebuked him saying, "You are a liar. The Almighty has pledged scholars to clarify it to people." Sulayman then asked him to visit him in the morning to obtain more knowledge and give him a gift, but he declined. When asked about the reason, he said, "I fear from inclining to you a little. In that case we should have made to taste equal punishment in this life, and in death." Sulayman asked his advice." He said, "Lo! Fear Allah! Indeed, He should not find you where He has forbidden, and miss you where He has commanded you."

Sulayman finally asked him to pray for him. Whereupon Abu Hazem said, "O Lord, if Sulayman is your friend, make goodness convenient to him. If not, guide him to goodness." Sulayman then ordered one hundred *dirhams* for him but Abu Hazem declined taking them. Az-Zuhry was attending and remarked, "He has been my neighbor for thirty years, but I have never spoken to him." Abu Hazem said to him, "Forgetting the Almighty, you have also forgotten me." Az-Zuhry wondered, "Do you revile me?" But Sulayman soon said, "You have reviled yourself. Do you not know that neighborhood command certain rights?" Abu Hazem then said, "When the children of Israel followed the law, their rulers used to reach their scholars who did their utmost to ward off them. Then the insidious people learned knowledge and reached rulers thereby. Later on, the Israelites unanimously committed sins. Hence, they fell and diminished. Had scholars preserved their religion and knowledge, rulers would have still respected them."

One day a Bedouin reached Sulayman ibn Abdul-Malik and addressed him saying, "O Caliph of the Believers, I will tell some words. You should bear them even if you detest them. Accepting them, you find them agreeable." Sulayman told him to proceed. The man said, "Some of your courtiers have substituted your worldly life for their life to come and your pleasure for Allah's wrath. They have feared you for Allah rather than Allah for you. Thus, they give you prosperity in this life and adversity in the Hereafter. Accordingly, never entrust them with what Allah has entrusted you, since they spare no effort in wasting their trust and undermining the whole nation. You are held responsible for their errors, not the vice versa. Thus, never flourish their worldly life at the expense of your life to come. Sulayman remarked, "You have unsheathed your tongue which is sharper than your sword." The man replied, "It is for, not against, you." Sulayman asked, "Do you have any need?" the man replied, "For me, I do not, but for all Muslims." Then he went away. Then Sulayman said, "How honorable his origin is! How sound his heart is! How eloquent his tongue is! How truthful his intention is! How pious he is! This is true honor and sensibility."

`Umar ibn `Abdul-`Aziz asked Abu Hazem (may Allah be pleased with him) to advise him. He said, when you go to bed, remember death. Then think of what you love to do, hence do it. And think of what you dislike, thus desert it.

Muhammad ibn Ka`b told `Umar ibn `Abdul-`Aziz (may Allah be pleased with him), "This life is like a market, wherefrom people have gone out with either benefits or detriments. Many are those who have been deceived by what we have now, till death suddenly overtook them. Thus, they departed blameworthy without being equipped for the Hereafter. Their properties have been distributed among their revilers. They have returned to Him [Allah] who admits no excuse. Thus, we should rather adopt their good deeds and discard their evil ones. Hence, fear Allah. Let your doors be open before all. Assist the oppressed and punish the offender. *Iman* -faith- becomes full-fledged through three traits. When pleased, a believer does not support falsehood. When angry, he does not overlook the truth. When triumphant, he does not seize what he does not possess."

`Ata' b. Abu Rabah visited Hisham b. Abdul-Malik. He welcomed him and said, "What is your need Abu Muhammad?" He then reminded him of the shares due to the people of *Makkah* and Al-Madinah, whereupon Hisham ordered their shares to be sent for them. Hisham then asked, "What else?" He reminded him of the shares of the people of Najd, Al-Hijaz and frontier states till he advised him not to overload the non-Muslim subjects. Hisham also asked, "What else?" He said, "Fear Allah for you have been created alone, and you will die alone, and you will be resurrected alone and you will be accounted alone."

Therefore Hisham cried strongly. Then `Ata' left. A man followed him with a purse telling him that the Caliph had ordered it for him. But `Ata' recited the *Qur'anic* verse which reads,

{*No reward do I ask of you for it: my reward is only from the Lord of the Worlds*}
(Ash- Shu`ara': 109)

Then he departed without even drinking a sip of water.

Muhammad ibn `Aly reported, "I was sitting with Abu Ja`far Al-Mansur –the Abbasid Caliph- along with ibn Abu-Dhi'b. Al-Hassan ibn Zaid was the mayor of Al-Madinah. Then the people of Ghaffar entered complaining to Abu-Ja`far from Al-Hassan ibn Zaid who said, "O Caliph of the believers, would you ask ibn Abu-Dhi'b about them?" Abu-Ja`far asked him and he said, "I testify that they defame peoples' honors." Abu-Ja`far told them, "Have you heard this?" They then asked him to inquire after Al-Hassan ibn Zaid. Doing so, ibn Abu-Dhi'b said, "I testify that he does not judge justly." Abu-Ja`far told him, "Have you heard this?" Al-Hassan ibn Zaid asked him to inquire after himself. Doing so, he said, "Pardon me."

But he insisted; therefore he said, "You have unjustly taken this property and given it to ineligible persons. Abu-Ja`far told him, "By Allah, but for my being the Caliph, the Romans, the Persians and the Turks would have seized even your seat." But ibn Abu-Dhi'b replied, "Omar and Abu-Bakr were Caliphs long before you, but they distributed properties justly and they ruled over the Romans and the Persians." Abu-Ja`far pardoned him saying, "Verily, had not I known that you are truthful, I would have cut off your head." ibn Abu-Dhi'b said, "Verily, I am more truthful to you than your son Al-Mahdy."

Al-'Awza`y narrates that Abu-Ja`far sent for him. He says, "Reaching him, he asked me to have a seat. And wondered, "Why are you so late?" I asked him for his intention. He replied, "I want to learn from you." "O Caliph", I said, "beware of listening to something and ignore it!" Ar-Rabi` was annoyed and tried to draw his sword but the Caliph reprimanded him saying, "Of our meeting, we seek reward rather than punishment."

Therefore, I became delighted and spoke freely. "Bishr reports that", I said, "Allah's Prophet (peace and blessing of Allah be upon him) said,

> *"Whenever a rulers dies cheating his subjects, he will never enter Paradise."*
>
> (Reported by Abu Na`im)

"You have been", I continued, "preoccupied with your own affairs rather than those of your diverse subjects. They all have their own share of justice. What will you do when they complain of your injustices inflicted upon them on the Last Day? Habib b. Salamah narrates,

> *"The Prophet (peace and blessing of Allah be upon*

him) asked a bedouin to retaliate from him due a tiny unintentional scratch. Gabriel visited him saying, "Muhammad, the Almighty has not sent you as a despotist nor as a tyrant. Whereupon he summoned the Bedouin and asked him to retaliate for himself. The Bedouin said, "I have pardoned you. I can never do so even if you had killed me." Then he prayed for him."

(Reported by Al-Baihaqi)

Al-'Awza`y then continued, "Reform yourself by your self and try to secure it from Allah's wrath. If your predecessors were alive, you would not have become a caliph. Allah says in the *Qur'an*,

⟨*They will say, Ah woe to us what a book is this it leaves out nothing small or great, but takes account thereof*⟩

(Al-Kahf: 49)

"O Caliph," he said, "your grandfather -ibn `Abbas- commented on this verse saying, "The small thing is a mere smile whereas the great is the laugh." Then tell me what about practical sins! I knew that Omar said, "I fear that I may be accounted for a sheep dying on Euphrates. How about those who underwent your injustice!"

"O Caliph", Al-'Awza`y continued, "Allah says in the *Qur'an*,

⟨*O David We did indeed make thee a vicegerent on earth: so judge thou between men in truth (and justice): nor follow thou the lusts*⟩

(Sadd: 26)

"This verse means that", he elaborated, "if two disputants ask you to judge between them, you should not wish to support one over the other due to your inclination to him. If not, you will be stripped of Prophethood and being vicegerent. O David, I have appointed my Prophets as shepherds due to their knowledge of protection and amiable politics to treat them gently and guide them."

Al-'Awza`y furthered his discourse saying, "Abu-'Umayrah Al-Ansari reports that Omar ibn Al-Khattab (may Allah be pleased with him) appointed an Ansari man to distribute charity. After some days, he found him at home. So he asked him, "Why did you not go to work today? Do not you know that you receive the same reward as a fighter in Allah's cause?" He answered in the negative. Omar wondered how come this! He replied, I was informed that Allah's Prophet (peace and blessings of Allah be upon him) said,

> *"Whoever undertakes a power will come on the Day of Resurrection having his hands tied up to his back. He will be stationed on a path over Hellfire. It will strongly shake him so much that his organs would shatter away. Then he will be brought for reckoning. If his deeds are good, he will be saved. Otherwise, he will fall in Hellfire for seventy years."*

Hearing this, Omar asked, who told you so? He said, Abu-Dharr and Salman (may Allah be pleased with all of them). Omar (may Allah be pleased with him) summoned them and they affirmed hearing it from the Prophet (peace and blessings of Allah be upon him). Whereupon Omar wondered; Who can undertake it? Abu-Dharr answered, "He who is humble and modest before the Almighty". Abu-Ja`far then cried so strongly that he caused Al-'Awza`y to cry.

Then Al-'Awza`y told him, "Your grandfather ibn `Abbas (may Allah be pleased with him) asked Allah's Prophet (peace and blessings of Allah be upon him) for an office. But he remarked,

> *"Uncle, to save soul is better than an office that you fail to manage"*
> (Reported by Al-Baihaqi)

In that way, he (peace and blessings of Allah be upon him) was very kind to his uncle, informing him that he avails naught for him before the Almighty. He was ordered by Allah in the Qur'an,

> ﴿*And warn your nearest Kinsmen*﴾
> (Al- Shu`ara': 214)

Abu Huraira reports, When this verse was revealed: "And warn your nearest kindred (Al- Shu`ara': 214), the Messenger of Allah (peace and blessings of Allah be upon him) called the Quraish; so they gathered and he gave them a general warning. Then he made a particular reference to certain tribes and said,

> *"O sons of Ka'b ibn Luwayy, rescue yourselves from the Fire; O sons of Murra ibn Ka'b, rescue yourselves from the Fire; O sons of Abd Shams, rescue yourselves from the Fire; O sons of Abd Manaf rescue yourselves from the Fire; O sons of Hashim, rescue yourselves from the Fire; O sons of `Abd Al-Muttalib, rescue yourselves from the Fire; O Fatimah, rescue thyself from the Fire, for I have no power (to protect you) from Allah in anything except this that I would maintain relationship with you."*
> (Reported by Al-Bukari)

After that Al-'Awza`y asked for permission to leave for his home. Abu-Ja`far permitted him to go and said, "I accept your admonition as such. May Allah guide me and assist me. For me Allah suffices, and he is the best Disposer of affairs. You should never sever me. We accept the advice of the truthful." Al-'Awza`y replied in the affirmative. Abu Ja`far ordered a gift for him, but he declined it saying, "I do not need it. I never sell my words for worldly gains. Knowing him, Abu Ja`far silenced himself.

When Ar-Rashid performed *Hajj* he was told that Shayban was in Makkah too. He summoned him. Reaching him, he asked for his advice. He said, "I am stuttering in Arabic. Would you get someone to translate what I am to say." He brought a translator. Then he said, "He who advises you before reaching security is better than the vice versa." Ar-Rashid asked about its meaning. Shayban said that he refers to a man who advises you, saying, "fear Allah for you are responsible for this nation. Allah has appointed you as its shepherd and its ruler. Thus, treat its people justly in all affairs. Such a person threatens you. Reaching security, later on, you taste its sweetness. He is more sincere than him who sedates by claiming, "You are forgiven due to your relation to the Prophet (peace and blessings of Allah be upon him). He anesthetizes you till reach perils where you fade away." Harun cried till his courtiers sympathized with him. He asked him for more but Shayban declined.

`Alqamah ibn Marthad narrates that when Omar b Hubayrah entered Iraq. He sent for Al-Hassan and Ash-Sha`by. He appointed a house for them where they stayed for about a month. He visited them. He said, "The Caliph sent me letters which if I fulfill I would incur Allah's wrath. If not, I would suffer his indignation. Do you find any way out for me?

Hence, Al-Hassan said, "Abu `Amr, answer the *Amir*." Ash-Sha`by stated that the *Amir* might be pardoned and excused because it is out of his hand. But the *Amir* said, "What do you think, Abu Sa`id?" Thus, Al-Hassan replied, "Lo! There is a mighty unbiased angel obeying his Lord. So he is about to drive you out from your great palace to your very narrow grave."

If you fear Allah, he will protect you from Yazid b. Abdul-Malik. But Yazid will never guard you against Allah. Beware that Allah may not forgive you due to your obedience to Yazid. I have met some early Muslims detesting this world while it inclines to them more than you. Beware of this state declared by Allah in this verse,

⟪*This for such as fear the Time when they shall stand before My tribunal- such as fear the Punishment denounced*⟫

(Ibrahim: 14)

O Ibn Huabyrah, if you obey Allah, He will guard you against Yazid. But if you obey Yazid, Allah will renounce you to him. Hence, Ibn Huabyrah cried and adhered to his admonition. Later on, he sent some gifts for them. But those of Al-Hassan were greater. Then Ash-Sha`by addressed people in the mosque saying, "Let Allah be your first priority. I have sought to please ibn Hubayrah, but Allah has determined to severe me from him."

Muhammad ibn Wasi` visited Bilal b. Baradah on a very hot day while he had ice. He asked him about his opinion of his house. He replied, "Your house is good, but. Paradise is better. Remembering the Hellfire make you forget all about it." He asked him about destiny. He said, "Your neighbors are the dead. Think of them. He asked him to pray for him. He wondered, "What avails you of my supplication while you have complainants by your door whose prayer is heard long before mine. Avoid injustice, then you will not need my prayer."

We hereby presented in brief some tales regarding admonishing rulers. These scholars used to adopt this approach in commanding the good and forbidding the wrong. They were totally indifferent to rulers' influence preferring the Almighty's right to compromising with their rulers. On the other hand, rulers recognized the virtue of knowledge. Thus they endured the severity of the scholars' admonitions. However, rulers should be avoided. If perchance one meets them, he should advise them gently. This is due two reasons, namely,

1- The first reason has to do with the scholar himself. He may have bad intention and inclination to worldly gains. Therefore, he may compromise his admonition to meet with the conduct of the ruler.

2- The second deals with the person admonished. Many persons have become busy with worldly gaieties disregarding the Hereafter. This has lead to degrading scholars.

Listening to Songs and Music

Satan has employed this evil to spoil people's hearts and seduce innumerable scholars and mystics, let alone the ordinary individuals; so much that some falsely claim unity with Allah during listening to songs and music. They even wrongly claim their joy to be related to ecstasy of the Hereafter.

Trying to know the truth, consider the first century of Islam. Has the Prophet (peace and blessing of Allah be upon him) or any of his Companions (may Allah be pleased with them) done such a thing. Then consider lives of jurists and the successors such as Malik, Abu Hanyfah, Ash-Shafi`y and Ahmad (may Allah be pleased with them). They all have condemned music. Malik stated that if man buys a slave girl and finds out that she is a singer, he should gave her back. Questioned about singing, he replied, "it is done by the obscene persons".

Imam Ahmad was asked about a man who died leaving a son and a slave girl. The boy needed to sell the girl. He viewed that she should be sold as a naïve and an artless girl. Telling him that as a singer she costs about thirty thousand, but as naïve she costs twenty thousand. He replied, she will not be sold but as a naïve. All jurists have agreed to disclaim singing.

Abu At-Tayyb At-Tabary has also compiled a book where he strongly condemned singing. Some mistaken and mislead persons have falsely presumed its permissibility. Hearing an itinerant, *Imam* Ahmad said, "it is not bad." He accredited poetry, which encourage good manners, wisdom, noble qualities and pious traits as long as no instruments, clapping or dancing are there.

In that way, `A'ishah's report (may Allah be pleased with her) that two girls were chanting beside her the poems of Buath (a story about the war between the two tribes of the Khazraj and the Aus, before Islam) come under this category. It is quite known that early Muslims did not have things such as mandolin, lute and cymbals that agitate latent lusts in a way misleading ignorant persons due to their false joy and ecstasy.

They do not claim that its some sort of lawful amusement, but rather consider it some kind of spiritual attachment calling it ecstasy. In fact, this practice is totally detached from that of early Muslims. It is overt distraction. True ecstasy comes through reciting the *Qur'an* and contemplating over it. It is when one's heart moves due to fear of punishment and longing for reward. The scope of ecstasy is not so narrow that we would resort to singers. Truly, such songs may arouse ecstasy a little bit, but most of them instigate carnal lusts.

Therefore, desiring to derive therefrom benefit for the Hereafter is similar to gazing at a beardless person to meditate over Allah's creation. But this is untrue, since his lust would preoccupy his thinking. He should rather follow the verse which reads,

> {*Do they not look at the sky above them? How We have made it and adorned it, and there are no flaws in it?*}
>
> (Qaf: 6)

Furthermore, presuming that it does not affect oneself or agitate his latent desires is a sheer pretence.

IX. Manners of the Prophet (peace and blessings of Allah be upon him)

We should know that outward manners are indicative of inward ones, in the sense that man's practical deeds are guided by spiritual contemplation and his knowledge. Inward secrets implant deeds and adorn it.

We will now highlight some manners of the Prophet (peace and blessings of Allah be upon him) in order to strengthen our *Iman* through observing his holy manners.

`A'ishah (may Allah be pleased with her) was once asked about his manners (peace and blessings of Allah be upon him). She replied, "He adopted manners of the *Qur'an*." The Almighty has praised his manners stating,

{And you stand on an exalted standard of character}

(Al-Qalam: 4)

He (peace and blessings of Allah be upon him) was very clement even with his enemies,

"Jabir ibn `Abdullah (may Allah be pleased with him) reports that some people from amongst the Jews said to Allah's Messenger (may peace be upon him), Abu'l-Qasim! As-Sam-u-'Alaikum –death overtakes you-, whereupon he said, Wa 'Alaikum – the same to you-, `A'ishah was enraged and asked him (Allah's Messenger) whether he had not heard what they had said. He said, I did hear and I retorted to them (and the curse that I invoked upon them would receive response from Allah), but (the

curse that they invoked upon us) would not be responded."

(Reported by Muslim)

He (peace and blessings of Allah be upon him) was also very generous and kind to all. He (peace and blessings of Allah be upon him) used to mend his shoes, patch his clothes and help his household. He (peace and blessings of Allah be upon him) was shyer than a virgin in her wedding night. He (peace and blessings of Allah be upon him) accepted invitation of slaves, visited the sick, walked alone, accepted gifts, ate therefrom and rewarded therefore. He (peace and blessings of Allah be upon him) never accepted charity nor approached it. He (peace and blessings of Allah be upon him) never ate bread for three consecutive days. He (peace and blessings of Allah be upon him) tied up a stone on his belly because of hunger. He (peace and blessings of Allah be upon him) never marred any food. He never ate while leaning on the ground. He (peace and blessings of Allah be upon him) used to eat from his front.

He (peace and blessings of Allah be upon him) also ate the pumpkin, vinegar and pressed dates. He (peace and blessings of Allah be upon him) sometimes rode a camel, mule or a donkey. He (peace and blessings of Allah be upon him) even walked on his bare feet. He (peace and blessings of Allah be upon him) loved perfumes and detested ugly winds. He (peace and blessings of Allah be upon him) received the graceful generously. He (peace and blessings of Allah be upon him) never treated any one harshly. His laugh was a gentle smile only. He (peace and blessings of Allah be upon him) was engaged all the time in righteous deeds. He (peace and blessings of Allah be upon him) never reviled a woman or a servant. He (peace and blessings of Allah be upon him) never hurt anyone except while fighting in Allah's cause. Whenever he (peace and blessings of Allah be upon him) was made to choose between two things, he always opted for the easier one unless it be a sin. 'Anas b. Malik (may Allah be pleased with him) reports,

> *"I served the Prophet (peace and blessings of Allah be upon him) for ten years, and he never said to me, "Uf" (a minor harsh word denoting impatience) and never blamed me by saying, "Why did you do so or why didn't you do so?"*
>
> (Reported by Muslim)

In the Torah, he (peace and blessings of Allah be upon him) was described as "Allah's chosen Prophet. He is neither stiff nor harsh. He does not raise his voice in markets. He does not retaliate mischief, but rather pardons and forgives." He (peace and blessings of Allah be upon him) used to greet people first. He (peace and blessings of Allah be upon him) never parted people first, even when shaking hands. He (peace and blessings of Allah be upon him) used to seat himself wherever he finds a room. He (peace and blessings of Allah be upon him) preferred silence for long periods. When he (peace and blessings of Allah be upon him) speaks, he used to repeat his words thrice. He never embarrassed anyone.

He (peace and blessings of Allah be upon him) was quite loyal and trustworthy. Seeing him (peace and blessings of Allah be upon him), people naturally revered him. Dealing with him (peace and blessings of Allah be upon him), they loved him very much. Anas highlighted,

> *"When fighting became fierce, we warded it off by Allah's Prophet."*
>
> (Reported by Al-Bukhari)

Furthermore, he describes the Prophet (peace and blessings of Allah be upon him) saying,

> *"The Prophet was of medium height amongst the people, neither conspicuously tall nor short. He had a rosy color, neither absolutely white nor deep brown. His hair was neither completely curly nor quite lank"*
>
> (Reported by Al-Bukhari)

The Prophet (peace and blessings of Allah be upon him) had broad shoulders, (long) hair reaching his ear-lobes. His face was like the moon. He had deep-black and large eyes with long lashes, dense beard, smooth checks and silky hands.

The Prophet's Miracles

Considering his life and manners in dealing with people and managing their different affairs as well as elaborating Shar`i Rulings, one becomes totally convinced that all these were purely divine. He was divinely guided and supported. Thus, his life proves his veracity beyond any doubt.

Practically speaking, the *Qur'an* presents the greatest and everlasting miracle granted to him (peace and blessings of Allah be upon him) by the Almighty. All people through ages have failed to produce a single verse of the like. All previous prophets (peace and blessings of Allah be upon them) had miracles which ended with the end of their message. But the *Qur'an* remains forever.

Furthermore, the moon was split for him, water gushed out between his fingers and innumerable people became full with little food of his. The stem of a palm-tree moaned longing for him, along with many other miracles.

Chapter Three

DESTRUCTIVE FLAWS

I. Within the Heart

The heart is the most honorable part of man's body, for it is the part that knows Allah, works for Him, seeks to draw near to Him, and feels the value of His bounties and favors. The other organs are only followers of the heart, which utilizes them as kings utilize their slaves.

Whoever knows his heart, knows his Lord, yet most people are ignorant of their hearts and souls. Allah, Most High, comes in between a man and his heart, and this "coming in between" is represented in His preventing him from knowing Him and being conscious of Him. Thus, knowing the heart and its qualities and functions is an integral part of the religion and a basis for those who seek the right way to Allah.

The heart is prepared to accept guidance, with regard to its nature but it may not accept it with respect to its desires and wishes. In this way, the heart remains a field of struggle between angels (the soldiers of good) and devils (the soldiers of evil) until it chooses either of them and then the chosen party settles therein, while the heart still have to resist the other party. The only way to get devils, the soldiers of evil, out of the heart is to mention Allah, as they cannot remain in a place where Allah is mentioned. Allah, the Almighty, states,

> {*From the mischief of the Whisperer (of Evil), who withdraws (after his whisper).*}
> (An-Nas: 4)

The heart is like a fort and devil is like an enemy who seeks to enter this fort to own and control it. The best way to protect a fort is to safeguard its gates, and none can safeguard its gates except a person who is well aware of them. By the same token, no one can push Satan away except one who knows the means that Satan uses to penetrate the fort of his victim. Satan's means of penetration are man's qualities, which are so many, but we are going to mention only the odious means, which are much and always used by the soldiers of Satan.

Among these heinous means are envy and covetousness. Once a man covets something his desire blinds the light of his heart with which he would recognize Satan's evil means of penetration. Satan finds more support if this covetous person is envious, as this enables the former to make good in his eyes everything that may help him to satisfy his desire, no matter if it is abominable or offensive.

Anger, craving, and wrathfulness represent other evil means of Satan against man. Anger destroys recognition, and once a man is no longer able to recognize things, Satan attacks him with his evil whispers. It is reported that Satan said, "When a man becomes heedlessly angry, we play with him as boys play with a ball".

Eating one's fill also constitutes an evil means of Satan, for it strengthens man's desire and distracts him from obedience to Allah.

There is also haste, about which the Prophet (peace and blessings of Allah be upon him) said,

> *"Haste is from Satan and deliberation is from Allah, the Almighty."*
> (Reported by At-Tirmidhi)

Love of wealth is another means, which, if inculcated in a man's heart, ruins it and drives him to seek wealth even through unlawful means and makes him stingy and afraid of poverty. He, in turn, holds the due rights of others.

Another Satanic means against man is fanaticism, especially on the part of the common people, regarding schools and doctrines, without acting according to their good requirements. Moreover, the common people may be interested only in thinking about Allah's Entity and Attributes as well as matters that are beyond the ability of their minds, and thus they may doubt the origins of the religion.

Thinking ill of Muslims is another destructive means of Satan. This is because when a Muslim thinks ill of his Muslim brother he may despise him, say and spread evil things about him, and believes that he is better than him. Still, the believer does not think ill of his Muslim brother because he always seeks excuses for him, but the hypocrite seeks defects and flaws of others. Man should keep away from suspicious situations so that others may not think ill of him.

These are only some examples of the means that Satan uses to lead man to the way of evil. The remedy of these flaws is to block the means that lead to them, by purifying the heart from all dispraised qualities. These qualities will be discussed later in detail, Allah willing.

When a man's heart is void of these evils, which represent the main instrumentality of Satan against man, nothing significant remains to support Satan against him, so he is driven away just by mentioning the Name of Allah. Adversely, if a man whose heart is controlled by vain desires and lusts remembers Allah, his remembrance does not settle in his heart, as Satan has already established himself therein.

A man may experience the truth of this by observing his own *Salah* and how Satan keeps reminding him while he is performing it of worldly matters, such as the market, clients' accounts, and the like. However, man's inner discourses are forgiven, including the evil things that he has intended to do. So if he does not do an evil thing that he has intended to do out of fear of Allah, it is written down for him as one good deed, but if he has made up his mind to do it, it is a sin, as the Prophet (peace and blessings of Allah be upon him) said,

> "When two Muslims meet each other with swords (i.e., fight each other), both the killer and the one killed are in the Fire."

The Prophet (peace and blessings of Allah be upon him) was then asked, "What is the sin of the one killed?" and he answered,

> "He was keen on killing the other one."
> (Reported by Ahmad ibn Hanbal)

Determination and keenness are condemned here because man's actions are judged according to his intentions; is it not that pride, hypocrisy, and ostentation are inner matters? That is why if a man saw in his bed a woman that he thought of to be his wife and copulated with her, he did not commit a sin by this copulation, but if he saw his wife and thought her to be a foreign woman he would commit a sin if he cohabited with her. All this refers to the intention of the heart.

It was reported in a *Hadith* that the Prophet (peace and blessings of Allah be upon him) used to say,

> "O You Who turns hearts, keep our hearts adherent to Your religion! O You Who guides hearts, guide our hearts to (showing) obedience to You!"
> (Reported by At-Tirmidhi)

And in another *Hadith*,

"The likeness of the heart is as the likeness of a feather that the wind is turning over in a desert."
                                (Reported by Ahmad)

With regard to their compliance with good and evil, the hearts are of three categories:

First: a heart that is filled with consciousness of Allah, purified with obedience to Him, and void of bad morals, so it is apt to receive Divine guidance.

Second: a forsaken heart that is charged with vain desires and stained with evils and bad morals, so it is ready to be supervised and controlled by Satan who turns it to a blinded heart that is unable to recognize the truth or be effected by admonition.

Third: a heart that is being seduced by evil thoughts and desires, but in the mean time faith-oriented thoughts and wishes are calling it to the way of good.

To illustrate this, Satan may wage an attack against a man's mind to seduce it and strengthen the vain desires within him, giving examples of people who are enjoying such desires freely and specifying some scholars of that kind; so he inclines to the Satanic seduction. Then the caller to the way of good within him wages a counter attack and reminds him how destruction goes only to those who forget the Hereafter, advising him not to be seduced by people's heedlessness. The caller to good keeps admonishing him in this way until this man's soul inclines to his advice and admonition. By then, the heart becomes hesitated between the soldier of good and that of evil, until it is completely attached to the side of which it is worthier. Thus, whoever is created for good, the way of good is made easy for him, and whoever is created for evil, its way is facilitated for him:

> ❲*Those whom Allah (in His plan) willeth to guide, He openeth their breast to Islam; those whom He willeth to leave straying, He maketh their breast close and constricted, as if they had to climb up to the skies...*❳
>
> (Al-An`am: 125)

May Allah guide us all to that which He likes!

II. Spiritual Exercise for the Soul, Gaining Good Morality, and Remedying the Heart Diseases

Good morals have always been connected to Prophets and the sincere people, whereas bad morals are destructive poisons that lead those who have them to the path of Satan. Therefore, one should know the diseases causing such ill morals and then work persistently to remedy them. In this connection, we will highlight a number of diseases and the way to remedy them, but without indulging into details, as these will be discussed later, Allah willing.

Good Morals Are Praiseworthy and Bad Morals Are Blameworthy

People tackled good morals from the perspective of their consequences, not in view of their nature, and even their consequences were not completely comprehended, as each one mentioned only what came to his mind. As a matter of fact, as far as this subject is concerned, it should be stated that every person may be good as regards both his morals and his creation, i.e., he may be good both in essence and in appearance.

The soul that recognizes things through insight is greater than the body that recognizes them through sight. That is why Allah (Glory be to Him) says,

> ⦃*Behold, thy Lord said to the angels: 'I am about to create man from clay: when I have fashioned him (in due proportion) and breathed into him of My spirit, fall ye down in obeisance unto him.*⦄
> (Sadd: 71-72)

Here, Allah draws attentions to the fact that the body is attributed to clay while the soul is attributed to Him. Consequently, morals are a reflection of the soul through which actions are brought out easily without need of thinking and meditation. So, if actions are good, they are called "good morals"; otherwise, they are called "bad morals".

Some idle people who find it difficult to practice spiritual exercises have claimed that morals are not supposed to be changeable, just as appearances are not supposed to be changeable.

In reply to this claim, it may be said that if morals were unchangeable, admonition and advice would be meaningless. Besides, how can it be alleged that morals are unchangeable while wild beasts are tamable, dogs are taught to stop eating when they are ordered to, and horses are taught how to walk properly and be easily led. Still, some natures can be effortlessly rectified while some others are not easy to rectify.

However, the belief that temperaments are unchangeable is not the crux of the matter here, since what is required from a spiritual exercise is to put one's desires and appetites to a moderate position between extravagance and negligence. Therefore, it is not acceptable to suppress desires entirely, as they have been created for certain necessary benefits which are inculcated in one's nature. If man loses the appetite of eating, he would die; if he loses the sexual appetite, there would not be any more reproduction; and if he entirely loses the feeling of anger, he would not be able to push away any harm that may attack him. Allah, the Almighty, says, {... *(Muhammad and the believers are) strong against unbelievers...* } (Al-Fath: 29) This strength does not appear except as a result of anger, so if there was no anger, strife against unbelievers would come to an end. Also, Allah, the Almighty, says, {... *who restrain anger...*} (Al

`Imran: 134) and does not say, "who loses anger".

Correspondingly, moderation is also required when dealing with the appetite of eating, as there should be neither overeating nor over lessening of the food usually needed by the body. Allah the Almighty commands,

❴... *eat and drink: but waste not by excess...* ❵
(Al-A`raf: 31)

However, if a sheikh finds that any of his followers tends to anger and satisfaction of his desires, he may exaggerate in dispraising them in order to bring him back to moderation.

Among the *Shar`i* proofs confirming that moderation is a good moral that is demanded by the *Shari`ah* and that stands between miserliness and wastefulness, is that Allah praises it when He says,

❴*Those who, when they spend, are not extravagant and not niggardly, but hold a just (balance) between those (extremes).*❵
(Al-Furqan: 67)

Sometimes man has this merit of moderation by nature and sometimes by acquisition through exercise, by training himself to do acts that bring about the prospective good moral. Accordingly, whoever wants to have the good moral of "generosity" should undertake spending-in-charity acts until this good moral becomes a habitual nature within him.

Likewise, whoever seeks to become humble should adhere to actions that reflect humility, and so on with regard to all praiseworthy morals. This is because habituation has a great effect in this regard, just as when someone seeks to learn writing, *Fiqh*, or any other field of knowledge, he keeps doing what writers or *Fuqaha'* usually do until he acquires the quality of being a writer or a *Faqih*. This is to be perfectly achieved through repetition and persistence, and it should not be expected that it may be realized in two or three days.

Just as adherence to matters that lead to virtues affects the soul and changes its nature, also adherence to laziness turns to be a habit that deprives the lazy person of all good.

Good morality may be required by keeping company with the righteous people, for natural disposition is like a thief that can steal both good and evil things.

This may be supported by the Prophet's saying,

> *"Man is affected by the morals of his friends, so let each one of you find out whom he should take as a friend."*
>
> (Reported by Abu Dawud)

The Way to Good Morality

You have already known that moderation in morals is a health in the soul and that leaving moderation is a disease. Now you should learn that the remedy of the soul is like the remedy of the body. Just as the body is not created completely, but is completed through raising and nutrition, also the soul is created incomplete and is apt to be completed. Completion of the soul is realized through purification, good morality, and knowledge.

Just as when the body is sound the doctor works to keep it sound and when it is diseased he works to cure it, also when the soul is pure and has noble morals man should seek to keep it uncorrupt and bring more strength to it, and when it is imperfect he should seek to bring it perfection.

Just as the cause of a disease in the body cannot be treated except with its anti-medication – if it is caused by heat, its medication is to be with cold and *vise versa* – also ill morals, which are caused by diseases of the heart, are to treated with their opposites; so ignorance is to be treated with knowledge, stinginess with generosity, pride with humility, and greed with avoiding the desired object.

Just as one should bear the bitterness of medicine and resist one's craving for certain things in order to have one's body cured, also one should bear the bitterness of resisting one's vain desires and keep patient while trying to remedy the diseases of one's heart. The latter is worthier of sacrifice and endurance, as physical diseases end with death whereas a disease of the heart is a suffering that lasts even after death.

In this respect, it is quite notable that the person who is entitled to treat the souls of those who seek his medication should not demand them to practice a certain spiritual exercise before knowing the reality of their morals and spiritual diseases. This is because one medicine is not necessarily suitable for all people. Therefore, if the patient is ignorant of the *Shari`ah*, he may teach him, if he is prideful, he may ask him to do things that turn him to humility, and if he is easily enraged, he may teach him how to be forbearing.

Unrelenting determination is the most important instrument for a person who is training himself to get rid of a bad moral or the like, as hesitation prolongs the period of medication. Consequently, whenever such a person finds that he has weak determination he should resist this feeling and keep patient even if he should punish himself with such means as observing long fasting and the like.

The Signs of the Heart Diseases, Remedying Them, and Discovering One's Shortcomings

Every organ in man's body is created for a certain function. One can discover that there is a disease in an organ of his body when it stops to do its function or if there is any deficiency in the organ as a whole. Accordingly, the heart becomes diseased when it no longer does the function for which it is created, that is, knowing, loving, and worshiping Allah, the Almighty, and preferring Him to every thing and every desire.

The sign of knowing Allah is to love Him, and the sign of loving Him is not to give preference to anything over Him. Therefore, whoever prefers anything to Allah has a diseased heart. Yet, the problem goes beyond this because that the diseases of the heart are concealed or secret, and one who suffers from any of them may not be aware of its existence at all. That is why people are usually heedless of such diseases. Even if they know it, they find it difficult to endure its bitterness, for its remedy is to contradict one's desires; and even if they can bear its bitterness they may not find a clever doctor who can remedy it, because doctors here are scholars and many of these have already been afflicted with the same diseases.

In order that a man remedies his diseased heart, he should treat the disease concerned moderately. So, if the disease is miserliness, for example, he should treat it by giving in charity, but without wastefulness; otherwise the medication of the disease would lead to another disease that may be more dangerous. Man may realize the reality of moderation, which is required here, by watching over himself: if he finds that keeping wealth is dearer to himself than spending it, then he is miserly and should resist this miserliness by spending from his wealth in charity, and if he finds that spending his wealth is dearer to himself than keeping it, then he is wasteful and should resist this wastefulness by keeping his wealth properly, until keeping and spending wealth become the same to him. By then he will have realized the required moderation.

The Muslim may apply this method in treating all the other morals, so that he will leave this worldly life while his heart is not attached to any of its pleasures and meet his Lord with a soul that will be in complete rest and satisfaction.

In fact, real moderation is not obviously realizable and is like the straight path. Because it is not easy for man to be straight, the Muslim is commanded to repeat every day in his Prayers,

{*Show us the straight way.*}

(Al-Fatihah: 6)

He who is not straight should make effort to draw near to straightness, as it is the way to salvation and salvation is not obtained except through righteousness. Righteous deeds in turn cannot be produced except through good morals. Consequently, every Muslim should examine his own morals and try to remedy any ill moral that he may find out in himself.

There are four methods that may help the Muslim find out his shortcomings:

First: he may consult a well-versed scholar who is aware of the defects of the human soul so that he will tell him about the defects of his soul and how to redress them.

Second: he may accompany a truthful pious friend who will watch his actions and help him find out his ill morals. `Umar ibn Al-Khattab, the Commander of the Believers, (may Allah be pleased with him) used to say, "May Allah have mercy on whoever guides us to our faults!" This denotes how the righteous predecessors used to love and appreciate those who warned them against their faults, but nowadays those who are most disliked by people are those who guide them to their shortcomings; this is a sign of weakness of faith.

Third: he may discover his own shortcomings through what his enemies and opponents say about him, because vices and failings emerge with enmity and wrath.

Fourth: the Muslim may mingle with people and avoid every blameworthy act he may see them doing.

We have already cited that desires are created for certain benefits, but it should be born in mind that what is condemned here is that desires control man instead of benefiting him. Still, he should not deprive himself totally of satisfying his desires according to Allah's commands, as this is unjust and contradicts the *Sunnah* of Prophet Muhammad (peace and blessings of Allah be upon him). After all, man should have mercy on and be gentle to his own self so that it may be able to act properly and soundly.

The Signs of Good Morality

A person who is seeking to rectify his morals may avoid indecent acts and other forms of disobedience and think that, by doing so, he has got good morality and a noble character. Actually, this is not true, because good morality consists of the qualities of the believers. Allah portrays their qualities in the Qur'an, for example, in the verses,

> *(For, Believers are those who, when Allah is mentioned, feel a tremor in their hearts, and when they hear His Signs rehearsed, find their faith*

strengthened, and put (all) their trust in their Lord; who establish regular Prayers and spend (freely) out of the gifts We have given them for sustenance: Such in truth are the Believers...﴾

﴿*Those that turn (to Allah) in repentance; that serve Him, and praise Him; that wander in devotion to the cause of Allah; that bow down and prostrate themselves in Prayer; that enjoin good and forbid evil; and observe the limits set by Allah- (these do rejoice). So proclaim the glad tidings to the Believers.*﴾

(At-Tawbah: 112)

﴿*The Believers must (eventually) win through, those who humble themselves in their Prayers; who avoid vain talk; who are active in deeds of charity; who abstain from sex, except with those joined to them in the marriage bond, or (the captive) whom their right hands possess, for (in their case) they are free from blame, but those whose desires exceed those limits are transgressors; those who faithfully observe their trusts and their covenants; and who (strictly) guard their Prayers; these will be the heirs.*﴾

(Al-Mu'minun: 1-10)

So, whoever finds it difficult to know to what extent his morality is good, may compare his qualities to those of the believers: if he enjoys all these qualities, then it is a sign of good morality; if he does not have any of them, it is a sign that he is of ill nature; and if he has some of them and does not have some others, he should strive persistently until he has all of them.

The Prophet (peace and blessings of Allah be upon him) dubbed the believers with many qualities, which are always connected to good morality. In a *Hadith* reported on the authority of Anas (may Allah be pleased with him) the Prophet said,

> *"By Him in Whose hand my soul is, no servant (of Allah) (truly) believes unless he loves for his brother what he loves for himself."*
> (Reported by Al-Bukhari and Muslim)

And, in another *Hadith* reported on the authority of Abu Hurayrah (may Allah be pleased with him), he said,

> *"Let him who believes in Allah and the Last Day be generous to his neighbor, and let him who believes in Allah and the Last Day either speak good or keep silent."*
> (Reported by Al-Bukhari and Muslim)

And in a third *Hadith*, he said,

> *"The person who is of the most perfect belief among the believers is one who is of the best good morals among them."*
> (Reported by Al-Bukhari and Muslim)

Forbearance in facing harm inflicted by the others is also a sign of good morality. It was reported that a Bedouin dragged the garment of the Prophet (peace and blessings of Allah be upon him) so strongly that the hem of the garment hurt the Prophet's shoulder. Then the man said, "O Muhammad, order that I should be given out of Allah's wealth which you are entrusted with!" The Prophet turned around towards him, then he laughed and ordered a gift for him.

Whenever children threw Uways Al-Qarani with stones he would say, "My brothers! If you should do so, please do it with small stones so that you may not bleed my legs and I become unable to perform Prayer (easily)."

These are examples of people who enjoyed such good morals because they trained themselves on endurance for the sake of Allah, so He granted them the quality of pleasure with their destinies, whether pleasant or unpleasant. Anyone who wants to have such noble qualities should follow their examples.

Raising Children on Good Morality

A child is a trust in the hands of his parents and his heart is a pure vessel that may be filled with both good and evil. Muslim parents should make their children used to good morals from the very beginning of their lifetime.

A father should inculcate good morality in his child in all aspects of life: in eating, drinking, clothing, speaking, and contacting with the others in general, etc. He should teach him the Qur'an, the *Sunnah*, and stories of the pious people, so that he can learn good morality through practical examples and learn to love and respect the people of righteousness and piety.

A father should reward and praise his child for every praiseworthy act he does. This is apt to encourage him to keep steadfast in the way of goodness. However, if the child commits some mistake, it is not necessary to punish him in the first time, but if he repeats it he may be blamed, but privately.

A child should be prevented from sleeping during the daytime because it leads to sloth and inactivity. For the same reason, he should be familiarized with exercise and action.

He should be prevented from doing certain blameworthy acts, which are widespread among ill-raised children, such as spitting and yawning in the presence of others, talkativeness, indecent words and impolite expressions, and the like. He should also be taught how to obey and respect his parents and teachers.

Sahl ibn `Abd Allah reported that when he was only three years old his maternal uncle, Muhammad ibn Suwar, taught him how to mention Allah in his heart, by saying the following words without pronouncing them factually, "Allah is with me; Allah is looking at me; Allah is witnessing my actions!" Sahl's uncle told him to say these words repeatedly every day, always in the same way. Sahl said he did so and in a short time he began to feel a special kind of sweetness stimulated by the repetition of these words. From them he learned how to be conscious of Allah all the time and this helped him to be a good worshiper of Allah throughout his lifetime.

Whoever witnesses the Hereafter through his heart and by means of certainty, his attention becomes entirely attached to it and he pays no attention to worldly life and its pleasures. Anyone who experiences this certainty-based witnessing of the Hereafter should exert his effort to keep on straightly in his way to it. Still, this requires that he should fulfill three conditions: to abandon wrongdoing completely, to seek a well-versed scholar to be his guide in the way lest devils should distract him from it, and to adhere to privacy (in matters of worship).

This is a brief account of the method that should be applied by those who seek the Hereafter. More details will be portrayed later, Allah willing.

III. The Appetite of Eating and Drinking and the Sexual Appetite

The appetite of eating and drinking is one of the most heinous means of destruction. It caused Adam to leave Paradise, and it stimulates the sexual appetite and the desire for collecting wealth, in addition to so many flaws that emerge as a result of the satisfaction of this appetite.

It was reported that the Prophet (peace and blessings of Allah be upon him) said,

> *"A believer eats in one intestine (i.e., is satisfied with a little food), and a disbeliever eats in seven intestines (i.e., eats much food)."*
> (Reported by Al-Bukhari and Muslim)

`Uqbah Ar-Rasibi said, "Once I entered upon Al-Hasan while he was having lunch. He asked me to join him but I said, 'I have eaten my fill so I cannot eat any more.' 'Glory be to Allah! Should a Muslim eat until he cannot eat (any more)?' he commented."

Some ascetics went beyond limits in suppressing their desire for food and resisting the pain of hunger. Of course, this is not fair, because what man is entitled to do is to satisfy this desire moderately. This moderation is realized in its best form when the Muslim follows the Prophet's instructions in this regard, namely, to make a third of his belly for food, a third for drink, and a third for breath. This makes his body healthy and protects it from diseases.

A person who is used to gratifying his appetite of eating and drinking should start to lessen his food and drink little by little until he reaches the limit of moderation to which we have just referred. He is also recommended to take of foods and drinks the quantities that maintain his strength and with which he neither feels hungry nor fed up. In this way he will get a sound body and a clear mind. If, however, he eats too much, he starts to sleep much and becomes thick-witted.

Interestingly enough, whenever someone avoids satisfying any appetite, he should avoid ostentation as well. Bearing this in mind, some righteous people would keep at home things that they had already avoided for the sake of asceticism, lest this avoidance be taken as something contradicting their asceticism. No one can stand for such an act except a sincere person, because, by doing so, he tastes the bitterness of patience twice.

As for the sexual appetite, it was originally created in man for two reasons: first, for the continuation of human reproduction, and second, for man to taste a special form of pleasure through which he would conceive the pleasures of the Hereafter. Yet, if man does not satisfy this appetite moderately, it causes him numerous horrendous problems and tribulations. That is why women are Satan's traps that he uses against men. How truthful are the words of the Prophet (peace and blessings of Allah be upon him),

> *"After me I have not left any affliction more harmful to men than women."*
> (Reported by Al-Bukhari and Muslim)

And, a righteous man once said, "If I am to be entrusted with a public treasury, I believe I will render back the trust, but if I am to be asked to stay alone with a black woman (even) for an hour, I cannot be sure that she will be safe with me."

This personal testimony may find support in the Prophetic

Hadith, in which the Messenger of Allah (peace and blessings of Allah be upon him) said,

> *"Whenever a man is in privacy with a woman Satan makes the third of them."*
> (Reported by Al-Bukhari and Muslim)

Exceeding the proper bounds in satisfying this appetite may distract the Muslim from the Hereafter and lead him to commit indecent acts. Consequently, man should avoid reaching this dangerous degree of inclination and addiction from the very beginning; otherwise it may be very difficult for him to cure it. After all, protection is better than cure.

IV. The Flaws Pertaining to the Tongue

There are various flaws, which are related to the tongue and for which man finds special inclination in his heart stimulated by his human temperament. Silence is the only way with which man can escape from or get rid of such flaws. Therefore, it may be better to speak first about the virtue of silence, before dealing with the flaws pertaining to the tongue.

First of all, it should be known that silence comprehends man's determination and rids his mind of wasteful thoughts.

It was reported that the Prophet (peace and blessings of Allah be upon him) said,

> "Whoever can guarantee (the chastity of) what is between his two jaw-bones and what is between his two legs (i.e., his tongue and his private parts), I guarantee Paradise for him."
>
> (Reported by Al-Bukhari)

Moreover, in the well known *Hadith* reported on the authority of Mu`adh ibn Jabal (may Allah be pleased with him), the Prophet (peace and blessings of Allah be upon him) took hold of his tongue and said, "Restrain this!" Mu`adh said, "O Messenger of Allah, will what we say be held against us?" He said,

> "May your mother be bereaved of you, Mu`adh! Is there anything that topples people on their faces – or he said on their noses – into Hell-fire other than the jests of their tongues?"
>
> (Reported by At-Tirmidhi)

Ibn Mas`ud said, "There is nothing that is in more need of

imprisonment than my tongue."

And, Abu Ad-Darda' said, "Be just to your ears as (you are) to your tongue. You have been provided with two ears and (only) one tongue so that you may hear more than you speak."

Flaws Pertaining to Speech

The first flaw: speaking about meaningless and insignificant matters

Whoever realizes the true value of his time and that it is his capital in life does not spends it in trifling matters. This is because such recognition prevents his tongue from indulging into meaningless speeches. The Prophet (peace and blessings of Allah be upon him) was reported to have said,

> *"Part of someone's being a good Muslim is his leaving alone that which does not concern him."*
> (Reported by At-Tirmidhi)

The second flaw: indulging into falsehood, by speaking about acts and things reflecting disobedience to Allah, the Almighty, such as places where intoxicants are taken and where indecent acts are committed.

There are many forms of disobedience to Allah. It was reported on the authority of Abu Hurayrah (may Allah be pleased wit him) that the Prophet (peace and blessings of Allah be upon him) said,

> *"A servant (of Allah) may say a word because of which he may fall into the Fire (a distance that is) more than that is between the east and the west."*

An example of such a form of words may be a person's hot

argumentation that he launches against some other person in order to prove that he is right and the other is wrong; this may stimulate and reflect pride and showing off. In order to remedy this flaw, the Muslim should suppress "pride" that drives him to show his superiority over the others. The Prophet (peace and blessings of Allah be upon him) said,

> *"The most hated person in the sight of Allah, is the most quarrelsome one."*
> (Reported by Al-Bukhari)

This refers to quarrel that is originally stimulated for the sake of falsehood or out of ignorance. In passing this, it is worth noting that even a person who has some right and seeks to get it should avoid disputation and quarrel as possible as he can, as they normally cause wrath, animosity, and hatred.

The third flaw: speaking gutturally

However, this does not include manners of speech and expressions that orators use when preaching people without exaggeration or indulging into strange or awkward words. This is because such manners, words, and expressions are used in this connection for addressing the hearts and feelings of the audience directly, so that they may be affected by the preaching positively.

The fourth flaw: insulting, and uttering indecent words

A person is afflicted with this flaw when he expresses embarrassing matters with explicit words and phrases, especially expressions related to sexual intercourse and the like. Pious and righteous people often avoid such expressions and get to the point concerned indirectly.

The fifth flaw: extravagant joking

There is no harm, however, if a man jokes politely and saying only the truth. The Prophet (peace and blessings of Allah be upon him) would joke but would never say anything that was not true.

It was reported that once he said to an old woman,

> "*No old woman will enter Paradise,*" *then he recited,* ⟨*We have created (their Companions) of special creation, and made them virgin pure (and undefiled),*⟩ *(Al-Waqi`ah: 35-36).*
> (Reported by At-Tirmidhi)

As far as the Prophet's joking is concerned, everyone should know three facts:

1. that it was handled through true statements,

2. that he used it mostly with women and kids, as well as men who needed a special kind of discipline through this way,

3. and that the Prophet used it rarely; so, anyone who seeks to jokes much should not seek proof in the *Ahadith* dealing with the Prophet's joking..

The sixth flaw: mockery and ridicule

A person is afflicted with this flaw when he seizes the attentions of people to the vices and shortcomings of someone by means of mockery and ridicule. This may be done through imitation, gesticulation, or inkling. Undoubtedly, Islam forbids and condemns such acts.

The seventh flaw: revealing secrets, breaking promises and oaths, and lying

This is entirely forbidden, except in cases where man's intention is directed towards some good goal, as in war.

As long as they are needed, indirect speech and gesticulation are recommended as better ways than direct and explicit speech. The Prophet (peace and blessings of Allah be upon him) said,

> *"Indirect speech (and gesticulation) helps man to avoid lying."*
>
> (Reported by Al-Bayhaqi)

If, however, one is not obliged to use indirect speech, it becomes detestable, since it resembles lying.

The eighth flaw: *Ghibah*

Ghibah, or backbiting, is forbidden in the Glorious Qur'an where a person who commits it is given the similitude of a person who eats the flesh of his dead brother.

It is also condemned in the *Sunnah*. We read in a Prophetic *Hadith*,

> *"Verily, your blood (i.e., life), your property, and your honor are inviolable (and sacred) among you..."*
>
> (Reported by Muslim)

And, on the authority of Abu Barzah Al-Aslami, the Prophet (peace and blessings of Allah be upon him) also said,

> *"O you who have believed (only) with their tongues*

while (true) belief has not visited their hearts! Do not backbite Muslims nor pursue their defects (and faults), because whomever Allah pursues his defects (and faults) He disgraces him even though inside his house."

(Reported by ibn Abi Ad-Dunya)

Ghibah is that a Muslim mentions his Muslim brother in a manner that the latter dislikes, whether by referring to a defect in his body, such as shortness and squint; or in his lineage, as to say, for example, that his father is immoral or indecent; or in his morality, as to say, for instance, that he is dirty.

All this is involved in the Prophetic *Hadith* where it was reported that when the Prophet (peace and blessings of Allah be upon him) was asked about *Ghibah*, he answered,

"To mention your brother in a manner which he dislikes". Then he was asked, "What if my brother actually has (this failing) that I made a mention of?" The Prophet said, "If (that failing) is actually found in your brother, you in fact backbit him, and if that is not in him it is a slander."

(Reported by Muslim)

It is also worth mentioning that whatever involves the meaning of insulting is included in *Ghibah*, whether it is in the form of words, gestures, or writing. Additionally, whoever listens to *Ghibah*, is regarded as a participant therein unless he denies it either with his tongue, or with his heart if he fears to do so in public; he may also leave the place where it is being committed or turn the speech being circulated into another subject. In all situations, he must deny backbiting. This is, of course, part of the Muslim's duties towards his fellow Muslim brothers.

The Causes and Remedy of *Ghibah*

There are many things that lead to *Ghibah*, including the following:

1. Alleviation of or response to one's anger: A person may be led by his anger with another person to backbite him.

2. Compliance with one's guests or fellows: By means of compliment, a person may share his fellows or guests in backbiting others, thinking that this is a requisite of good social relations or that they may deny his act if he does not do so.

3. Upgrading one's position by degrading that of another person: For example, a person may say that so-and-so is ignorant or narrow-minded, aiming to show that he is knowledgeable and broad-minded and, consequently, better than him.

4. Joking and jesting: A person may backbite some people just for the sake of making some others laugh; this even represents a means of livelihood for some persons.

As far as the remedy of *Ghibah* is concerned, the backbiter should know that, by backbiting people, he subjects himself to the wrath and punishment of Allah, the Almighty, and that his good deeds will be paid to those whom he backbites, and if he has no good deeds their evil deeds will be loaded on him. It is a very effective remedy for any backbiter to remember and comprehend these facts. Furthermore, whenever he is about to backbite someone, he may think about his own shortcomings and how to rectify himself. In this way, he may feel ashamed of himself when realizing that he himself has defects that others can see. Even if a backbiter thinks that he has no defects, he may show gratitude to Allah for His uncountable favors and bounties by not defiling himself with one of the ugliest flaws, i.e., *Ghibah*. Moreover and more important still, he should remedy *Ghibah* by overpowering the cause or causes leading to it. So, if he knows that he backbites someone because he is, for example, angry with him, he should suppress his anger, and so on.

Before moving to another point, it is worth noting to highlight the fact that *Ghibah* may be committed by the heart, and this is what may be called "thinking ill of the others". A Muslim should not think ill of another Muslim unless he explicitly knows about him some evil thing that cannot be interpreted as meaning otherwise, especially when he knows it through a trustful, faithful Muslim. Nevertheless, a Muslim is generally recommended not to respond to ill thoughts as regards his Muslim brothers. He may instead invoke Allah on their behalf whenever Satan pushes him to think evil of them, for this enrages Satan and drives him away, fearing that he may be accustomed to invocation through his evil whispers.

Legal Excuses for Using *Ghibah*, and Expiation for It

In the *Shari`ah* of Islam, there are certain matters which drive away the sin of *Ghibah*. They may be presented as follows:

First, complaining about oppression or injustice: It is lawful for an oppressed or wronged person to mention the evil things committed against him by one who has oppressed or wronged him, in the presence of someone who is supposed to bring him his right back.

Second, seeking the help of others for changing something wrong and bringing an oppressor back to the way of righteousness.

Third, asking for a *Fatwa* regarding a certain matter: However, it is recommendable for the person who wants to do so to use hints or indirect references when telling the *Mufti* about his legal opinion concerning "someone" who has wronged him.

Fourth, warning a Muslim against some evil: One, for example, is permitted to warn a pious person against some wicked or immoral person whom he visits frequently without knowing about his wickedness or immorality. This is also recommendable in consultation regarding matters such as marriage and entrusting money and the like. However, if the consulted person here has to warn against some evil, he must do so out of good advice, and not calumniation and slander.

Fifth, if a person is known with a special title such as "the lame" or "the blear-eyed," it is not an act of *Ghibah* to call him as such. But, if he can be recognized with another means, it is preferable to use this means instead of calling him with such titles.

Sixth, if a person commits immoral and indecent acts in public and does not feel shy of doing so, it is not an act of *Ghibah* to tell the others about these acts.

As for expiation for *Ghibah*, it should be known that a backbiter commits two sins: one is violation of Allah's right, as he has committed something that He has forbidden him to do; the expiation for this sin is repentance and regret. The other sin is committed against the honor of the backbitten person; if the latter has known about the backbiter's act against him, he should ask him for forgiveness. It was reported on the authority of Abu Hurayrah (may Allah be pleased with him) that the Messenger of Allah (peace and blessings of Allah be upon him) said,

> *"Whoever has wronged his brother with regard to wealth or honor, should ask for his pardon (before his death), before he pays for it (in the Hereafter) when he will have neither a Dinar nor a Dirham. (He should secure pardon in this life) before some of his good deeds are taken and paid to this (his brother), or (if he has no good deeds) some of the bad deeds of this (his brother) are taken to be loaded on him."*
> (Reported by Al-Bukhari and Muslim)

If, however, the backbitten person has not known about the backbiter's act against him, the latter should keep asking Allah to forgive him (the backbitten person), so that he may not know about it and thus become angry with him (and that he himself may forgive him if he is to know about it).

The ninth flaw: *Namimah* (Calumniation)

It was reported that the Prophet (peace and blessings of Allah be upon him) said,

> *"A calumniator will not enter Paradise."*
> (Reported by Al-Bukhari and Muslim)

Namimah is generally commited when a person tells someone about the evil speech said about him by someone else, but it is also connected to the revelation of anyting that is dislikeable to be revealed, be it a saying or a deed.

Whoever receives a *Namimah*, as for example when someone tells him that someone else has said such-and-such words against him, has to do six things:

1. not to believe the person who has told him, because a

calumniator is an immoral person whose testimony is to be rejected,

2. to advice him not do so again,

3. to hate him for the sake of Allah, because Allah hates him,

4. not to think ill of his fellow Muslim brother who has been accused of saying those evil words about him,

5. not let this evil claim drive him to spy on his brother to investigate the truth, for Allah, the Almighty, commands, ﴾... *and spy not on each other...*﴿ (Al-Hujurat: 12),

6. and not to do himself that which he has forbidden the calumniator to do, i.e., to tell others about what he has told him.

It was reported that once Sulayman ibn `Abd Al-Malik said to a man, "I have been told that you said such-and-such evil words about me". The man assured he did not say so and Sulayman commented, "But the person who has told me is truthful". "A calamniator cannot be truthful," said the man. "You have told the truth! You can leave peacefully," said Sulayman.

Here, we recall that Yahya ibn Abi Kathir said, "A calumniator ruins in an hour what a magician cannot ruin in a whole month."

The tenth flaw: the speech transformed by a double-faced person among disputants

Such a person tells each party what he has heard from the other party against them, adding to this speech what conforms with the party concerned and promising that he would help them. Such is the worst amongst people, as the Prophet (peace and blessings of Allah be upon him) said;

> *"The worst amongst people is the double-faced one; he comes to some people with one face and to others with another face."*
> (Reported by Al-Bukhari and Muslim)

The eleventh flaw: praising

Prasing may produce a number of flaws, some of which are connected to the one who praises and some others are related to the praised one.

A person who praises another person may say things that he cannot make sure whether they are true or not. Moreover he may exaggerate in his praiseing so much that he may lie, or he may praise someone who is worth dispraising.

As for the praised person, he may be negatively affected by this praise and turns into a prideful person and thus becomes subject to destruction. That is why the Prophet (peace and blessings of Allah be upon him) said to a man when he heard him praising another,

> *"Woe to you! You have cut off your fellow's neck (i.e., the praised one)..."*
> (Reported by Al-Bukhari and Muslim)

Moreover, when a person is praised he may become self-admired and think that he has perfectly carried out what he is entitled to do and thus starts to adhere to idleness. That is why the Prophet (peace and blessings of Allah be upon him) said to the man, *"... You have cut off your fellow's neck..."*

If praising is free from these flaws, then there is no harm, because the Prophet (peace and blessings of Allah be upon him) praised Abu Bakr and `Umar (may Allah be pleased with them both) and other Companions (may Allah be pleased with them all).

On his part, the person who is praised should not let praising lead him to pride, arrogance, or inactivity. The only way to save himself from these flaws is to remember what he really is and that if the one who has praised him were to know about him what he himself knows, he would never praise him.

The twelfth flaw: mistaking the content of words regarding religious matters, especially those connected to Allah, the Almighty. Only eloquent scholars can use such words properly, so whoever is not eloquent and knowledgeable enough to do so is not free from committing mistakes in this regard. The Prophet (peace and blessings of Allah be upon him) was reported to have said,

> *"None of you should say, 'My bondman and my slave-girl,' for all of you are the bondmen of Allah, and all your women are the slave-girls of Allah; but let him say, 'My young man and my young girl'."*
> (Reported by Al-Bukhari and Muslim)

By contemplating what we have said so far about the flaws pertaining to the tongue, it becomes clear that the more man speaks, the more he is subject to fall into these flaws. So it may be true that silence is much better than speaking on many occasions.

Before moving to another subject, we may conclude this subject by highlighting the fact that among the flaws which are widespread among the common people is asking (so much) about the Attributes of Allah, the Almighty. It should be realized that Satan may whisper to a common person that by indulging into matters that concern scholars he becomes a scholar and one of the people of superiority. Satan may also keeps making this "indulging" likeable in his eyes until he says words that lead him to disbelief while he does not perceive it. The Prophet (peace and blessings of Allah be upon him) said,

> *"People will not stop asking questions until they say, 'This is Allah, the Creator of everything, then who created Allah?'"*
>
> (Reported by Al-Bukhari and Muslim)

What the common people are entitled to do in this regard is to avoid indulging into such serious matters, to believe in them as they are, to accept what is mentioned in the Qur'an and the *Sunnah* thereabout, and to occupy themselves with worshiping Allah as they are commanded.

V. Anger, Malevolence, and Envy

Anger is a flame of fire, and when man is angry he has some relation to the accursed Satan who said, as the Qur'an tells,

> ❨... *Thou didst create Me from fire, and him from clay.*❩
>
> (Al-A`raf: 12)

Anger is condemned in Islam because it produces malevolence and envy.

> *Once a man said to the Prophet (peace and blessings of Allah be upon him), "Advise me!" and the Prophet said, "Do not become angry". The man asked (the same) again and again, and the Prophet said in each time, "Do not become angry".*
>
> (Reported by Al-Bukhari)

It was also reported that Allah's Messenger (peace and blessings of Allah be upon him) said,

> *"The strong person is not the one who overcomes the people by his strength, but the strong person is the one who controls himself while in anger."*
>
> (Reported by Al-Bukhari and Muslim)

Again, it was reported that once Iblis (Allah's curse be upon him) said to Prophet Musa (peace and blessings of Allah be upon him), "O Musa! Beware of fury, for I play with the furious man as children play with the ball..."

As a matter of fact, anger is a feeling that drives man to take revenge on whosoever has enraged him. With respect to the strength of anger, people are classified into three categories: excessive, negligent, and moderate.

Excessiveness in anger is blameworthy, because it causes the angry person to lose his ability to think. Negligence is also dispraised with regard to anger, because a man who does not show any kind of anger has no enthusiasm or interest, and is unable to restrain his own vain desires, because they are to be overpowered by the strength of anger within man, as he feels angry with himself when he has tendency towards futile lusts. Thus, as both excessiveness and negligence are dispraised as regards anger, moderation is the only means with which man can get the benefit of anger.

The Causes and Remedy of Anger

It has already been mentioned that the remedy of any defect mainly depends on the elimination of its cause or causes. Self-admiration, joking, argumentation, and betrayal are among the primary causes of anger. Undoubtedly, these are ill morals which the *Shari`ah* condemns, and in order to get rid of them, man should treat each of them with its opposite.

As far as the remedy of anger is concerned, the Muslim should fulfill certain matters, as follows:

First: he should get himself well-acquainted with the virtues of forgiveness, forbearance, endurance, and restraining anger. Al-Bukhari reported on the authority of ibn `Abbas (may Allah be pleased with them both) that a man asked for permission to meet `Umar (may Allah be pleased with him) and he was permitted to do so. Then the man said to `Umar, "O ibn Al-Khattab! By Allah, you do not give us much (from the public treasury) nor do you judge between us with justice." Thereupon `Umar (may Allah be pleased with him) became so angry that he was about to punish the man, but Al-Hurr ibn Qays said, "O Commander of the Believers! Allah, Glorified and Exalted be He, said to His Prophet, Muhammad, (peace and blessings of Allah be upon him), ❴*Hold to forgiveness; command what is right; but turn away from the ignorant*❵ (Al-A`raf: 199), and this is one of 'the ignorant'". Immediately, `Umar (may Allah be pleased with him) complied with the instruction in the verse, as he always used to do with the instructions of the Book of Allah.

Second: he should frighten himself with the punishment of Allah, the Almighty, by saying to himself, "Allah's might over me is much greater than my might over that person (who has enraged me), so if I punish him now, I cannot be sure I will be safe from Allah's punishment on the Day of Resurrection, and I am much more in need of His forgiveness (than His punishment)!"

Third: he should warn himself against the consequences of enmity, revenge, and glee at the misfortune of his disputants, for he is not free from calamities that may afflict him at any time, just like them.

Fourth: the Muslim should meditate how ugly his image seems when he is angry, and that he should not lead himself to such a terrible image.

Fifth: he should think over the cause that invites him to take revenge; for example, the cause of his anger may be because Satan says to him, "You should not stand still after hearing such humiliating words (that he may have just heard from someone), otherwise you will become humble in the sight of people." At that moment, he should say to himself, "Do you fear that you should become humble in the sight of people and do not fear of being humble in the sight of Allah, the angels, and Prophets?" In this way, he may restrain his anger and escape from the destructive traps of Satan.

Sixth: the Muslim should remember that his anger has been caused by something that happened according to Allah's will and not his own will, so how can he comply with his own will other than the will of Allah, the Almighty?

This is how the Muslim should act when being inflicted with the flaw of anger, so that he may avoid its ruinous and baleful consequences.

Restraining Anger

Praising the pious people, Allah, the Almighty, says,

❴*... who restrain anger...*❵

(Al `Imran: 134)

And, the Prophet (peace and blessings of Allah be upon him) said,

> *"Whoever restrains his anger though able to release it, Allah will call him in front of creatures (on the Day of Resurrection) and make him choose whichever (he would like to have) of the Hur Al-`In (female companions with beautiful, big, and lustrous eyes)."*
>
> (Reported by Abu Dawud)

Also, `Umar (may Allah be pleased with him) said, "Whoever is conscious of Allah, does not release his anger and whoever fears Allah does not do whatever he wants..."

Forbearance

Once the Prophet (peace and blessings of Allah be upon him) said to Ashajj ibn Qays,

"You have two (good) morals that Allah and His Messenger love: forbearance and deliberateness."

A man insulted ibn `Abbas (may Allah be pleased with them both) and when he finished ibn `Abbas said, "O `Ikrimah, if this man (who had insulted me) has any need, fulfill it for him". Thereupon the man felt ashamed and lowered his head.

Once a slave of Abu Dharr came to him with a sheep whose leg had been broken. On asking him who had broken its leg, the slave answered, "I have done this deliberately in order to enrage you so that you may hit me and commit a sin as a result." "I shall enrage the one who drove you to do so (i.e., Satan)," commented Abu Dharr then set the slave free!

One night, `Umar ibn `Abd Al-`Aziz entered a mosque when it was so dark that he stumbled upon a man who was sleeping there. The man raised his head and exclaimed, "Are you crazy?" "No," said `Umar. The soldiers of `Umar were about to punish the man when `Umar prevented them, saying, "He just asked me, 'Are you crazy?' and I said, 'No'."

A man said evil words about `Ali ibn Al-Husayn (may Allah be pleased with him) so his slaves were enraged, but he told them to calm down and said to the man, "What you do not know about us is much more that what you have just said. Do you have any need that we can fulfill for you?" The man felt ashamed and said nothing, so `Ali gave him a garment that he himself was just wearing and ordered his slaves to give him a thousand *Dirhams*. After that the man used to say, "I testify that you are a descendant of the Messenger!"

A man told Wahb ibn Munabbih that so-and-so had abused him and Wahb said to him, "And you are the only postman that Satan has found (to let me know about it)!"

Forgiveness and Leniency

The meaning of forgiveness appears when a person has a right over another but he does not take it. This is different from forbearance and restraining anger. Allah, the Almighty, says about the pious,

> ❨... and (they) pardon (all) men...❩
> (Al `Imran: 134)

He, Most High, also says,

> ❨... but if a person forgives and makes reconciliation, his reward is due from Allah...❩
> (Ash-Shura: 40)

And, the Prophet (peace and blessings of Allah be upon him) said,

> "... and Allah does not increase a servant (of His) as a result of his forgiveness except in glory..."
> (Reported by At-Tirmidhi)

It was also reported by Al-Bukhari and Muslim on the authority of `A'ishah (may Allah be pleased with her) that the Prophet (peace and blessings of Allah be upon him) said,

> "Surely Allah, the Almighty, loves that one should be kind and lenient in all matters."

And, in another *Hadith* he said,

> *"He who is deprived of tender feelings is in fact deprived of good."*
>
> (Reported by Muslim)

Malevolence and Envy

If a person restrains his anger only because he is unable to release it at once, it settles within him in the form of malevolence. The sign of this is that he starts to hate the person who has enraged him. Therefore, malevolence is the fruit of anger and malevolence in turn may lead to envy.

It was reported on the authority of Az-Zubayr ibn Al-'Awwam (may Allah be pleased with him) that the Messenger of Allah (peace and blessings of Allah be upon him) said,

> *"The disease of the nations before you has crept into you: envy and hatred."*
>
> (Reported by Muslim)

And, Al-Bukhari and Muslim reported that the Prophet (peace and blessings of Allah be upon him) said,

> *"Do no hate one another, and do not cut (your relation) with one another, and do not envy one another, and do not turn away from one another; and O Allah's worshipers! Be brothers (as Allah has ordered you!)"*

In another *Hadith*, the Prophet (peace and blessings of Allah be upon him) said,

> *"Verily, envy eats good deeds as fire eats firewood."*
>
> (Reported by Ahmad)

Ibn Sirin said, "I have never envied anyone for anything related to this worldly life, because if he is to be one of the residents of Paradise, how can I envy him for something pertaining to worldly life while he is going to Paradise? And if he is to be one of the residents of the Fire, how can I envy him for something pertaining to worldly life while he is going to the Fire?"

When Allah bestows some blessing on a Muslim, the others react to this blessing in either of two ways: to hate this blessing and wish that it may be removed, and this is the *Hasad* or envy; or they may not hate it nor wish that it should be removed, but rather wish that they could just receive a blessing like it, and this is *Ghibtah* or rejoicing.

Sometimes envy can be remedied with contentment with one's destiny, other times with turning away from worldly pleasures, and sometimes with thinking over what is connected to these bounties of grief in this life and accountability in the other life. By any of these methods, man can restrain his desire for the bounties that the others enjoy.

Yet still, it should be borne in mind that it is not from envy that a person likes to exceed his fellows or counterparts by accomplishing something good that they have not yet accomplished. This is because he does not wish that the good things they have should be taken away from them but wants to excel them, looking forward to receiving Allah's good reward for his effort. Allah, the Almighty, says,

﴾... *and for this let those aspire, who have aspirations.*﴿

(Al-Mutaffifin: 26)

And, Al-Bukhari and Muslim reported on the authority of

ibn 'Umar (may Allah be pleased with them both) that the Prophet (peace and blessings of Allah be upon him) said,

> *"There is no envy except in two: a person whom Allah, Glorified and Exalted be He, has given (knowledge of) the Qur'an and he recites it during the night and during the day (and acts upon it), and a person whom Allah has given wealth and he spends it in the cause of truth during the night and during the day."*

Causes of Envy

Envy generally appears as a result of enmity, pride, self-admiration, love of leadership, and impurity of the soul. However, enmity is the most serious one among these causes, because it leads to malevolence and this in turn causes man to be thirst for revenge and drives him to gloat over any calamity that may afflict his enemy and, of course, grieve if he receives any blessing.

As for the relationship between pride and envy, it is that when a person obtains some wealth or high standing, someone may fear that he may consequently be greater than him and starts to show off before him; and this is something that he would not be able to stand. The disbelievers envied the Prophet (peace and blessings of Allah be upon him) for similar reasons; Allah, the Almighty says,

> ﴾*Also, they say: Why is not his Qur'an sent down to some leading man in either of the two (chief) cities?*﴿

(Az-Zukhruf: 31)

Allah, Most High, also tells what they said about the believers,

❮... *is it these then that Allah hath favored from amongst us?...*❯

(Al-An'am: 53)

And, in another verse, He says,

❮... *Ye are only men like ourselves...*❯

(Yasin: 15)

and,

❮*If ye obey a man like yourselves, behold, it is certain ye will be lost.*❯

(Al-Mu'minun: 34)

Thus, the disbelievers did not like that the Message should be given to a mere human being just like themselves, so they envied Allah's Messengers.

As for love of leadership and glory, its likeness is that a man dislikes having a match in anything that he perfectly masters, especially when he is fond of being praised and believes that he is the only one of his kind. So, when he hears about any equivalent of him even in the remotest part of the world, he is upset and wishes that this equivalent may be destroyed or that he may lose the blessing in which he shares him.

As for impurity of the soul, it stimulates the person who is inflicted with it to rejoice at the calamities afflicting people and grieve if they are granted any favors. It is quite difficult to remedy this impurity of the soul, because it has no accidental cause that may be eliminated as a means of remedy, but its cause is impurity of nature, which is not easy to change.

Perhaps, it is obvious from the above presentation that love of worldly life and its pleasures is the main driving power that produces and motivates the causes of envy. Therefore, worldly life, what is praised and what is dispraised therein will be tackled in detail in the following pages.

Worldly Life

The Qur'an contains many verses that highlight the true nature of worldly life and encourage people not to indulge into its trivial pleasures. For example, we read,

> ❴Fair in the eyes of men is the love of things they covet: women and sons; heaped up hoards of gold and silver; horses branded (for blood and excellence); and (wealth of) cattle and well-tilled land. Such are the possessions of this world's life; but in nearness to Allah is the best of the goals (to return to). Say: Shall I give you glad tidings of things far better than those?...❵
> (Al `Imran: 14-15)

> ❴... for the life of this world is but good and chattels of deception.❵
> (Al `Imran: 185)

> ❴The likeness of the life of the present is as the rain which We send down from the skies: by its mingling arises the produce of the earth which provides food for men and animals...❵
> (Yunus: 24)

> ❴Know ye (all), that the life of this world is but play and amusement, pomp and mutual boasting and multiplying, (in rivalry) among yourselves, riches and children. Here is a similitude: how rain and the

growth which it brings forth, delight (the hearts of) the tillers; soon it withers; thou wilt see it grow yellow; then it becomes dry and crumbles away...⟩
(Al-Hadid: 20)

Also, the *Sunnah* provides a great deal of *Ahadith* covering the same subject. Al-Bukhari and Muslim reported on the authority of Al-Musawwar ibn Shaddad that the Prophet (peace and blessings of Allah be upon him) said,

"The likeness of this worldly life in the Hereafter is as the likeness of what any of you (gets when he) puts his finger into the sea; so let him see that which he gets!"

In another *Hadith*, the Prophet (peace and blessings of Allah be upon him) said,

"The worldly life is a prison on the part of the believer and a garden on the part of the disbeliever."
(Reported by Muslim)

Truly, worldly life is a transitional abode through which one gets to the Hereafter, the abode of eternal settlement. The keys of worldly treasures were offered to Prophet Muhammad (peace and blessings of Allah be upon him) but he refused them, as he disliked taking something that his Lord detests.

Examples of Life

Worldly life has been given many examples, of which we may present the following.

Yunus ibn `Ubayd said, "Worldly life has been given the likeness of a sleeping man who is viewing, during his sleep, both what he likes and what he dislikes, then he suddenly awakes."

It was said that Prophet `Isa (peace be upon him) saw worldly life in the form of a toothless old woman who had been adorned with all kinds of adornments. He asked her, "How many men did you marry?" "They are uncountable," she replied. "Well. Did they all die or did they all divorce you?" asked Prophet `Isa. "No. I killed them all," the old woman answered. Thereupon Prophet `Isa commented, "How miserable your would-be husbands are! How can they not take admonition from what happened to your ex-husbands? How can it be that you destroy them, one after another, while they pay no attention to this?"

Here is another example indicating what life is, but it may be a different one: konw that man experiences three conditions with regard to worldly life: a condition in which he is nothing, and that is before his existence in life; another condition is experienced from the moment he dies up to endless existence; and between these two conditions is a halfway condition represented in man's days in worldly life. Man's lifetime is nothing when compared to the time of the other two conditions; it is simply less than the twinkling of an eye in the time of the world.

Whoever looks at the world from this perspective will never adhere to it nor will it ever concern him as to whether he spends his lifetime in ease or in adversity. That is why the Prophet (peace and blessings of Allah be upon him) did not pay attention to it and said,

> *"I have nothing to do with the (pleasures of) worldly life. It is only that my likeness and the likeness of this worldly life is that of a traveler who*

takes a nap under a tree and then leaves it away."
(Reported by At-Tirmidhi)

Prophet `Isa (peace be upon him) said, "Worldly life is (like) a bridge, so cross it and do not populate it." This is an explicit example of worldly life, for it is only a "bridge" on which man crosses to the Hereafter; his cradle is the first part of this bridge and his grave is its second and last part.

It was said, "The similitude of a person who seeks worldly pleasure is as the similitude of a person who drinks from a sea: the more he drinks the more he feels thirsty, until drinking kills him."

Finally, Al-Bukhari and Muslim reported on the authority of Abu Musa (may Allah be pleased with him) that Allah's Messenger (peace and blessings of Allah be upon him) said,

> *"My example and the example of the message with which Allah has sent me is like that of a man who came to his people and said, 'I have seen with my own eyes the enemy forces, and I am a naked warner (to you) so save yourselves!' A group of his people obeyed him and went out at night, slowly and stealthily and were safe, while another group of them did not believe him and thus the army took them in the morning and destroyed them. This is the likeness of those who obey me and follow the message that I have brought and those who disobey me and deny the truth that I have brought."*

Worldly Life Between Praise and Dispraise

Many people hear about the dispraising of worldly life in general, so they refrain from things they naturally need such as food and drink, thinking that this dispraising includes even the beneficial things in worldly life.

Allah, the Almighty, has inculcated in the souls of human beings yearning for things that are useful to them. However, such people prevent their souls from satisfying their needs whenever they long for any of these things, believing that this is true asceticism and out of ignorance of the human rights and needs. This is absolutely wrong, as given facts prove. Worldly life consists of certain things and objects that were originally created for the use of man. This includes the earth and all things it contains and bears of foods, drinks, clothing, etc. Man is commanded to make good use of all these things, which are to help him to fulfill his job on earth, i.e., being Allah's vicegerent thereon, and to assist him in his way to the Hereafter. In order to make good use of these things which have been made subservient to him, man should take of them only what he needs; otherwise they may distract him from the Hereafter and turn him into a mere pursuer of worldly pleasures; this, of course, contradicts the goal of his existence in life. Therefore, there should be neither extravagance nor negligence in dealing with things that Allah has created and subjected to the benefit of man in this worldly life.

Wealth between Miserliness and Geed, and Generosity and Contentment

Wealth is not to be dispraised or condemned in its own right. What is blameworthy is man's bad use of this wealth, represented in culpable qualities and acts such as avarice, hoarding of wealth, showing off with it, and gaining it unlawfully. That is why Allah, the Almighty, says,

{*Your riches and your children may be but a trial...*}

(At-Taghabun: 15)

And that was also why the righteous predecessors used to fear the "trial" of wealth.

Yahya ibn Mu`adh said, "Wealth is a scorpion: if you do not (intend to) deal with it properly so do not take it (from the beginning), because if it stings you, its poison will kill you." Someone asked, "And how can we deal with it properly?" He answered, "Gain it (i.e., wealth) by lawful means and spend it where it should be legally spent."

The Advantages and Disadvantages of Wealth

You have already learned that wealth is not to be dispraised in its own right, because it is a means that helps man in his worldly and religious affairs. So it is a "means of support" for man, as Allah, the Almighty, states,

> ❴To those weak of understanding make not over your property, which Allah hath made a means of support for you...❵
>
> (An-Nisa': 5)

Sa`id ibn Al-Musayyab said, "There is no goodness in a person who does not gain property through lawful means in order to protect himself from (the humiliation of) begging people, keep good relations with his kinship, and give out its dues (i.e., *Zakah*)."

Wealth has worldly and religious advantages. All people are aware of its worldly advantages and that is why they are busy seeking them. As for its religious advantages, they are restricted into three forms:

The first form: what man spends on himself in acts of worship such as *Jihad* and pilgrimage, or in things that help him fulfill some acts of worship such as food and drink.

The second form: what he spends on people, and this is classified into four categories: charity, hospitality, safeguarding one's honor and dignity, and hiring others.

The third form: what he does not spend for certain people or certain objects but produces a common benefit or a public interest, such as constructing mosques and bridges, and eternal endowments.

Moreover, wealth has worldly and religious disadvantages. Its religious disadvantages are the following three:

1. it almost leads man to commit acts of disobedience to Allah,

2. it drives him to seek enjoyment through lawful pleasures, until he addicts them and becomes under their control,

3. and it distracts him from remembrance of Allah, and this is the most dangerous disadvantage with which most people are afflicted.

Perhaps a person who has little money that only suffices his necessary needs day by day, is free from fear, grief, worry, and discomfort from which the wealthy people suffer. So in order for man to avoid such grievances and flaws, he should take from wealth only what he needs moderately and gives what is beyond this for charitable purposes, as this surplus part may be just a poison that ruins his life, if it remains in his possession.

Avarice and Contentment

Poverty is sometimes praiseworthy, especially when the poor person is contented with what Allah has given him and does not pay attention to what the others possess. Muslim reported on the authority of `Amr ibn Al-`As (may Allah be pleased with him) that the Messenger of Allah (peace and blessings of Allah be upon him) said,

> "He is successful who has accepted Islam, has been provided with what is sufficient for his want, and has been made contented by Allah with what He has given him."

In this respect, Abu Hazim said, "Whoever does three things is apt to have a perfect mind: to know what he really is, to safeguard his own tongue (from lying, backbiting, and the like), and to be contented with that with which Allah has provided him."

Adversely, avarice and greed are blameworthy flaws that the Prophet (peace and blessings of Allah be upon him) forbade, stressing the fact that no one will get except that which Allah has written down for him.

It was said, "If it were that someone asked "greed," 'Who is your father?' it would answer, 'doubting about destinies;' and if it were to be asked, 'What is your profession?' it would reply, 'humiliation acquisition;' and if it were to be asked, 'And what is your goal?' it would say, 'Deprivation!'"

How to Remedy Avarice and Greed and Acquire Contentment

The remedy of avarice and greed consists of three components: patience, knowledge, and action, and these three are to be acquired through five things:

1. Man should deal with his livelihood and financial needs economically and be contented with any available food, drink, clothing, etc. The Prophet (peace and blessings of Allah be upon him) was reported to have said,

> *"Economization is half of livelihood."*
> (Reported by Ad-Daylami)

2. If he is provided with sufficient livelihood, he should not worry about the future; rather, he should be certain that his provision would come to him as Allah has predestined.

3. He should be aware of the meaning of independence, which is involved in "being content," and of humiliation, which is involved in avarice and greed.

4. He should contemplate much about the life of ease that the disbelievers and the foolish enjoy then meditate the conditions of the Prophets and the righteous people and how content and patient they were. This will encourage him to be content with his provision, no matter how little it is, and not to be seduced by the enjoyment of those disbelievers and fools.

5. He should understand the dangerous effects of collecting wealth, as we have pinpointed earlier, and think over the good rewards that the patient poor people receive. He is also recommended to look at those who are poorer than him. The Prophet (peace and blessings of Allah be upon him) said,

> *"Look at those who are below you and do not look at those who are above you, for this is more becoming that you do not despise Allah's favor(s) upon you."*
> (Reported by Muslim)

Examples of Generous Persons

The Prophet (peace and blessings of Allah be upon him) was the most generous of people and never said 'No' to any one who asked him for something in charity. Once a man asked him (for something in charity) and the Prophet (peace and blessings of Allah be upon him) gave him (a flock of) sheep between two mountains. Then the man went to his people and said, "O my people, convert to Islam, because Muhammad gives (in charity) as a man who does not fear poverty."

`Uthman owed Talhah (may Allah be pleased with them both) fifty thousand *Dirhams*. Then once when he entered the mosque Talhah came to him and said, "Here is your money, so take it". But `Uthman said, "It is yours, Abu Muhammad, to help you in your hospitality."

`Urwah said, "I saw `A'ishah (the Prophet's wife, may Allah be pleased with her) distributing seventy thousand (*Dirhams* or *Dinars*) while patching her hauberk."

It was also reported that once `A'ishah distributed a hundred thousand and eighty (*Dirhams* or *Dinars*) among the people only in one day. When she came upon the evening, she asked her slave-girl to bring her something to break her fasting with and the latter brought her bread and oil. So Umm Darrah said to `A'ishah, "Could you not keep a *Dirham* of the money you distributed today to buy us some meat with which we would break our fasting?" "Had you reminded me, I would have done so," replied `A'ishah (may Allah be pleased with her).

Once Sa`d ibn Qays fell ill but none of his friends visited him. On asking about the reason, it was said to him, "They are shy of the debts you owe them." He said, "May Allah humiliate a wealth that prevents one's brothers from visiting him!" Then he commanded someone to call out among the people, "Whoever is indebted to Qays with something, is free from it." It was said that the steps leading to the entrance of his house were broken as a result of the numerous feet of his visitors that trod them.

And, once someone asked Sa`id ibn Al-`As for something in charity and he gave him a hundred thousand *Dirham*s. Then the man burst into tears, and when Sa`id asked him why he did so he said, "I am weeping (out of my grief) that the earth will eat someone like you (when you will be buried after death)!" So Sa`id gave him another hundred thousand *Dirham*s!

Miserliness

Abu Sa`id (may Allah be pleased with him) reported that the Prophet (peace and blessings of Allah be upon him) said,

> *"Two qualities are not found together in a believer: miserliness and bad morality."*
> (Reported by Al-Bukhari)

Muslim reported that he (peace and blessings of Allah be upon him) used to say,

> *"O Allah! I seek refuge with You from cowardice and miserliness!"*

Salman Al-Farisi said, "Whenever a generous person dies the earth says, 'O Allah, please forgive Your servant because of his generosity,' and whenever a miserly person dies it says, 'O Allah, please deprive this servant of Paradise, just as he deprived Your servants of the provisions You gave him in worldly life.'"

A Bedouin described a man saying, "He is "insignificant" in my eyes because worldly life is "significant" in his eyes."

Examples of Miserly Persons

It was reported that ibn `Abbas (may Allah be pleased with them both) said, "Al-Hajib, a miserly Arab man, used not to kindle fire during the night lest someone should observe it and benefit from its light. But if he was obliged to start fire and then saw someone using its light, he would put it out."

It was said that Marwan ibn Abi Hafsah was a very miserly person and once when he was about to go out to meet Al-Mahdi (a Caliph) his wife asked him, "What will you give me if he gives you a gift?" Marwan said, "If he gives me a hundred thousand *Dirhams*, I will give you one *Dirham*." Al-Mahdi gave him sixty thousand *Dirhams* so he gave his wife less than a *Dirham*!

It was also said that once a very miserly man, who was also very rich, needed a porter to carry some staff for him. "How much will you take from me for carrying this staff?" he asked the porter. "A *Dirham*," answered the porter. "No, you should take less than that," objected the miserly man. "But what is supposed to be less than a *Dirham*?" asked the porter. The miserly man said, "We may buy some carrots with a *Dirham* and then eat them together!"

Ithar (Preferring Others to Oneself)

Ithar is the highest degree of generosity. It is that a person prefers others to himself, especially when he is in need of the thing with which he prefers others to himself. Allah, the Almighty, praises the Companions of His Prophet Muhammad with this great good character, saying,

> *(... but (they) give them preference over themselves, even though poverty was their (own lot)...)*
> (Al-Hashr: 9)

During the Battle of Yarmuk, `Ikrimah ibn Abi Jahl, Suhayl ibn `Amr, Al-Harith ibn Hisham, and a group of the Banu Al-Mughirah were wounded. Someone brought them water and whenever it was offered to anyone of them to drink he wanted that his brother who was next to him should drink first, and so on until they all died and none of them drank a drop of the water.

Once a Companion of the Prophet (peace and blessings of Allah be upon him) was given a head of a sheep as a present, but he said, "My (Muslim) brother (so-and-so) needs it more than me." Then he sent it to the man, who sent it to another, and it was circulated among seven houses until it came back to the first one!

And, once `Abdullah ibn Ja`far met a black slave-boy in a palm garden where the latter was working. Then someone brought food to the slave but he gave it all to a dog that had just entered the garden. `Abdullah asked the slave-boy, "What is the quantity of food that you usually receive every day?" "The quantity that you have just seen me receiving," answered the slave. "So why did you gave it all to the dog?" asked `Abdullah. The slave replied, "This is not a land where dogs are always seen around, so it must have come from a distant land, and he was hungry so I disliked to let him go back without food." "But what will you eat today?" asked `Abdullah. "I will fast for the rest of the day," said the slave. Thereupon `Abdullah ibn Ja`far said, "People blame me for being over generous while this slave-boy is much more generous than me!" Then he bought the palm garden and all the equipment therein and bought the slave-boy, set him free, and dedicated the palm garden and its equipment to him.

In these great examples of the generosity and *Ithar* of the Prophet (peace and blessings of Allah be upon him) and his honorable Companions (may Allah be pleased with them all) are valuable lessons for those who seek to obtain such high good morals.

VI. *Jah* (Prominence and Prestige) and *Riya'* (Ostentation and Loving to Be Seen by People): Analysis and Remedy

Jah

Jah is loving to be prominent, famed, and famous and to have prestige among people. This is a very dangerous flaw, and that is why the people of righteousness and piety never mean to be celebrated, nor do they ever try to approach any means leading to fame. They always prefer to keep themselves out of people's sight, especially when doing acts of worship and the like, lest this should be counted as ostentation or showing-off.

To illustrate this, Abu Al-`Aliyah (may Allah have mercy on him) used to leave his sitting if more than four people gathered around him to learn from him.

Once a man asked Bishr Al-Hafi (may Allah have mercy on him) to advise him and Bishr said, "Do not seek to be celebrated among people..." He also said, "A person who likes to be celebrated and famed in worldly life does not taste the sweetness of the Hereafter."

Muslim reported on the authority of `Amr ibn Sa`d who said that he went to his father Sa`d while he was in the fold of his sheep outside Madinah. When Sa`d saw him he said, "I seek refuge with Allah from the mischief of this rider." And as he got down he said to him, "O my father, you are busy with your sheep while the people are contending with one another for kingdom (i.e., sovereignty)." Sa`d struck his chest and said, "Keep silent. I heard Allah's Messenger (peace and blessings of Allah be upon him) saying,

> '*Allah loves the servant who is conscious of Allah and is free from want and is hidden (from the view of people).*'"

However, someone may wonder: if fame is such condemned, what about the fame of the Prophets and leading Imams and scholars? In reply to this, we say that what is blameworthy here is "to seek fame," but if it exists according to Allah's will and without man's pursuing it, then it is not condemned. Yet still, it may be a source of trial and seduction for those who are weak in faith.

Jah and Wealth

Jah and wealth are the main pillars of worldly life, and the love of both of them is naturally inculcated in the hearts of men, but *Jah* is much more loved than wealth. This is because wealth is just a mere means that is used for getting something likeable or desirable, but *Jah* provides man, in addition to this, with respect, esteem, and high position amongst people, to such a degree that wealth cannot provide.

Nevertheless, it should be put in mind that *Jah* may be praiseworthy, in the sense that, just as man needs wealth to secure for him such necessities of life as food and drink, he may also need some kind of prominence and prestige that enable him to lead a sound and safe life amongst the people; it is quite known that some people need guards to protect them, servants to fulfill their needs, and the like. This is not blameworthy as long as it is sought within legal limits.

The Remedy of *Jah*

The remedy of *Jah* depends on both knowledge and action. As for knowledge, the person who loves *Jah* should know that the reason why he loves it is to have a certain characteristic with which he can control both the persons and hearts of people. He should also learn that even if he can get such a characteristic, he will finally die, just like any other creature, and by then he will be asked about his deeds in worldly life, including those resulting from such *Jah*. He should also pay attention to the dangers that afflict the people of *Jah* in worldly life, such as being all the time subjected to envy and harming, and being always afraid of losing their prominence and prestige.

The remedy of *Jah* also depends on action. This is to avoid being famed or celebrated in the eyes of people. For example, an ascetic may mingle with people, walk at the markets, buy his needs himself, and carry them; for if he covers himself from people, this "covering" is apt to create some kind of *Jah* for him in their hearts, and this in turn may cause them to be bewitched by him. Therefore, "action" should be considered along with "knowledge," as far as the remedy of *Jah* is concerned.

Riya'

Riya' is dispraised both in the Qur'an and in the *Sunnah*. In the Qur'an, Allah, the Almighty, says,

> ⟨*So woe to the worshippers who are neglectful of their Prayers; those who (want but) to be seen (of men).*⟩
>
> (Al-Ma'un: 4-6)

and,

> ⟨*... whoever expects to meet his Lord, let him work righteousness, and, in the worship of his Lord, admit no one as partner.*⟩
>
> (Al-Kahf: 110)

And, in the *Sunnah*, it was reported that the Prophet (peace and blessings of Allah be upon him) reported from his Lord (Glory be to Him) the following *Hadith Qudsi*,

> *"Whoever does something in which he associates someone else with Me, then this (thing) is (done) for whom he associates (with Me), and I am free from it."*
> (Reported by Malik)

In another *Hadith*, the Prophet (peace and blessings of Allah be upon him) said,

> *"The thing of which I am most afraid (that it should afflict) you is the minor polytheism."*

They (the listeners) said, "O Messenger of Allah, what is the minor polytheism?" The Prophet (peace and blessings of Allah be upon him) answered,

> *"(It is) Riya'. Allah, Glorified and Exalted be He, says to those (who commit Riya' in worldly life) on the Day of Resurrection, when He rewards people for their deeds, 'Go to those of whom you wanted to be seen in worldly life, (and see if) you (can) find (any) good with them.'"*
> (Reported by Ahmad)

The *Riya'* Pertaining to One's Religion

The flaw of *Riya'* may afflict the Muslim in his religion. This takes five different forms:

The first form: to be through one's physical appearance, by showing thinness and paleness of the body, so that people may know how active in worship of Allah he is and how scared of the Hereafter he may be.

The second form: to be through one's clothing and outer movements, such as lowering one's head while walking to show humility and submission, leaving a mark of prostration on the forehead, and wearing rough and woolly clothes. However, some of those who do *Riya'* in this form fear to attend the sittings of kings and the elite in such clothes lest they should despise them. Therefore, they are scattered between wearing rough clothes in order to please the common people and wearing smooth, fancy clothes in order to please kings and the elite. In no way can any of these please both sides all the time.

The third form: to do *Riya'* in the form of words; for example, a person may show off in the presence of the people of religiosity by preaching the people and reminding them of Allah, His Messenger, and the Hereafter, etc., using a lot of news and traditions, only to show how knowledgeable he is.

The fourth form: that *Riya'* is done in the form of deeds; for example, a person may stay bowing or prostrating for a long time during Prayer in order to show how a submissive worshiper he is.

The fifth form: that *Riya'* is done through friends and visitors; a person may deliberately visit and plan to be visited by people of special positions such as scholars and Sheikhs so that people may say that he has good "relations" with such people.

Still, someone may wonder: is *Riya'* prohibited, detestable, or permissible?

If *Riya'* is connected to acts of worship, then it is prohibited, since the person who does it in this divine area commits a great sin because he is in fact seeking someone other than Allah, the Almighty, Who is the only one worthy of worship. If, however, *Riya'* is in something that is not related to worship, such as collecting wealth and seeking prominence and prestige, then it is prohibited only if done with unlawful means.

In this connection, it is worth noting that people's intention may originally be directed to something good when doing such acts as beautifying their clothes and decorating their houses, for it is part of man's nature to dislike that any deficiency should be seen of him. Muslim reported on the authority of ibn Mas`ud that once the Prophet (peace and blessings of Allah be upon him) said,

> *"He who has in his heart the weight of an atom of pride shall not enter Paradise."*

A man said, "Verily a person loves that his dress should be fine, and his shoes should be fine." He (the Prophet) remarked,

> *"Verily, Allah is Most Beautiful and He loves beauty. Pride is to disdain the truth (out of self-conceit) and to contempt people."*

Besides, some people prefer to rehearse and proclaim Allah's favors upon them. The Prophet (peace and blessings of Allah be upon him) himself was ordered by Allah to do so (See the Qur'an: Surat Ad-Duha: 11).

The Degrees of *Riya'*

Riya' has different degrees, some of which are more serious than the others.

The first and most gangrenous degree of *Riya'* is that one who commits it does not originally seek to get a good reward for his deed, as in the case of a person who performs Prayer only when people can see him and neglects it when being away from their sight.

The second degree is that he seeks to get a good reward for his act but his deed is a little bit absorbed with *Riya'* to such an extent that if he was alone he would not do it. This degree is near to the first one, and both are detestable in the sight of Allah, the Almighty.

The third degree of *Riya'* is that his intention is equally directed towards both getting a good reward for his act and taking it as a means to be seen by people. In this case he ruins his good deed, as he is not free from sin.

The third degree is that being seen by people encourages him to do such religious acts, but he does not neglect worship when being out of people's sight. In this case he is rewarded for his good intention and punished for his bad intention.

The Hidden *Riya'*

Riya' may be either obvious or hidden.

The obvious *Riya'* is that which drives man to do some act.

There is another degree of *Riya'* that is not as obvious as this one, and it is that which does not drive man to do some act but undervalues the act that is done for the sake of Allah. For example, a man may be accustomed to offering voluntary Prayers every night but he feels that it is hard to bear, so whenever he has a pious guest who would spend the night with him, he offers such Prayers with him actively.

Then comes another degree of hidden *Riya'*, that is, that which neither affects man's doing the act nor makes it easier for him to do it, yet it is inculcated in his heart.

Another form of *Riya'*, which is more hidden than the latter, is that with which a man does not like to be seen by people when doing some act, but whenever he meets any of them he likes that he should greet him first and show him respect and veneration. If people do not do this to him, he does not feel well, as if his soul should be paid for the acts of worship that he does secretly.

The hidden *Riya'* is so dangerous that the faithful people are always afraid of it and take heed not to fall into its abyss. They unceasingly do their best to distract people from observing their good deeds, especially those ones which are to be done in secret. They are even keener on hiding their righteous deeds than people on hiding their evil deeds. By doing so, they only wish that their deeds would be most faithfully done for the sake of their Lord, so that He may reward them for faithfulness and sincerity in the Hereafter.

Riya' May or May Not Make One's Deeds Fruitless

If a *Riya'*-oriented thought visits the mind of someone after fulfilling some act of worship without this thinking being translated into an action of showing-off or attracting the attention of others to himself, then his act is not rendered fruitless by this thought. This is because he has already done the act sincerely, before *Riya'* comes to his mind. If, however, a thought of *Riya'* comes to him before finishing an act of worship, it does not make his act fruitless on the condition that it is a mere feeling of satisfaction, but if it is of that kind of *Riya'* that drives man to do an act, as in prolonging the period of prostration in order to let people see him, then his act is fruitless.

The Remedy of *Riya'*

Two elements constitute the remedy of *Riya'*: first, to uproot it form the heart, and second, to ward it off immediately whenever it comes to one's mind when doing an act of worship.

As for the first element, that is, uprooting *Riya'* from the heart, it should be realized that love of prestige and high position is the primary root of *Riya'*. There are three signs of such love: to love the pleasure produced by being praised, to flee from the pain caused by being dispraised, and to look greedily at what the other people possess.

This finds support in the Prophetic *Hadith* reported by Al-Bukhari and Muslim on the authority of Abu Musa (may Allah be pleased with him) that a man came to the Prophet (peace and blessings of Allah be upon him) and said, "O Messenger of Allah, a man may fight to show his position (i.e., bravery), another may fight out of pride and wrath, and a third may fight so that he may be mentioned by the people; which of these is regarded as fighting in Allah's Cause?" The Prophet (peace and blessings of Allah be upon him) replied,

> *"He who fights so that Allah's Word (i.e. Islam) should be superior, fights for Allah's Cause."*

A person may not like being praised or mentioned by people yet he does not like either to be dispraised by them, as in the case of a person who, though a coward, does not flee from the battlefield lest he should be accused of cowardice. The best remedy for such a person as well as the person who likes to be praised by people is to think over the whole thing that leads him to commit *Riya'* and to recall the tremendous consequences of this terrible flaw. He will then realize that in spite of its being pleasant at the moment it is harmful in the end, so it is quite rational that he should avoid it from the beginning. This rational and logical thinking may help him get rid of the inner desire that drives him to act with *Riya'*.

As pinpointed above, looking greedily at what other people possess constitutes one of the main roots of *Riya'*. Man can remove this root by comprehending the fact that it is only Allah, the Almighty, Who provides bounties and wealths, and that whoever looks greedily at the possessions of others is not free from humiliation and loss, even if he gets any of these possessions; how can he then leave that which in the hands of Allah for the sake of a deceptive desire for that which in the hands of people?

The second element constituting the remedy of *Riya'* is to ward it off immediately whenever it comes to one's mind when doing an act of worship. This should be acquired through much practice and strife against one's vain desires. This strife requires that the person who is afflicted with *Riya'* habituates himself to contentment with Allah's bounties and not seeking to get what the others have. He should also pay no attention to people's praising or dispraising him, for Satan never leaves him alone when worshiping Allah and always attacks him with *Riya'*-oriented thoughts, so that they may render his worship fruitless. If, for example, he is distracted by the idea that people are observing his worship, he may say to himself, "It does not matter whether they know or do not know about my worship, for Allah knows best about it. So, what is supposed to be gained by anyone else's knowing about it?"

Showing Good Deeds and Hiding the Evil Ones May Be Legally Permissible

There is a great benefit in hiding one's good deeds, as it secures sincerity and freedom from ostentation. Likewise, showing one's good deeds may be beneficial, in the sense that it may encourage others to follow one's example and act righteously. Besides, there are certain deeds that cannot be hidden, such as pilgrimage and *Jihad*.

Interestingly enough, a person who is to show his good deeds should be careful not to be just attracting the attention of others to himself; rather, he should "intend" that he will do so only in order that others may follow his example in doing good. Of course, there are some people who are so sincere and pious that they do not care whether people should praise or dispraise them; there is no harm if such people show their good deeds in public, because encouraging others to do good is good in its own right. It was reported that some of the righteous predecessors would let people know about some of their righteous deeds in order that they might follow their examples.

On the other hand, hiding one's evil deeds should not be counted as a sign of double-dealing. The Muslim is recommended to hide his evil deeds, as Allah, the Almighty, does not like that sins and acts of disobedience should be proclaimed in public; rather, He likes that they should be hidden. The Prophet (peace and blessings of Allah be upon him) was reported to have said,

> *"Let him whoever commits any of these dirty acts cover himself under the cover of Allah, Glorified and Exalted be He."*
> (Reported by Al-Hakim)

This is because such a person, though disobedient, still loves Allah (Glory be to Him), as faith is still inculcated in his heart.

Acts of Worship Stimulated by the People's Observation of Them

A Muslim may spend most of the night with some Muslims offering voluntary Prayers, although he usually does so not for more than an hour every night. Had it not been that he was in their company, he would not have done so.

Someone may think that this is part of *Riya'*, while it is surely not. Every believer craves after worshiping Allah, the Almighty, but he may be distracted from this by some means of distraction. When seeing other believers worshiping Allah, he may automatically get rid of those hindrances, as the love of worship is originally implanted in his heart. As a matter of fact, there is an immense difference between such a person and a person who imitates the others' worshiping only for the sake of *Riya'*.

A man may be distracted from offering voluntary Prayers during the night by being in a luxurious house, in a comfortable bed, and beside a beautiful wife. Yet when it happens that he spends a night away from this atmosphere, these obstacles may disappear, especially when being in the company of devoted worshipers who would encourage him to be like them. This should not be taken as a sign of *Riya'*. However, it is worth mentioning here that in such a case, he should "test" his conscience with regard to this participation in worship; he may do like them but in a place where he can see them while they cannot: if he is faithfully devoted to the acts of worship he is doing, then he is doing them for the sake of Allah, and if he experiences such faithful devotion only in their presence, then it is *Riya'*.

VII. Pride, Arrogance, and Self-admiration

Pride and Arrogance

Allah, the Almighty, says,

> ⟪Those who behave arrogantly on the earth in defiance of right them will I turn away from My Signs...⟫
>
> (Al-A`raf: 146)

and,

> ⟪... verily He loveth not the arrogant.⟫
>
> (An-Nahl: 23)

Muslim reported that the Prophet (peace and blessings of Allah be upon him) said,

> "He who has in his heart the weight of an atom of pride shall not enter Paradise."

Al-Bukhari and Muslim reported that the Prophet (peace and blessings of Allah be upon him) said,

> "The Fire said, 'I have been favored with the arrogant.'"

Al-Bukhari and Muslim also reported that the Prophet (peace and blessings of Allah be upon him) said,

> "Allah will not look on the Day of Judgment at him who drags his robe (behind him) out of pride."

Then, Abu Bakr said, "O Messenger of Allah, one side of my robe slacks down unless I get very cautious about it." The

Messenger of Allah (peace and blessings of Allah be upon him) said,

"But you do not do that out of pride."

Pride is an inner bad moral that makes the person who is afflicted with it see himself "above" the others due to the perfect qualities and attributes that he "believes" to have. This is a very dangerous flaw that afflicts so many people, even some ascetics, scholars, and worshipers of Allah. Surely, it is so dangerous because the Prophet (peace and blessings of Allah be upon him) stated that he who has in his heart the weight of an atom of pride will not enter Paradise. Pride covers the prideful person from Paradise because it prevents him from acquiring the qualities of the believers, for he cannot like for the believers that which he likes for himself, nor can he be humble, or avoid animosity, envy, or wrath, or restrain his anger, or accept good advice, or refrain from despising and backbiting people. In short, he is subject to all blameworthy morals.

Among the worst forms of pride is that which prevents man from benefiting from knowledge, accepting the truth, and complying with it. However, a prideful person may have some knowledge, but his prideful soul does not let him comply with the truth, as Allah, the Almighty, says,

{*And they rejected those Signs in iniquity and arrogance, though their souls were convinced thereof...*}

(An-Naml: 14)

{*They said: Shall we believe in two men like ourselves?...*}

(Al-Mu'minun: 47)

❬... *Ah! Ye are no more than human, like ourselves!...*❭

(Ibrahim: 10)

And, the Prophet (peace and blessings of Allah be upon him) explained the meaning of pride when he said,

"Pride is to disdain the truth (out of self-conceit) and contempt people."

(Reported by Muslim)

The Degrees of Pride

As far as pride is concerned, scholars and worshipers of Allah are of three degrees:

The first degree is that pride is inculcated in the heart of any of them, so he sees himself better than the others, but he tries to rectify himself and act humbly.

The second degree is that any prideful person among them shows pride and arrogance in public sittings through such acts as proving how he is more excellent than his counterparts and devaluating whoever does not show him respect. Such a person forgets the divine command to the Prophet (peace and blessings of Allah be upon him):

❬*And lower thy wing to the Believers who follow thee.*❭

(Ash-Shu`ara': 210)

The third degree is that he shows pride and arrogance through words; for example, he may show how proud he is of himself, his accomplishments, his lineage, etc., aiming to show how he is better and more significant than the others or than a certain person.

Some Qualities of the Prideful Person

1. That he likes that people should stand up for him, whether on his coming or while he is sitting. However, the Muslim scholars view that it is recommendable to stand up for parents, just rulers, and virtuous people.

2. That he does not walk except with someone walking behind him.

3. That he does not visit anyone because he feels that he is better than people (and thus it is they who should pay him visits).

4. That he does not like that anyone should sit or walk beside him.

5. That he refuses to carry even his own staff under any circumstances.

6. That he does not help his wife in any of the house affairs, contradicting what the Prophet (peace and blessings of Allah be upon him) used to do.

How to Remedy Pride and Acquire Humility

The remedy of pride, which is also a means to require humility, mainly depends on the removing of its source from the heart. This requires that the prideful person should know himself and his Lord.

By knowing himself, he realizes that he should never have been prideful. It is sufficient for him to know that "clay" is the origin of his existence then he was created out of a sperm that came out of the same place where urine comes out of the body, then out of a clot of blood, then out of a morsel of flesh, then he was given life, along with the gifts of hearing, sight, and understanding. Allah, the Almighty, refers to this fact in the Qur'an, saying,

❨*From what stuff hath He created him? From a sperm drop: He hath created him, and then mouldeth him in due proportions.*❩
(`Abasa: 18-19)

Then He favors him,

❨*Then doth He make his path smooth for him.*❩
(`Abasa: 20)

❨*... so We gave him (the gifts) of Hearing and Sight.*❩
(Al-Insan: 2)

Thus, Allah gives man life, moulds him in due proportions, and brings him to the world where he provides him with food, drink, clothing, guidance, and strength.

Therefore, if this is the reality of man's existence and creation, why should he be prideful or arrogant?

Having realized this, the prideful person should remember that his life may be taken from him at any time and in any place, and that by then he will be buried in his grave where his body will be worn out, then on the Day of Resurrection he will receive his "record" and it will be said to him,

❨*... read thine (own) record: sufficient is thy soul this day to make out an account against thee.*❩
(Al-Isra': 14)

Recalling such scenes every now and then is apt to decrease one's feeling of pride and arrogance until it finally fades away,

Allah willing.

As for knowing his Lord, it is enough for the prideful person to contemplate about the signs and effects of His might and greatness, to realize that no one is to show pride or arrogance in the Kingdom of this All-Mighty Lord, Glory be to Him.

Self-admiration

It was reported on the authority of Abu Hurayrah that the Prophet (peace and blessings of Allah be upon him) said,

> *"While a man was strutting in two gowns out of self-admiration, Allah caused the earth to swallow him up, and he has been submerging therein up to the Day of Resurrection."*

And, it was reported that ibn Mas`ud (may Allah be pleased with him) said, "Destruction lies in two things: self-admiration and despair." Ibn Mas`ud gathered self-admiration and despair together because happiness cannot be obtained except with exerting much effort; the despairing person does not make any effort because of his despair and the self-admired person believes that he has got what he wants so he feels he does not have to make any effort either.

Self-admiration leads to pride, as it is originally one of its causes, and pride leads to many destructive flaws.

The Remedy of Self-admiration

Allah, Glorified and Exalted be He, favored man when He created him and provided him with all the blessings he has. Therefore, no one should be self-admired because of his actions, knowledge, beauty, or wealth, as these are bounties provided by Allah out of His Grace. Even man's being favored with such bounties is another favor from Allah upon him!

Moreover, even a person's righteous deeds will not admit him to Paradise, because it is Allah Who guides him and enables him to do them. It was reported on the authority of Abu Hurayrah that the Prophet (peace and blessings of Allah be upon him) once said,

> *"The good deeds of any person will not make him enter Paradise."*

They (the Prophet's Companions) said, "Not even you, O Messsenger of Allah?" He said,

> *"Not even myself, unless Allah bestows His favor and mercy on me."*
> (Reported by Al-Bukhari and Muslim)

It should also be known that the causes of pride are also from amongst the causes of self-admiration. They have already been mentioned earlier, so they may be referred to where they are cited above.

Someone may say: a noble man may be self-admired because of his noble lineage, and he may wish that his noble relatives will intercede for him on the Day of Resurrection.

Commenting on this, we can say that all Muslims wish for intercession on their behalf, and it is true that intercession may not be accepted when one's sins are very great. Allah, the Almighty, declares,

> ❨... *Verily the most honoured of you in the sight of Allah is (he who is) the most righteous of you...*❩
> (Al-Hujurat: 13)

And, the Prophet (peace and blessings of Allah be upon him) said to his daughter,

> "O Fatimah, I have no power (to protect you) from Allah in anything."
>
> (Reported by Al-Bukhari)

Therefore, it is only man's righteous deeds and good qualities that make him "noble" or "honorable" in the sight of Allah. Besides, Al-Bukhari and Muslim reported on the authority of Abu Hurayrah (may Allah be pleased with him) that Allah's Messenger (peace and blessings of Allah be upon him) said,

> "I should not find that any of you should come on the Day of Resurrection with a growling camel mounted on his neck, and should appeal to me for help saying, 'O Messenger of Allah, help me,' and I should say, 'I have no authority to help you; I already communicated to you'."

So, whoever knows and comprehends these facts will start occupying the rest of his life with as many acts of worship and obedience as he can, as this is the only rope to salvation.

VIII. *Ghurur*

Ghurur denotes "conceit, conceitedness, self-conceit, self-importance, self-deceit, and self-seduction" all together.

Some people are seduced by worldly life, though its time is nothing if compared to the time of the Hereafter. Some of those who disobey Allah are seduced by false wishes and vain desires, saying, "Allah is Most Generous, and we depend on His forgiveness." They may also be seduced by the righteousness of their parents.

These should know that, just as Allah is Most Merciful, He is also strict in punishment. He (Glory be to Him) has decreed that disbelievers will remain eternally in the Fire although their disbelief does not harm Him in the least; He also inflicts some of His creatures with diseases and tribulations in worldly life although He is able to remove them; meanwhile, He warns us against His punishment, so how should we not fear Him?

Still, fearing Allah should be connected with wishing for His mercy, so that man is always keen on working righteousness. Wishes alone cannot secure salvation. Had it been that a person could get salvation by mere wishing, so why did the Prophets and pious people do their best to gain Allah's pleasure? Indeed, the People of the Book were dispraised because they let themselves be seduced by false wishes and neglected working for the Hereafter; Allah, the Almighty, says,

> ⟨... *but they chose (for themselves) the vanities of this world, saying (for excuse): (everything) will be forgiven us...*⟩
>
> (Al-A`raf: 169)

Some people think that their good deeds exceed their evil

ones, because they only pay attention to the former and completely forget about the latter. Surely, this is manifest error.

The Categories of Those Afflicted with *Ghurur*

In most cases, *Ghurur* afflicts four categories of people: scholars, worshipers, the *Mutasawwifah* (those who pretend to be true Sufis), and the rich. Each category will be dealt with in some detail, as follows.

The First Category: Scholars

Ghurur may strike scholars in different forms. Some of them are well versed in *Shar`i* and rational sciences but neglect guarding their organs against committing acts of disobedience and making them adhere to acts of obedience, thinking that they have a high position in the sight of Allah because of their knowledge. Were such knowledgeable-ignorant people to have true insight, they would have realized that knowledge is fruitless without action. That is why Allah, the Almighty, said, ⟨*Truly he succeeds that purifies it,*⟩ (Ash-Shams: 9) and did not say, "Truly he succeeds that "learns" how to purify it".

Another section of this category have perfect knowledge and act perfectly only in manifestation, i.e., they do not try to examine their hearts and remove the blameworthy qualities inculcated therein, such as pride, envy, ostentation, love of fame, and the like. These persons have "decorated" their appearances and neglected their inner entities, forgetting that the Prophet said,

> "Verily Allah does not look to your bodies nor to your faces but He looks to your hearts and your deeds."
>
> (Reported by Muslim)

Another section of the scholars who are afflicted with the flaw of *Ghurur* do not know that these inner morals are dispraised, yet they, out of self-admiration, believe that they are free from them and that they are too high in the sight of Allah to be inflicted with such evil morals. To illustrate this, one of them may show pride and arrogance but he would say, "This is the glory of religiosity" or "This is the honor of knowledge"!

Another section of them preach people and some of them mostly concentrate on the good morals of the soul and qualities of the heart, such as fearing Allah, yearning for His forgiveness, patience, gratitude, dependence on Allah, asceticism, certainty, and sincerity, thinking that they have such qualities and good morals simply because they speak about them and call people to acquire them, while they actually do not have any of them. These are the most afflicted with *Ghurur* from among this category, or perhaps from among all people.

The Second Category: Worshipers

Ghurur may also beset some worshipers of Allah. Some of them may be too meticulous in fulfilling some acts of worship to the extent that counterproductive results may be the only fruit they can ever get from their worshiping. For example, one of them may be so meticulous concerning the *Takbirat Al-Ihram* (saying *Allahu Akbar* [Allah is Greater] at the beginning of Prayer) that he may miss the first *Rak`ah* of congregational Prayer.

Other worshipers may be very picky when reciting the Qur'an to the extent that one of them may totally concentrate on the recitation itself, especially the correct pronunciation of sounds which he is always not sure if he has made it correctly or not. Due to this over-carefulness, this worshiper may not pay any attention to the meaning of the Qur'anic verses he is reciting. This is one of the worst forms of *Ghurur*, since the Muslim is not commanded to undergo such affectation when reciting the Qur'an.

Another section of worshipers are very keen on reading the Qur'an so much that one of them may finish the whole text twice a day, but their hearts are filled with vain wishes and not with the meanings of the Qur'an. In other words, they read the Qur'an but do not follow its instructions, thinking that the Qur'an is only for recitation. The case of such readers of the Qur'an resembles that of those who read it only to enjoy the sweetness of their voices when reading it or to let others enjoy it, forgetting about its meaning.

Another section of worshipers observe so much Fasting but they harm people with their tongues, break their Fasting with unlawful food and drink, and their Fasting is not free from *Riya'*.

Others go on pilgrimage more than once but do not give heed to the duties that must be fulfilled before and during the pilgrimage, such as paying one's debts, taking lawful provision, refraining from obscenity, wickedness, and wrangling. In spite of this, they believe they are doing good!

Another section of worshipers enjoin the right and forbid the wrong but forget to do what they call people to enjoin and to refrain from the wrong they forbid them to do.

Others are keen on performing voluntary and supererogatory acts of worship more than the obligatory ones, thinking that this brings them nearer to Allah. Such people forget what Allah, the Almighty, says, in the *Qudsi Hadith* reported by the Prophet (peace and blessings of Allah be upon him):

> *"Those who seek to draw near to Me do not do so with anything that equals (the religious) duties that*

I have prescribed for them."

(Reported by Al-Bukhari)

The Third Category: The *Mutasawwifah*

Some people pretend to be true Sufis merely by imitating the latter in uniform, words, and appearance, without making any effort to strive against their own vain desires; rather, they indulge into prohibited and doubtful matters and quarrel with one another for the sake of any trivial worldly matter.

Another group of them claim that they have knowledge of Allah, the Almighty, and the ability to reveal the truth, and that they are specially close to Allah, and the like, while they do not know anything about such matters except their names. Though, one of them may think that he has acquired all knowledge and despise true scholars and leading Imams, let alone the common people.

Others reject the rulings of the *Shari`ah* and count the lawful and the prohibited as being the same, saying that Allah does not need their good deeds so why should they annoy themselves with doing such deeds? Others may say that it is only hearts that should be considered here, and their hearts are filled with love for Allah, while they actually deceive themselves.

The Fourth Category: The Rich

The rich are the fourth category of those who are mostly afflicted with the flaw of *Ghurur*.

Some of them are keen on constructing mosques, schools, and the like, but they insist that these buildings should be named after them, so that their names may remain in worldly life forever. If any of them is asked to construct any of such buildings without naming it after him, he will not accept it in any way.

Some of the rich people do not spend from their wealth in charity out of miserliness and are keen on performing physical acts of worship that do not need spending money such as Fasting, Prayer, and recitation of the Qur'an, forgetting that miserliness is such a destructive flaw that cannot be overcome by such voluntary acts of worship. On the contrary, spending money itself may be the best means to overcome miserliness.

Another group of the well-to-do people attend religious lectures and lessons but do not translate the preaching they receive into actions, thinking that mere attendance is sufficient for them to be dutiful worshipers. These forget that religious lectures and lessons are originally delivered to drive people to "work" righteousness.

The Remedy of *Ghurur*

Ghurur can be remedied with three things:

1. A mind with which man realizes the realities of things.

2. Knowing oneself, one's Lord, worldly life, and the Hereafter.

3. Knowing the way to Allah, the Almighty, and how to pass it over and deal with the obstacles that may hinder one from reaching the prospective destination at the end of it.

These three components of the remedy of *Ghurur* are tackled in detail in this book, so they may be referred to where there are cited in the book.

Here we have reached the end of the chapter dealing with the destructive flaws and bad morals that hinder the Muslim from going on safely and soundly in his way towards the Hereafter. May Allah protect all of us from their danger!

Chapter Four

MEANS OF SALVATION

I. Repentance

Conditions and Prerequisites

One should know that sins stand as a barrier between the servant and his Beloved, Most High Allah. So, avoiding all acts that the Beloved, Most High, hates is a duty.

This will be maintained by means of knowledge, repentance, and determination. Thus, unless one is aware that sins are the reasons behind keeping him away from his Beloved, he will neither regret for these sins nor feel pain for his misbehavior. And, unless he feels pain, he will not repent.

In relation to repentance, we can quote the following Qur'anic verses,

⟨... *And O ye Believers! Turn ye all together towards Allah, that ye may attain Bliss.*⟩

(An-Nur: 31)

⟨*O ye who believe! Turn to Allah with sincere repentance...*⟩

(At-Tahrim: 8)

⟨*For Allah loves those who turn to Him constantly and He loves those who keep themselves pure and clean.*⟩

(Al-Baqarah: 222)

Abu Hurayrah (may Allah be pleased with him) reported the Prophet (peace and blessings of Allah be upon him) as having said,

"*O people, seek repentance from Allah. Verily, I*

seek repentance from Him one hundred times a day."
(Reported by Al-Bukhari and Muslim)

On the authority of Ibn Mas`ud (may Allah be pleased with him) that the Messenger of Allah (peace and blessings of Allah be upon him) said,

"Allah is more pleased with the repentance of His slave-servant than a man who encamps at a place where his life is jeopardized, but he has his riding beast carrying his food and water. He then rests his head and sleeps for a short while and wakes to find his riding beast gone. (He starts looking for it) and suffers from severe heat and thirst or what Allah wished (him to suffer from). He then says, 'I will go back to my place.' He returns and sleeps again, and then (getting up), he raises his head to find his riding beast standing beside him carrying his provisions of food and drink. Allah is more pleased with the repentance of His servant than the recovery of this riding beast along with the provisions (of food and drink)."
(Reported by Al-Bukhari and Muslim)

In this context, there are many *Hadiths* discussing this issue and the obligation of repentance is also confirmed by the consensus of Muslim scholars. As long as sins inevitably lead to destruction, one should steer clear of them.

Man, in fact, should incessantly declare his repentance to Allah, for no one is ever free from committing mistakes and sins either by organs or heart.

Moreover, if one could be free of doing wrong by his

hand and heart, he would hardly escape the insinuations of Satan, which divert him from *Dhikr* (Remembrance of Allah the Almighty).

Again, if he is free of all these, he may be heedless and negligent of Allah and His Attributes. Indeed, no one is free of such imperfection, but people are of different degrees in this regard.

It was reported on the authority of the Prophet (peace and blessings of Allah be upon him) that he said,

> *"My heart may be covered. I, therefore, ask Allah's forgiveness each day and night seventy times."*
> (Reported by Al-Bukhari and Muslim)

Accordingly, Almighty Allah has honored him saying,

> ❴*That Allah may forgive thee thy faults of the past and those to follow...*❵
> (Al-Fath: 2)

Wonderfully, if this was the condition of the Prophet (peace and blessings of Allah be upon him), what others should do? Know that when the conditions of repentance are met, it will be sound and acceptable. Almighty Allah says,

> ❴*He is the One Who accepts repentance from His Servants and forgives sins...*❵
> (Ash-Shura: 25)

The Messenger of Allah said,

> *"Indeed, Allah accepts the repentance of His slave unless he is not in death-rattle."*
> (Reported by At-Tirmidhi)

Categories of Sins

One should know that man has many characteristics and ethics. But sins fall into four qualities:

First, the overbearing quality: there branches from it pride, conceit, vanity, arrogance, etc. These sins are destructive and some people are unfortunately unaware of.

Second, the satanic quality: there branches from it envy, deceit, trickery, hypocrisy, mischief, etc.

Third, the animal quality: there branches from it greed, niggardliness, lust for sexual and physical desires which leads to adultery, homosexuality, theft, etc.

Fourth, the vicious quality: there branches from it anger, hatred, physical violence, murder, prodigality, etc.

Truly, these qualities have some kind of graduation in their nature. The animal quality dominates first, then, it is followed by the vicious quality. If these two qualities are joined together in one person, they will make his mind resort to the satanic qualities such as trickery and deceit. Then, the overbearing qualities prevail.

Eventually, these are the springs of sins which then turn into the parts of the body. Some of them stay in the heart such as disbelief, *Bid`ah* (Innovation in matters of religion), and hypocrisy. Likewise, some others are connected to the faculties of hearing, sight, tongue, hands, feet, stomach, private parts and all one's extremities. Then, sins are divided as follows: What is related to the rights of people and what comes between the servant and his Lord. However, what is related to the rights of people is more repulsive. As for what comes between the servant and his Lord, there is more hope of being pardoned unless it is associating others in worship with Allah, may Allah forbid, which is not forgiven.

One should know that sins are of two kinds: minor and major. The scholars and the *Hadiths* are in disagreement concerning the number of the major sins. The authentic *Hadiths* regarding heinous sins amounts to five and they are as follows:

It was reported on the authority of Abu Hurayrah (may Allah be pleased with him) that the Prophet (peace and blessings of Allah be upon him) said,

> *"Avoid the seven major destructive sins." The people enquired, "O Allah's Messenger! What are they?" He said, "To associate others in worship along with Allah, to practice sorcery, to kill the life which Allah has forbidden except for a just cause, (according to Islamic law), to eat up Riba (usury), to appropriate an orphan's wealth, to flee from the battlefield at the time of fighting, and to slander chaste believing women who are unexpected to be accused with adultery."*
> (Reported by Al-Bukhari and Muslim)

Ibn Mas`ud (may Allah be pleased with him) narrated,

> *"I asked the Prophet, (peace and blessings of Allah be upon him), 'What is the greatest sin in the Sight of Allah?' He said, 'That you set up a rival unto Allah though He Alone created you.' I said, 'That is indeed a major sin.' I then asked, 'What is next?' He said, 'To kill your son lest he should share your food with you.' I asked, 'What is next?' He said,*

> *'To commit illegal sexual intercourse with the wife of your neighbor.'"*
>
> (Reported by Al-Bukhari and Muslim)

Ibn `Umar (may Allah be pleased with him) reported that the Prophet (peace and blessings of Allah be upon him) said,

> *"The major sins are: To join others in worship with Allah, and to be undutiful to one's parents."*
>
> (Reported by Al-Bukhari)

Anas Ibn Malik (may Allah be pleased with him) reported that the Messenger of Allah (peace and blessings of Allah be upon him) said,

> *"Shall I inform you of the biggest of the major sins? That is the forged statement or the false witness."*
>
> (Reported by Al-Bukhari and Muslim)

According to Abu Bakrah (may Allah be pleased with him) the Messenger of Allah (peace and blessings of Allah be upon him) said,

> *"The biggest of the major sins are: To join others in worship with Allah, to be undutiful to one's parents." The Prophet then sat up after he had been reclining (on a pillow) and said, "And I warn you against giving a false witness, and he kept on repeating that warning until we wished he would stop saying it."*
>
> (Reported by Al-Bukhari and Muslim)

Scholars disputed regarding the exact number of the major sins and the *Hadiths* regarding them did not enumerate their exact number. By this, the Legislator may aim at making the people fearful of sins, to know the essence of major sins and know also the most grievous ones among them. As to the smallest among the minor ones, it is not known exactly. But the scholars have discussed the number of the major sins as follows:

Ibn Mas`ud (may Allah be pleased with him) said that they are four. Ibn `Umar said that they are seven. When Ibn `Abbas (may Allah be pleased with him) was told that the major sins are seven, he said that they are nearer to seventy than seven.

Abu Salih reported that Ibn `Abbas said, "A major sin is what deserves the *Hadd* (prescribed penalty) in this world."

Ibn Mas`ud also said, "Major sins start from the beginning of *Surat* An-Nisa' to Allah's saying,

⦃*If ye (but) eschew the most heinous of the things which ye are forbidden to do...*⦄
(An-Nisa': 31)"

Sa`id Ibn Jubayr and others said, "Major sins are all the sins which Allah has promised their doers with entering Hellfire."

Finally, Abu Talib Al-Makki said, "Major sins are seventeen: Four lie in the heart and these are: Associating others in worship with Allah, insistence on committing a sinful deed, despondence of Allah's Mercy and feeling secure against Allah's devising. Another four are associated with the tongue and these are false witness, slandering chaste women with adultery, false swearing and sorcery. Three stay in the stomach: Drinking *Khamr* (alcoholic beverages), appropriating an orphan's wealth wrongfully and devouring usury. Two stay in the private parts. They are: Adultery and homosexuality. Another two stay in the hand and these are: murder and theft. One stays in the feet, that is, fleeing from the battlefield. And finally, one stays in the whole body that is being undutiful to one's parents.

Distributing Degrees in the Hereafter on the Basis of Good and Bad Deeds in This Worldly Life

One should know that degrees of people will differ in the Hereafter as they differ in this world. In the Hereafter, people will be either perished, tormented, saved, or favored.

The similitude of this is like that of a king who invades a province, kills some of its residents, tortures others without killing them, setting others free, and showering favors on others who will be his favorite ones. If this king is just, he will divide them according to their deeds. He shall kill only whoever denies his right to kingship, inflict punishment on whomever fall short of paying him service while confessing his kingship, setting free only whoever confesses his right to kingship without any laxity in paying him good service and showering his favors only on those who spend their life in his service and support. With respect to the degrees of favors and punishment, each one of these divisions differs in accordance with its condition. This is confirmed by the *Hadith*, which reported that some people would pass on the *Sirat* (a bridge laid across Hell) like flying lightening while some others would fall and stay in Hell for seven thousand years. Indeed, there is a great variance between a single moment and seven thousand years.

As for the variance in the severity of punishment, the most grievous of which has no end while the least punishment will be in discussing one's deeds. The king may torment some slackers through discussing their acts and then he pardons them. He may flog them some lashes or may torture them with any other kind of punishment.

Likewise, the degrees of the people of happiness differ. These general matters are known by means of narration and the light of knowledge.

To take this topic in detail, we say: Whoever has a firm faith, avoids all major sins, performs all obligations well and only commits minor sins in isolation without insistence, there will be more hope of being pardoned. This is confirmed by the text of the Glorious Qur'an which states that refraining from major sins pardons minor ones.

Actually, either he will be in the company of the devout servants of Allah or the companions of the right hand in accordance with his faith. In other words, if one's faith weakens, his rank will be lowered but if it becomes stronger, his rank will be elevated or raised high.

Moreover, the devout servants of Allah vary according to the variance of their knowledge of Allah, Most High. Eventually, the degrees of the knowledgeable (of Allah) are countless. That is due to the fact that the sea of knowledge has no coast but divers dive in it in accordance with their abilities. For the highest degrees of the companions of the right hand are the lowest degrees of the devout servants of Allah and this is, indeed, the condition of those who refrain from major sins and at the same time perform the obligations.

As for the one who commits a major sin or neglects the pillars of Islam, if he turns to Allah with sincere repentance before death rattle, he will be joined to those who does not commit these sins. For the penitent from sins is like the one who does not commit sins.

But if he dies before declaring repentance, his condition will be dangerous. Insistence on committing sins may lead one to breathe his last while indulging in evildoing. Belief based on blind imitation, however, is more apt to deterioration even by means of minor doubts. Men of unswerving belief are safe from evil end of their life.

However, the punishment of the one who dies without repentance will be in accordance with the repulsiveness of the major sins he commits and the duration of insistence. Then the dimwitted imitators will be raised to Paradise and the knowledgeable (of Allah) will be raised to the highest places in Paradise. As we have mentioned before, the degrees of people on the Day of Judgment vary according to a clear ruling. The similitude of this is as the judgment of a physician on a patient that surely he will die because of his incurable disease, and his prescription concerning another patient that his disease will be easily treated. Unquestionably, this is in accordance with his thinking that is right in most cases. Perhaps the soul of the latter is ruined without the feeling of the physician and accordingly, he may breathe his last without the physician being certain of that. Indeed, this is because of the hidden secrets of Allah, Most High. Likewise, there is vagueness in the spirits of people alive concerning the causes that their creator arranged and no human being is able to know its intrinsic qualities. Also, enjoying the blessings of the Hereafter or suffering its torment has mysterious reasons that no human power has the ability to recognize their essence. And it is permissible that Allah pardons the sinner however grievous or numerous his sins are and afflicts His wrath on the obedient however numerous his visible good deeds are. That is because acts will be judged according to piety, which is an act of the heart. And, the conditions of the heart may be hidden to its possessor; so how is the case with others?

As for those who are saved, they are those who do not do services to the king and thereby do not deserve his favors on them. But, at the same time they do not fail to accomplish their obligations and thus they do not deserve punishment. Most probably, this is the case of the insane and children of the disbelievers who are not informed of the *Da`wah*. For they have neither consciousness, atheism, obedience, nor disobedience. There is also permissibility that they will be on *Al-A`raf* (the Heights).

As for the favored, they are the most devout to Allah, the nearest to Him, the foremost (in faith), those who do not know what delights of the eye are kept hidden (in reserve) for them and they are not keen to enter Paradise but they are keen to meet Allah, Most High, and look at Him. Now this is enough in showing the distribution of ranks according to good deeds.

What Turns the Minor Sins into Major Sins

The minor sin may turn into a major one according to the following:

Insistence and persistence: In the *Hadith*, which was reported on the authority of Ibn `Abbas (may Allah be pleased with him) who said that the Prophet (peace and blessings of Allah be upon him) said,

> *"There is no minor sin with insistence and no major sin with forgiveness."*
> (Reported by Abu Ash-Shaykh)

One should know also that the forgiveness of a major sin, which is not repeated, is more hopeful than the forgiving of a minor sin, which is insisted on.

An example of this could be the drops of water, which are frequently falling on a given stone. They will definitely affect it. But, if they are poured on it all at the one time, they will not affect it. Thus, the Prophet said,

> *"The most beloved deed to Allah is the most regular and constant even though it were little."*
> (Reported by Al-Bukhari and Muslim)

Amongst things which turn the minor sins into major sins is belittling the sin. The greater the sin is in the sight of the servant, the lesser it will be in the Sight of Allah and *vice versa*. That is because the magnification of the sin emanates from the aversion and hatred of the heart towards it.

Ibn Mas`ud (may Allah be pleased with him) said, "A believer perceives his sins as a mountain, which is about to fall upon him. While a profligate perceives his sins as a fly which when rests on his nose, he raises his hand towards it, consequently, it flies." (Reported by Al-Bukhari and Muslim)

The believer counts any sin as great because the glorification of Allah is firmly established in his heart.

It was reported on the authority of Anas (may Allah be pleased with) that,

> *"You people do (bad) deeds (commit sins) which seem in your eyes as tiny than hair while we used to consider those (very deeds) during the lifetime of the Prophet as destructive sins."*
> (Reported by Al-Bukhari)

Bilal Ibn Sa`d (may Allah bestow mercy on him) said, "Do not look at the minuteness of the sin, but look at the greatness of the One Whom you disobey."

Amongst these reasons also is that one becomes cheerful due to his committing of sins. As the person may say, have you not seen how I defamed the honor of such and such and how I mentioned his defects until he became very shy. A merchant might say, have you not seen how I duped and defrauded him. All of these examples turn the minor sins into major sins.

One of the reasons is to become careless about the concealment of one's sins by Allah and His forbearance and respite of His torture. But he does not realize that this may be a form of punishment in itself which will lead him to more sins.

Amongst the reasons also is to commit a sin and mention it in the presence of others. It was reported on the authority of Abu Hurayrah (may Allah be pleased with him) that the Prophet (peace and blessings of Allah be upon him) said,

> *"All the sins of my followers will be forgiven except those of the Mujahirin (those who commit a sin openly or disclose their sins to the people). An example of such disclosure is that a person commits a sin at night and though Allah screens it from the public, then he comes in the morning, and says, 'O so-and-so, I did such-and-such (evil) deed yesterday,' though he spent his night screened by his Lord (none knowing about his sin) and in the morning, he removes Allah's screen from himself."*
> (Reported by Al-Bukhari and Muslim)

Then if the sinner is a scholar by whom people are guided and his sin is known, it will be turned into a major sin such as wearing a silk garment, visiting oppressors without denying them their shameful acts, etc. That is because the sins of the scholar are followed by people. He, in effect, dies while his evil and corruption continue to fly far and wide. Thus, blessed be he whose evil ends with his death.

In the following *Hadith*, we find the Prophet (peace and blessings of Allah be upon him) saying,

> *"... And he who sets in Islam an evil precedent, there is upon him the burden of that, and the burden of him also who acts upon it subsequently, without any deduction from their burden."*
>
> (Reported by Muslim)

As for the scholar, he has two functions: the first is to abstain from committing sins and the second is to conceal it when falling into a shameful deed. It is also notification that as the burden of the scholars is doubled in case they are followed with respect to committing sins, their rewards also multiply in case they are followed in good deeds. Because of being followed by people, the scholar should be moderate in his style of clothing and expenditure. He, moreover, should be watchful in relation to what people used to follow from his footsteps. That is because if he is accustomed to visiting kings and is occupied with seeking the vanities of this world and thus being followed by people, he will bear their burden without their burden being diminished.

To exemplify this, we may narrate the previous mentioned story that there was a king who used to compel people to eat the flesh of swine. Once, a scholar was brought. The chamberlain said to him, "I have slaughtered a young goat for you so that you may eat from it." When he attended the feast the goat was brought to him but he did not eat. Subsequently, the king commanded him to be killed. Then, the chamberlain said to the scholar, "Have I not said to you that it is a goat." He replied, "How can those who follow my footsteps know that?"

Prerequisites of Repentance

Know that Repentance consists of a regret, which gives the person determination and resolve. This regret, in turn, will make the person know that sins stand as a barrier between him and his Beloved.

Regret is a pain in the heart when one feels that he will be separated from his Beloved. Prolonged grief and weeping are its signs. Is there anything dearer to him than his soul? Is there any punishment more severe than the Fire? Who is more truthful than the Messenger of Allah (peace and blessings of Allah be upon him)? When a person feels that a disease may catch his son or someone close to him then his weeping and sorrow is aggravated. If a physician tells him that his son's disease is incurable, then immediately his sorrow increases. Yet, son is not dearer to him than his soul, nor does the physician know better than Allah and His Messenger, nor is death more grievous than the Fire, nor does disease necessarily lead to death. What is sure is that sins lead to Allah's Wrath.

The penitent should turn his reflection and search in his memory if he has missed prayer or prayed in an unclean garment, or prayed without fully pure intention, because of his ignorance of the conditions with regard to intention he should make up for them.

As for fasting, if he has omitted some days of fasting he should strive to make up for them.

As for Zakah, he must calculate all his wealth and the number of years he has not performed it and pay it by estimating what is due.

As for pilgrimage, if he was able for some years, he must

perform it.

As for sins, he should turn his reflection to the first day he reached the age of puberty and search for all his sins until he finds all of them, both minor and major, then he should see what is between himself and Allah, Most High, then repentance for it comes by remorse and asking Allah's forgiveness. Then he should estimate it, then he should seek to do a good deed to atone for every sin. Then he should perform an equal number of good deeds to those of his sins according to Almighty Allah's saying,

❨*... For those things that are good remove those that are evil.*❩

(Hud: 114)

The Prophet (peace and blessings of Allah be upon him) was narrated to have said,

"*... and follow an evil deed with a good deed, for surely it will efface it.*"

(Reported by At-Tirmidhi)

An example for this is to atone for listening to diversion by listening to the Glorious Qur'an and remembrance meetings. He should atone for drinking wine by giving a lawful drink as charity.

As for oppressing people, it is also a sin and an aggression against the ordinance of Allah, Most High, as He has forbidden oppression. For the oppressor with regard to people has committed disobedience by his oppression. So, he should regret and resolve not to do it again. Added to that he should perform good deeds that are parallel to these kinds of oppression. As for causing harm to people, repentance for that would be by seeking their consent and being kind in relation to them. As for appropriating wealth, he should give some of his lawful property in charity. As for murder, repentance for that would be through manumitting some slave-servants (besides the assigned punishment in this world).

Actually, this is pertaining to the right of Allah. If one does so, he will not be pardoned until he clears himself of the obligations owed to people.

Their obligations would be either in souls, properties, chastity and honor, or hurting hearts.

As for the first, if one kills a person by mistake, he shall pay blood money to its due person. But if he kills him premeditatedly, *Qisas* (the law of equality) is obligatory. Thus, he should surrender to the guardian of the killed who will have the very right either to kill him or to pardon him. It is not permissible for the killer to conceal the matter. This is in contrast with adultery or fornication, theft or drinking wine. Repentance in these cases does not require one to uncover his offenses. Rather he should veil himself. But if the case is raised to the ruler, he will be punished due to his offence and his repentance will be valid and accepted by Allah. This was proven by the story of Ma`iz and Al-Ghamidiyyah (who committed adultery and then repented and were punished for their offence. Afterwards, the Prophet (peace and blessings of Allah be upon him) gave glad tidings that their repentance was valid and accepted).

As for the second obligation that is connected with properties such as appropriation of wealth, trickery and deception, one must return these obligations to its owner and thus clearing himself of these rights.

He should talk with the owners of these obligations and

return them their rights and then seek their forgiveness one by one. But in case he cannot return back all their rights, he must return back according to his ability and the sin of the rest will only be overcome by increasing his good deeds so that on the Day of Judgement some of them will be taken from him and put over the deeds of the owners of the obligations as a compensation. If he has not enough good deeds, some of their bad deeds will be taken from them and put over his evil deeds. If he has properties for someone who has died or is not known for him nor his heirs, he should give these properties in charity instead of him. If the lawful and the prohibited are mixed, one should endeavor to estimate the measure of the prohibited and then give its equal in charity.

The third is connected with offences against chastity and honor and causing harm to hearts. The sinner should search for the offended and seek their forgiveness one by one. He, moreover, should make the offended know his offence against him unless mentioning it may cause harm to the offended. In this case he should seek his forgiveness without making him know his offence against him. And whoever of them has died, the sin of this will only be overcome by increasing good deeds so that on the Day of Judgement a compensation may be taken from them for it and there is no salvation without the superiority of good deeds.

Among the prerequisites of valid repentance is that one should make a firm pledge to Allah that he intends never to return to such these sins and the like of them in the future.

The similitude of this is as the patient who knows that eating fruit causes him harm because of his disease. Thus, he intends firmly not to eat any kind of fruit as long as he is patient. His resolve is ascertained immediately however he may imagine that he will be overcome by his desire after a while. But he is not a penitent unless his resolve is ascertained immediately. Firstly, the penitent should be silent, eat and sleep little, have good earning, avoid doubtful matters, and abstain from vain desires.

It was said: "Whoever is truthful in abstaining from vain desires and endeavors to fulfill his resolve for seven years he will not be tried with this sin again." Others said, "Whoever repents from an offence and follows the straight way for seven years, he will never return to that offence."

Types of People Who Are in Continual Repentance

One should know that the repentant are of four types:

First: One who repents from all sins and is constant in repentance until his death and does not intend to return to committing sins but only falls into small faults that are never disjoined from people. In other words, this represents straightforwardness in repentance and its owner is foremost in good deeds. This kind of repentance is called sincere repentance and this soul is called the satisfied soul (in complete rest).

Second: One who repents and follows the straight path in the core of matters pertaining to the religion and refrains from shameful deeds, but he persists in some sins unintentionally, and he is tested by it in the course of his life without having intention to commit them. This type of soul is self-reproaching which reproaches its holder when falling into sins. This is also a high level even if it is lower than the first type. Surely, its owner has a great reward. In this context, Allah, Most High, says,

《*Those who avoid great sins and shameful deeds,*

only (falling into) small faults, verity thy Lord is Ample in Forgiveness.

(An-Najm: 32)

Third: One who repents and continues without committing sins for a period, then his desire overtakes him and he commits some sins, which he inclines toward intentionally because of desire, this is due to his inability to overcome his desire. But in spite of the sins he commits, he is constant in performing good deeds and refrains from some sins whenever he is able to control his desire which he cannot break. He wishes if Almighty Allah could give him the capacity to control and break his desire. On doing a sin, he prepares himself to repent and relinquish that sin. The holder of that soul is as the likeness of Almighty Allah's saying,

Others (there are who) have acknowledged their wrong doings: they have mixed an act that was good with another that was evil.

(At-Tawbah: 102)

In other words, there is more hope for being forgiven because of his insistence on doing virtuous acts and hating shameful deeds. This is in accordance with Almighty Allah's saying concerning them,

...Perhaps Allah will turn unto them (in mercy)...

(At-Tawbah: 102)

Eventually, he should be mindful that he is in danger because of his delay and respite of repentance. For death may attack him before repentance. Verily, the (results of) deeds done depend upon the last actions. Thereupon, he should care about his last actions.

Fourth: The one who repents and continues for a while then returns back to commit sins without thinking of repentance nor remorse for what he has done. He is a confirmed sinner and his soul is that which incites him to do evil.

If he dies while believing in the Oneness of Allah, there is more hope of being saved from the fire of Hell even if this is after a while. And, it is not impossible that Allah, Most High, may forgive and pardon him because of a hidden cause that no one knows but Allah. However, it is not permissible for the sinner to depend on this.

As we have mentioned, the penitent should perform good deeds that are opposite to the evil ones he has committed to nullify them and blot out its effect. The atoning good deeds would be by means of heart, tongue, and other organs in accordance with the sin.

It was reported on the authority of Abu Bakr (may Allah be pleased with him) that the Messenger of Allah (peace and blessings of Allah be upon him) said,

> *"No one commits a sin and follows it by performing ablution well, then performs two Rak`ahs and asks Allah for forgiveness without being pardoned."*
> (Reported by Abu Dawud)

The Treatment for Repentance and the Way to Break the Habit of Sin

One should know that one couldn't decide the cure unless he diagnosed the disease. There is no meaning in medicine except in that which counters the causes of disease, and the only thing, which nullifies a thing, is its opposite. The cause for persistence in sin is heedlessness and desire, only knowledge can counteract heedlessness and desire can be countered by patience and blotting out the causes.

Heedlessness is the head of the sin. Therefore, there is no treatment for repentance except by a mixture of sweetness of knowledge and the bitterness of patience.

Surely, scholars are the physicians of this disease. For it is among the diseases of the heart that exceed these of the body. It became one of the diseases of the heart because of the following:

First: The patient does not know that he is patient.

Second: Its upshot is not visible in this world unlike diseases of the bodies whose consequence is real death and what is after death is invisible. Thus, you see one depends on Allah's favors with regard to diseases of the heart while he endeavors in treating physical diseases without dependence.

Third: The incurable disease, which is losing a physician. Physicians are scholars and they are diseased in this era. Most physicians are overtaken by seeking vanities of this world. Consequently, they cannot warn people against diseases lest they should be replied, "Do you enjoin having treatment and forget to practice it yourselves?" That is why the incurable disease prevailed and having treatment came to an end.

If it is said, "What is the way a preacher should follow in the way of preaching with the people?"

You can reply that it is an intensive subject, which cannot be covered. But we indicate here the useful methods, which can be employed to untie the knot of insistence. They are four methods:

1- To remind of the verses in the Glorious Qur'an that warn sinners, and to remind of with what has been narrated from the sayings of the Prophet and the Companions. This should be accompanied with praising the penitent.

2- To remind with the Prophets and the righteous ancestors and what came to them of catastrophes because of their sins. As what happened to Adam (peace and blessings of Allah be upon him) when he disobeyed his Lord and how he suffered for his sin by being ejected from Paradise. Also, what happened to Dawud, Sulayman and Yusuf (peace and blessings of Allah be upon them all). The Glorious Qur'an mentions these stories to be taken as admonition. Since the chastisement of Allah is more painful in the Hereafter, these stories should be mentioned repeatedly on the hearings of those who persist in committing sins for they are useful in motivating causes of repentance.

3- To explain to them that hastening punishment in this world is expected and that every affliction, which besets any servant, is because of the shameful acts he has committed. There are those who are unconcerned about the punishment of the Hereafter while they are afraid of the punishment of Allah in this world because of their ignorance. The effect of a sin may be hastened in this world. This is proven by the *Hadith* of the Messenger of Allah (peace and blessings of Allah be upon him) in which he said,

> *"Surely a servant may be deprived of the bounty because of a sin he has committed."*
> (Reported by Ibn Majah)

Once Al-Fudayl Ibn `Iyad said, "When I commit a sin I can recognize this in the behavior of my monkey and slave-servant."

Abu Sulayman Ad-Darani said, "Dry dream is a kind of punishment and no one missed a prayer except because of a sin he has committed."

According to Abu Hurayrah (may Allah be pleased with him), the Prophet (peace and blessings of Allah be upon him) said,

> *"When a believer commits a sin, a black spot forms on his heart. If he repents and mends his ways and seeks forgiveness, the spot is purged from his heart. But if he goes on sinning, the spot will grow until it covers his heart all over. That is rust, which Allah (Glorified and Exalted be He) mentions in His Book, ⟨By no means! But on their hearts is the stain of the (ill) which they do.⟩ (Al-Mutaffin: 14)"*
>
> (Reported by At-Tirmidhi)

Al-Hasan (may Allah have mercy upon him) said, "The good deed is a light in the heart and a source of power in the body while a bad deed is a darkness in the heart and a source of weakness in the body."

4- To tell the people about the punishment for major sins such as intoxication, adultery (or fornication), murder, pride, envy, and backbiting. What is important here is that the learned people should be like a skillful physician who can diagnose the disease successfully so that he can treat it. It was reported that a man said to the Prophet (peace and blessings of Allah be upon him),

> *"Advise me! The Prophet said, 'Do not become angry and furious.'"*
>
> (Reported by Al-Bukhari)

Another man said to the Prophet (peace and blessings of Allah be upon him),

> *"Advice me! The Prophet (peace and blessings of Allah be upon him) said, 'You should be despondent of what is in the hands of people.'"*
>
> (Reported by Ibn Majah)

What has been mentioned is the treatment of heedlessness and here we discuss the treatment of sensual desire. In effect, the way of its treatment may be taken from what we have remarked in the chapter of exercising the soul. Undoubtedly, patience is of paramount importance for the treatment of sensual desire. To exemplify this, one's disease may prolong because of having something harm to his disease. Indeed, he is motivated to take these harmful matters by his ardent desire or his heedfulness. Therefore, one should feel the bitterness of patience. Also, this way can be used to treat desire with regard to committing sins. For example, if one is overtaken by his desire and consequently cannot keep his eye, heart, and his extremities away from seeking out vain desires, he should remind himself of the threatening statements (of Allah's punishment) that are mentioned in the Book of Allah, Most High, and the *Sunnah* of the Messenger of Allah (peace and blessings of Allah be upon him). Subsequently, if his fear increases, he will keep himself away from the causes that agitate his desire.

It is notification that what agitates desire externally is the presence of the desired and looking at him. The treatment for that is hunger and continuous fasting, which can only be achieved by patience. And, what motivates patience is fear (of Allah's punishment), which can only be attained by knowledge and sightedness. Thus, the first thing for the treatment of this disease is attending remembrance meetings and listening with a conscious heart. Then, one should ponder over what have been said and consequently fear will be produced. Whereupon, patience and causes of seeking treatment will be easy and available. And, all of these are due to Almighty Allah's Help and Support.

If it is asked: Why does a man commit sins even though he knows their shameful consequences?

To this question there are many answers:

1- The promised punishment is not existent at present.

2- If the believer committed a sin he should be determined to repent as he is promised that repentance pardons what is previously done. But the hope in long life is the dominant characteristic of human beings. So, he continued to delay repentance. And when repentance became something hopeful, he engaged in sins.

3- Man always inspires hope in Allah's forgiveness.

To treat all these diseases, man should be mindful that every coming is near, and he is not sure when this may attack him. Moreover, reminding one another that most of the torture of people in Hell is because of its delay and this can help the implementation of repentance. The one who delays builds the matter up on his existence, which is not actually the case, for he may die, and even if he lives for some time, he may be unable to relinquish sins as he is today. He also should be remembered that the reason for his inability to avoid sins lurks behind the dominance of his desires and it will accompany him thereafter. This matter is assured by habit. For this, those who delay have perished, because they thought that there is a difference between the two cases.

The similitude of the one who delays is like that of the one who wants to uproot a tree, but finds that it is very strong and will only be uprooted with difficulty. Thereupon, he said, "I will delay its uprooting for one year, then I will come to uproot it." But he does not know that the longer the tree lives, the more firmly rooted it will be, and that the more elderly he is, the more feeble he will be. What a wonder that he is unable to attack it, even though he uses his full strength, while it is very weak. How does he expect to overcome it if he grows faint, while it grows strong!

As for awaiting Allah's forgiveness, it is possible that the sinner may be forgiven, but the man should be serious. The likeness of this man is the one who spent all his property, impoverished himself and his children, and awaited Allah to guide him to a treasure in a ruin. This can be materialized but this person is foolish. And Allah, Glorified and Exalted be He, knows best.

II. Patience and Gratitude

Here, the book deals with two main subjects. First, it sheds light on patience, its meaning, and categories. The Arabic word "*Sabr*" – patience – has been quoted ninety times in the Qur'an. It has been joined with various bounties as its fruits. For example, Allah, Most High, says,

⟨*And We appointed, from among them, leaders, giving guidance under Our command, so long as they persevered with patience and continued to have Faith in Our Signs.*⟩
(As-Sajdah: 24)

⟨*On those who patiently persevere, their reward according to the best of their actions.*⟩
(An-Nahl: 96)

⟨*Say, O you My servants who believe fear your Lord. Good is (the reward) for those who do good in this world. Spacious is Allah's earth those who patiently persevere will truly receive a reward without measure.*⟩
(Az-Zumar: 10)

⟨*And we made a people, considered weak (and of no account), inheritors of lands in both east and west, lands whereon we sent down our blessings. The fair promise of thy Lord was fulfilled for the children odd Israel, because they had patience and constancy, and we leveled to the ground the great works and fine buildings which Pharaoh and his people erected (with such pride).*⟩
(Al-A`raf: 137)

All acts are measured in light of the proportion of patience accompanied therewith. Since *Sav m* (Fasting) is an aspect of patience, the Almighty in His *Qudsi Hadith,*

> "*Fasting is for Me Alone and I reward therefore.*"
> (Reported by Al-Bukhari)

He promised the patient His Company and blessed them with incomparable gifts, He says,

> {*They are those in whom (descend) blessings from their Lord and mercy, and they are the ones that receive guidance.*}
> (Al-Baqarah: 157)

On the other hand, many Hadiths have dealt with patience. For example, the Prophet (peace and blessings of Allah be upon him) said,

> "*Nobody can be given a blessing better and greater than patience.*"
> (Reported by Al-Bukhari)

Al-Hasan said, "Patience a valuable treasury of goodness, given by the Almighty to an honorable servant." Some righteous Muslims used to a piece of paper where he they have written write,

> {*Now await in patience the command of thy Lord: for verily you art in Our.*}
> (At-Tur: 48)

Scientifically, patience is a human trait. Animals are not expected to observe patience due to their inferiority. Angels do not also observe it because of their integrity. Angels are free from desire that distracts man.

As for man, in his early childhood, he is inferior, having only the instinct of eating. Then comes that joy. Then comes that of marriage without being supported with patience. When his mind grows and operates, lights of guidance find their way with maturity. However, this primary guidance needs a guide leading it to the Hereafter. Nature necessitate fulfilling what man yearns for, but *Shar`* and one's mind curb him. Hence, struggle between both of them begins within man's heart. Therefore, patience signifies the religious incentive against the carnal one. If patiently preservers, he joins the patient. If not, he follows Satan. In that way, patience turns out to be human quality.

Categories of Patience

Patience has two categories, namely,

1- Physical patience such as undergoing bodily hardships and doing difficult works.

2- Psychological Patience. It stands for resisting natural desires and whims. This type of patience covers many aspects of human endeavor, such as chastity, courage, clemency, content, and patience in case of calamity. In that way, all ingredients of *Iman* come under patience.

No one can do without patience in any way. Man's experience has two kinds,

1- What agrees with his desires of being healthy, rich, prestigious and so on and so forth. In all these aspects, man needs patience. He should not rely on them nor be indulged therein. He should observe the Almighty's right by giving charity and assisting others. If unable to control himself, he would lead a miserable life filled with disgust and greed. A righteous man said, "believers endure adversity, but only the truthful endure prosperity." Therefore, `Abdur-Rahman Ibn `Awf said, "We maintained patience in adversity, but failed to have it in prosperity." Allah says,

{O you who believe! Let not your riches or your children divert you from the remembrance of Allah. If any act thus, the loss is their own.}
(Al-Munafiqun: 9)

{And know you that your possessions and your progeny are but a trial; and that it is Allah with whom lies your highest reward.}
(Al-Anfal: 28)

{O you who believe! Truly, among your wives and your children are (some that are) enemies to yourselves: so beware of them.}
(At-Taghabun: 14)

Therefore, a *true* human is the one who endure prosperity. This kind of patience is closely attached to thanksgiving. In fact, it is fulfilled by it. This form of patience is quite hard since it is joined with facility, rather than a hungry person who has nothing to eat.

2- The second type contradicts one's desires. This is further subdivided into three kinds, namely,

ii) Obedience. Man needs to perform it patiently. Some rituals may be detested due to laziness such as *Salad*, due to greed such as *Zakah* or because of both reasons such as fighting in Allah's cause. An obedient person needs for patience in three instances. Before engaging in worship, he should purify his intention, be sincere and ward persistently off dissemblance. During worship where he should constantly remember Allah. He should be ready to observe complementary supererogatory rite and its manners. Thus, man should perseveringly resists indolence and laziness. Finally, he should observe patience after his worship. He should not propagate it, nor show it off. Giving a charity, if a man does not hide it patiently, he nullifies it.

iii) Shunning disobedience persistently. We all are actually in a dire need for this kind of patience. When an act is easily committed, such as backbiting, lying and argumentation, it becomes more difficult to avoid. Seeing someone wearing silky clothes, one condemns him. But he may indulge in backbiting without reproving him. If unable to have full control over one's tongue, solitude is the sole way out of this dilemma.

iv) Involuntary matters, i.e., adversities such as death of a dear person, loss of property, being inflicted with blindness, becoming infirm and so on and so forth. This type commands the highest level of patience, since certitude forms its cornerstone. The Prophet (peace and blessings of Allah be upon him) said,

> "Whenever Allah goodness to someone, He inflicts him."
>
> (Reported by Al-Bukhari)

One should also bear human's injury. This is the highest level of patience in this group. Allah says,

> ⟨*But if you persevere patiently, and guard against evil, then that will be a determining factor in all affairs.*⟩
>
> (Al-'Imran: 186)

❨*We do indeed know how thy heart is distressed at what they say.*❩

(Al-Hijr: 97)

❨*But if you show patience, that is indeed the best (course) for those who are patient.*❩

(An-Nahl: 126)

Many *Ahadith* have been reported clarifying the virtue of patience. `A'ishah reported that Allah's Prophet (peace and blessings be upon him) said,

> *"No trouble comes to a believer even if it is the pricking of a thorn that it becomes (the means) whereby his sins are effaced or his sins are obliterated."*

(Reported by Muslim)

In another *Hadith*, the Prophet (peace and blessings of Allah be upon him) said,

> *"Believing men and women still suffer adversities in their bodies, properties and children till they return sinless to Allah."*

(Reported by Al-Bukhari)

Sa`d Ibn Abu Waqqas (may Allah be pleased with him) narrates that he said,

> *"O Prophet of Allah, who suffers more adversities among human? He replied, "Allah's Prophets, then the righteous, then the best. Every one is inflicted in proportion to his faith. If it is firm, his infliction becomes severer and the vice versa. One still suffers adversities till he becomes sinless."*

(Reported by At-Tirmidhi)

Allah has also said in a *Qudsi Hadith*,

> *"Whenever I inflict any person in his body, property or children, and he endures it patiently, I decline holding him for accountability on the Last Day."*
> (Reported by At-Tirmidhi)

Manners of Patience

> *"Verily, the patience is at the first stroke of a calamity."*
> (Reported by Al-Bukhari)

We should also say to Allah we belong, and to Him is our return according to a *Hadith* reported by Umm Salamah (may Allah be pleased with her) in *Sahih* Muslim. We should also keep silent. We can shed tears without disgust, since it is futile and delights malicious persons. An adversity should be endured with good patience without its being wrongly reflected in man's behavior as did by Umm Salim.

Thabit Al-Banani said, "`Abdullah Ibn Mutraf died. Then his father appeared dressed in good clothes and applying perfumes. His people was outraged saying, `Abdullah dies and you do such and such? He replied, should I give in to distress? Allah has promised me with three traits all of which are very dear to me. Allah says,

> ❴*Who say, when afflicted with calamity: "To Allah we belong, and to Him is our return" -They are those in whom (descend) blessings from their Lord and mercy, and they are the ones that receive guidance.*❵
> (Al-Baqarah: 156-157)

Then he continued, verily I will spare everything taken from me in this world to have its reward in the Hereafter even if it were a cup of water.

Silah Ibn Ashim and his son joined a battle in Allah's cause. He addressed his son, "Go on son and fight so that I should sacrifice and be rewarded by Allah. Then his son fought till he fell a martyr. Then his father followed him. Then people reached his mother Mu`adhah Al-`Adawyah. She remarked, "Welcome, if you are actually coming to congratulate me. Otherwise, return back." If an adversity can be concealed, it is purely divine bless.

Abu Hurayrah (may Allah be pleased with him) reports Allah's Prophet (peace and blessings of Allah be upon him) as saying,

> *"When someone becomes ill, Allah sends two angels commanding them, "Observe what he tells his visitors. When he thanks Allah, they carry his words to the Almighty Who already knows. Hence, Allah says. "If I cause my servant to die, I will admit him into Paradise. But if recover him, I would restore him a better physique and forgive him his sins."*
> (Reported by Muslim)

Imam Ahmad was once asked, "How are you? He answered, "I am fine." The man said, "Did you suffer from fever yesterday?" He replied, I say I am fine. Do not bother me with what I detest. Imam `Ali (may Allah be pleased with him) remarked, "Out of reverence to Allah, you should never complain your pain to any one, nor mention your adversity." Al-Ahnaf said, I have lost my eyesight since forty years, but I have never mentioned it." "Disclosing one's adversity impairs the sweetness of *Iman* in one's heart," highlights Shaqiq Al-Balkhi.

In the same vein, a wise man said, concealing your calamity is a treasure of righteousness. Early Muslims were delighted with calamities due to the good rewards they receive therefore. For example, when `Abd Al-Malik Ibn `Umar Ibn `Abd Al-`Ziz (may Allah be pleased with him) died, `Umar buried him. He stood for a while and said, "May Allah be merciful to you, son! You have honored your father. By Allah I have been delighted with you since your birth. But now I am more pleased with you than ever before."

However, one may argue, patience requires us not to detest calamity, but this is untenable. How about being delighted therewith, which is completely unfeasible? In fact, we endure patience as to pleasing things and detestable ones. It does not repudiate natural feelings but rather alien practices such as tearing one's clothes and inveighing with one's tongue.

As for one's delight with a calamity, it is *Shar`i*, rather than biologically oriented. Human nature entails detesting adversities. For example, a sick man may seek a remedy, which is bitter. He would spend a lot of money to get this medicine. Taking it and getting recovered, he would be pleased with recovery rather than the drug itself. The same applies to a king telling a poor man I would strike you with this tiny stick and give you a thousand Dinar for each stroke. In fact, the poor man will be delighted with the money rather than the strokes.

Treatment of Patience

One should know that there is no disease that Allah has created, except that He also has created its treatment. Patience, though difficult, is tenable through knowledge and practice. They both formulate treatments for all spiritual illnesses. Every disease requires a certain aspect of knowledge and practice. Variation in diseases affects treatments. For example, if one is preoccupied by his sexual desire, and is unable to control himself, he should so three things, namely,

1- He should keep fasting and be satisfied with little food when breaking his fast.

2- He should avoid all means leading thereto such as gazing and contemplating. Solitude is the treatment as well as lowering one's gaze. In fact, gaze is a poisonous arrow shoot by Satan towards man's heart.

3- He should marry. This is the best treatment, since fasting undermines physical strength. It does not curb one's desire. You should get accustomed to combating lusts and whims, whereby you will overcome them easily.

Faithfully speaking, curbing premonition is actually the most difficult form of patience due to man's leisure and seclusion. Hence, scruples may burn man. Their sole treatment is solitude and thinking of the Almighty's prodigies in the universe. He should also keep remembering the Almighty through reciting the Qur'an and *Salah* with full presence of his mind. Premonition distracts man's mind.

As for divine gifts granted to man thereby, this is purely divine. Like fishing, man my exert his utmost efforts, but catches a little. Another one may do modest endeavors, but he catches more. This depends on Divine Providence. The same applies to human endeavors. Therefore, every one should elevate his soul yearning for Allah's blessings distributed throughout the whole life as indicated by the Prophet (peace and blessings of Allah be upon him) in At-Tabarani.

We should prepare our hearts to receive these blessings, just like a farmer preparing his land to saw seeds. Then it should be irrigated; water comes from rain. But none knows when does it fall. However, it certainly rains every year. The same applies to blessings.

Accordingly, we should purify our heart and fill it with sincerity and good will. We should expose it to Allah's showers of mercy. Just as rain is more likely to fall in winter and spring, we await for these blessings in their due times such as the in *`Arafah*, on Friday and in *Ramadan*.

Gratitude: Virtue and Blessings

Allah refers to gratitude in more than one instance in the Qur'an. For example, He says,

> {*And swiftly shall we reward those that (serve us with) gratitude.*}
>
> (Al `Imran: 145)

> {*What can Allah gain by your punishment, if you are grateful and you believe?*}
>
> (An-Nisa': 147)

> {*But few of My servants are Grateful.*}
>
> (Saba' : 13)

> {*If you are grateful, I will add more (favors) unto you.*}
>
> (Ibrahim: 7)

> {*And if you fear poverty, soon will Allah enrich you, if he wills, out of his Bounty.*}
>
> (At-Tawbah: 28)

> {*Allah forgives not that partners should be set up*

with him; but he forgives anything else, to whom he pleases.

(An-Nisa': 48)

For Allah will turn (in mercy) to whom he wills.

(At-Tawbah: 15)

If it be his will, he would remove (the distress) which occasioned your call upon him.

(Al-An'am: 41)

For Allah bestows his abundance without measure on whom he will.

(Al-Baqarah: 212)

Recognizing the virtue of gratitude, Satan assaulted humans saying,

Then will I assault them from before them and behind them, From Their right and their left: Nor will You find, in most of them, Gratitude (for Your mercies).

(Al-A'raf: 17)

Al-Mughirah (may Allah be pleased with him) narrates,

"*The Prophet (peace and blessings of Allah be upon him) used to stand (in the Prayer – Salah) or pray till both his feet or legs swelled. He was asked why (he offered such an unbearable Prayer) and he said, "Should I not be a grateful servant!"*

(Reported by Al-Bukhari)

Mu'adh Ibn Jabal (may Allah be pleased with him) reports, the Prophet (peace and blessings of Allah be upon him) told,

"I love you, so you should say, "O Allah empower me to remember You, to be thank to You and worship You properly!"

(Reported by Abu Dawud)

Gratitude with Heart, Tongue and other Organs

One's gratitude is entertained by his heart, expressed by his tongue and reflected by his organs. As for one's heart, one should wish good to all humans. Accordingly, one's intentions should be good.

One's tongue should also hymn the Almighty's praise. Other organs reflect one's gratitude practically through obedience and warding of sinful acts. Thus, gratefulness of one's eyes and his ears is to conceal human defects that one may see or hear. The same applies also to the tongue. It should express man's pleasure with the Almighty. The Prophet (peace and blessings of Allah be upon him) said,

"Murmuring blesses is gratitude, whereas neglecting them is ingratitude."

(Reported by Ahmad)

A man greeted `Umar Ibn Al-Khattab (may Allah be pleased with him). `Umar asked, "how are you today? He replied, "Fine, thanks Allah." `Umar remarked, "You have answered my question." Early Muslims used to ask each other the same question to thank the Almighty, thus; obeying Him in that way.

Knowledge of Allah's Law Fulfills Gratitude

One should know that gratitude is fulfilled through one's knowledge of what the Almighty loves and commands. Gratitude signifies employing His blesses the way He loves.

Ingratitude stands for the contrary. It either involves negligence of good deeds or adopting abominable ones. This latter is determined by two criteria, namely,

1- Listening, which is specified in accordance with the Qur'an

2- Considering with one's insight. This is quiet scarce. Therefore, the Almighty has sent His Messengers and Prophets to pave the way before humans to advance toward His pleasure. Knowledge of this aspect depends on learning *Shar`i* Rulings as to human endeavors. Ignorance of this criterion undermines man's gratitude to the Almighty. One should also try to sound the wisdom behind all creatures and their underlying objectives. This wisdom is either obvious or hidden, as follows,

Obvious wisdom, such as having day and night due to the sun's circulation. We work during daytime and go to bed at night. The sun also adorns the sky. The same applies to human organs, some of which have clear wisdom while others still conceal theirs. Eyes, for example are made to see, hands to give, take, etc. and legs to move on them. As for other physiological organs such as kidneys, veins, arteries, liver and other systems, only specialists have sound the wisdom behind their creation. However, they only know a scratch of it. Thus; employing any organ in anything other than what it has been created for signifies ingratitude. For example, hitting someone illegally, one becomes ungrateful to the Almighty as his hands. They have been created to do what is beneficial for him. Likewise, casting unlawful gazes signifies ingratitude to Allah as one's eyes as well as the sun.

In fact, things in this world are created to draw man nearer to the Almighty and guide him to Him. This end can be achieved only through loving Him, constantly remembering

Him and giving up worldly gaieties. Love of the Almighty is secured through knowledge of Him obtained through frequent contemplation. This state is attained only one's body is healthy. In its turn, physical health depends on the land, water and air. Likewise, they come from heavens, the earth as well as all other conspicuous components. They all are made for the human body, where the soul resides. The righteous soul will return back to the Lord, well pleased and well pleasing unto Him due to obedience and knowledge! Allah says,

❴*I have only created Jinns and men, that they may worship Me.*❵

(Adh-Dhariyat: 56)

Thus, using anything improperly signifies ingratitude. For example, Allah has blessed man with coins that are, in origin, mere useless stones. But all humans have to use them, since they need different necessities such as food, drink, and clothes among many other things. However, one possesses a redundant thing and is in a dire need for another important thing. At the same time may have that essential thing and seeks for your surplus. Hence, they both should exchange their things, but it should be fair according to each things value. I that way coins are created by Allah to determine the value of things and make humans' life convenient. Coins, or money as a whole, are not besought for their own sake, but rather for the benefit they lead to. Thus, they have obtained a specific status, rendering their owner an owner of many things. This being the wisdom behind his or her creation, if anyone behaves in contradiction to it is ungrateful to the Almighty. Thus, hoarding them renders them invaluable before the Almighty, since he has deprived people wherefrom. This is clearly expressed by Allah saying,

❴*And there are those who bury gold and silver and spend it not in the way of Allah: announce unto them a most grievous penalty.*}

(At-Tawbah: 34)

The same rule applies to making pots of the same stones of coins, i.e. gold and silver.

Another example is to employ the ruler in dressmaking and cleaning streets, which is done by people who are inferior to him. In fact, both copper and metal were designed to accommodate liquids. Thus they can never be replaced by gold or silver. Therefore, disclosing this great wisdom, the Prophet (peace and blessings of Allah be upon him) said,

> *"He who drank in vessels of gold or silver he in fact drank down in his belly the fire of Hell."*
> (Reported by Muslim)

Likewise, usurious transactions in currency signify outright ingratitude, since he spoils their original objective. This example is actually applicable to all man's affairs. Furthermore, the Almighty has gifted man with two hands, one of which is stronger than the other. Hence, it commands more honor. In addition, Allah has held you in need of certain deeds, some of which are honorable such as handling the Qur'an, while the other are not such as removing impurity. Therefore, if one juxtaposes both actions, as if cleansing oneself by his right hand and handling the Qur'an by the left hand, one would have reversed their original objectives. This is sheer ingratitude. The same applies to the feet. Wearing the left shoe before the right one is ingratitude to the right leg, since shoes are designed to protect the legs.

Furthermore, breaking a branch from a tree randomly, one has violated the wisdom of creating trees, i.e. public benefit. Breaking it for a rightful objective signifies gratitude. If it belongs to someone else, it is aggression, even if he was obliged to do so, until its owner permits him to.

Grace: Essence and Varieties

One should know that every wish is called a grace. However, the true grace is happiness in the Hereafter. Other wishes are figuratively called a grace. In fact, all our affairs come under four categories, namely,

1- What benefits man in this life and that to come, such as knowledge, good manners. This is the true grace.

2- What undermines man in both lives. This is actual affliction.

3- What benefits man in this life and damages him in that to come such as indulgence. Ignorant persons take it after a grace.

4- What undermines man in this life and prospers him in the Hereafter. This is regarded a grace by sensible persons only. For example, a medicine may be bitter now but curative in the future. A young boy considers it a distress, but a sensible man regards it a grace. Thus, a sensible enemy is better than a foolish friend. You should befriend your soul, but one's soul in an ignorant friend. Thus, you treat it harsher than you deal with an enemy.

Allah's Boundless Graces

A grace is either besought on their own right, being an end in itself, or lead to another desired end. As for the former, it is pleasure in the Hereafter. It achieved through four aspects, namely, immortality, eternal pleasure, lasting knowledge and endless prosperity.

As far as the second type is concerned, it stands for those means leading to the above-mentioned pleasure. In its turn, it commands four sub-categories, namely,

1- Virtues of the soul such as *Iman* (Faith) and good manners.

2- Virtues of the body such as power and health.

3- Surrounding graces such as wealth and authority.

4- The bonds interlacing these surroundings with virtues such as guidance, providence and divines assistance.

However, one may argue what do wealth and authority have to do with the Hereafter! In fact, these things act like a wing of a bird and a means leading to a certain objective. If a seeker of knowledge is not supported with enough financial means, he is like a fighter without a sword. If he is poor, he will totally busy earning his subsistence. As for authority, one ward thereby off humiliation and oppression. Otherwise, he would be preoccupied with defending himself. One's heart is his capital. Thus richness and authority subdue these concerns. Health, power and long life are also graces, since works and knowledge rely on them. The Prophet (peace and blessings of Allah be upon him) said,

> *"There are two blessings which many people lose: (They are) Health and free time for doing good."*
> (Reported by Al-Bukhari)

When asked about the best of people, he (peace and blessings of Allah be upon him) said,

> *"It is he whose life is long and deeds are good."*
> (Reported by At-Tirmidhi)

Though they are graces, we have already dealt with evils of wealth and authority. However, they are not always condemned. It is evident that guidance, divine assistance and providence are the greatest graces that man can receive.

Allah's Grace in Means of Obtaining Food

We have already cited physical health among the second virtues of grace. We cannot count those means leading to this grace. However, food is one of those means. In the coming few line, we will deal only with some means of obtaining food.

The Almighty has gifted man with a very delicate sensitive system and movement to seek nutrition. Let us consider these five sensory gifts, which enhance man's sense of perception.

As for the sense of touching, it is the first sense that man enjoys. Its least reflection is to feel what touches him. Feeling remote things actually signifies perfection of one's senses. Thus, man's need for senses to feel remote objects has appeared. Then, the Almighty has created the sense of smelling to feel scents.

But one still fails to determine the source of such a smell. Therefore, one still needs to search for the origin where it spreads. One may come across it or not. He may find his way or not. So he needs for eyes to guide him through his search and behold far objects. However, if this were the case, man would have been defect. Searching for something, one may be detected by an enemy. There may be a barrier between you and this enemy; but he may have approached you without your knowing. The barrier may be removed without affording you ample time either to escape or get prepared to defend yourself.

Therefore, the Almighty has gifted you with the sense of

hearing to scrutinize sounds far behind barriers. However, one is still imperfect. Without the sense of tasting, one would be unable to determine beneficial food from harmful one. Unlike a tree that absorbs whatever water it receives, be it salty or pure. This is, in fact, may be for its detriment.

Finally, one has been gifted with the supreme grace; it is the mind whereby one realizes different kinds of food, their nutritional value and their potential harm. With one's mind, one prepares various types of food, thus; enhancing one's health. However, this the least benefit that can be derived from one's mind. The greatest wisdom is to know the Almighty.

Nevertheless, these five senses are some of many. Faithfully, we have not dealt with them in details. Eyesight, for example, is one of these senses. The eye is the sight's tool. It is composed of ten different layers, some of which are juicy and others form various tissues. Each layer has its own description, appearance, function and composition. If there is any disturbance in any of these aspects, one's eyesight is undermined defying all physicians. This is only one sense, how about other senses?

We may consider the creation of power, will as well as the various tools of movement. If one is gifted with eyes to see food, but he is deprived if inclination thereto and is not naturally urged to seek for it, one's eyes will be useless. Many patients behold food but they do not approach due the absence of appetite. Thus, the Almighty has created an appetite for food.

Furthermore, if this instinct is not satiated with the reasonable amount of food, one will excessively and dangerously eat. Therefore, Allah created satiation to give up eating in time. The same applies to sexual intercourse for procreation.

Likewise, the Almighty has created man's organs as tools to receive food along with many other things. Hands are among these organs. They are composed of numerous joints to facilitate free movements in diverse directions. He has made one's wrest broad with five fingers; which command various length. He has lined them up starting with the thumb as a master over them. Had they been created like a chaotic bunch, their wisdom of creation would have elapsed. Fingers have been gifted with nails on their tips to support them and handle thereby tiny things.

Nevertheless, taking food in one's hand is not enough. Hence, He has created the mouth to carry it into one's belly. The mouth is composed of two bony jaws enhanced with teeth. The teeth have been classified according the need assigned to each of them. The lower jaw has been made free, while the upper stationary. Consider the Almighty's creation! In fact, each mill has its upper part free while its lower one stationary. But this mill created by Allah is not. Had the upper been free, those organs enhanced by it [i.e. eyes, ears, nose, brain ...etc] would have been undermined. Consider also the tongue! It roams around the mouth assisting one's teeth to chew food. It acts like a scoop to the mill, not to mention its miracle of speech. Suppose being unable to swallow a morsel after chewing it! It cannot be swallowed except with a softening material. Therefore, the Almighty has created salivary glands under the tongue to act as smoothers.

In addition, how can this chewed food be carried to the stomach? This cannot be done with one's hands. Hence, Allah has created both the pharynx and the larynx. The former has been made of valves, which allow food to pass but not to return till it reaches esophagus. Reaching the stomach, food cannot become blood, bones and flesh until it is properly digested.

Thus, the Almighty has designed the stomach as a pan where food is prepared. Then, four supervisors, namely; the liver, the spleen, the blood capillaries and the valves, handle it. Hence, food becomes a liquid and ready to be absorbed by veins. Then food moves to the liver where it spends some time to be cleaned. Then it spreads through the whole body. Some of it remains to be excreted.

We should think of the Almighty's Graces in order to be grateful to Him. We only know the blessing of food, which is the least in a long series. We even only recognize our hunger, thus we eat. Animals also do the same. If one does not know himself more than a donkey does of itself, how can he then be grateful to the Almighty!

All these graces revealed to us along with others are only a drop of water in an endless ocean. Allah clearly states in the Qur'an,

> *If you would count up the favors of Allah, never would you be able to number them: for Allah is Oft-Forgiving, Most Merciful.*

(An-Nahl: 18)

Marvels of Food and Treatment

Food is a collective noun under which come numerous varieties. The Almighty has assigned endless signs therein. Food generally covers three categories, namely; nutrients, treatments and fruits.

As for nutrients, having some barely, if you eat them, you will have nothing. Thus, you are required to search for a certain work whereby barely increases so much that it meets your needs. This work is agriculture. You need to saw in a land where it receives its due of water. However, the soil and water are not enough. It also needs air. But how can it penetrate the soil. It should, in its turn, be ploughed. Air also needs the wind to storm it within the soil. However, this is not enough. Heat of spring and summer are also necessary. Extreme cold hinders cultivation.

Let us consider water needed for cultivation. How has the Almighty created it? He has caused the earth to gush forth with springs, wherefrom He has caused rivers to flow. Since some parts of the earth are uneven, the Almighty has sent them clouds driven by the wind to different regions. Allah raises up the heavy clouds and sends to lands in need therefore. The Almighty has created mountains preserving rains. Wells gradually gush out therefrom. Had it sprung all at once, the whole world would have drowned.

We should consider also how the Almighty has created the sun and made it subservient. Though it is extremely far away from the earth, it nevertheless gives warmth to it proportionately in different times. The heat of the sun ripens fruits. Each heavenly body is designed to achieve certain wisdom and endless graces. Since items of food do not grow in one place, Allah has sent traders who are interested in accumulating wealth. Though are not usually satisfied, they are preoccupied with hoarding property. In that way, the Almighty has cause hope and negligence to influence them. Thus, undergoing perils and dangers to carry food and human's needs from the farthest ends of the world.

They have become ungrateful due to negligence and ignorance. They have been prevented thereby to sound the graces. Gratitude comes from knowledge. However, knowledge is not a passive aspect, such as murmuring with one's tongue, "Praise be to Allah," or "Thanks Allah." In fact, gratitude is a practical aspect, in the sense that a grace should be utilized to fulfill its designed wisdom.

Reasons of Negligence of Graces

Due to ignorance, people have a very narrow view on divine graces, disregarding whatever bless they have in their life. Thus, the do not express their gratitude therefor. Seeing that all humans enjoy the same blesses, they do not regard them graces, since all people share them. Hence, they do not thank the Almighty for giving them air, even though if it does not reach them for a moment, they will die. They are not grateful unless they suffer such an adversity then become rescued. This is sheer ignorance.

For example, enjoying eyesight, one does not recognize its grace unless he becomes blind. Restoring his eyesight once more, he sounds its grace and thanks Allah therefore. This person resembles an evil slave who is continually hit. When spared hurts for a while, he becomes grateful. If his master gives up hitting him altogether, he becomes ungrateful and discontented. Once someone complained of poverty to a righteous person. He replied. "Would you like to have ten thousand Dirhams and lose your eyesight?" He answered in the negative. The he asked him, "Would you like to be dump and possess ten thousand Dirhams?" he answered in the negative. Then, he asked him, "Would you like to be insane and have ten thousand Dirhams?" he answered in the negative. He then asked, would you like to have your hands cut and possess ten thousand Dirhams?" He also answered in the negative. Hence, he remarked, "Do you not feel shame complaining your Lord while He ahs given your goods worth of forty thousand Dirhams?"

One day a man suffered poverty so much that he fell in

despair. He saw I a dream that someone addresses him, "Would you like to forget *Surat Al-An`am* and be given a thousand Dinars?" He answered in the negative. Then he was made to choose between *Surat* Hud, Yusuf ... etc, be he declined. Hence he was told, "How do you complain of poverty while you have a treasure worth of a hundred thousand Dinars!"

Ibn As-Sammak visited Ar Rashid and counseled him. Therefore, Ar-Rashid shed tears. Then, Ibn As-Sammak asked for a cup of water and remarked, "O Caliph, if you are prevented to drink this cup of water unless you lay down your office, would you do so?" He answered in the affirmative. Then, Ibn As-Sammak gave him the cup of water to drink. Drinking it, he remarked, "If you are unable to excrete this water unless you give up your office and property, would you do so?" He answered in the affirmative. Then, he highlighted, "What does it avail for a thing less worth than a cup of water!"

In that way, the grace of drinking water in thirst is even greater than the whole universe. Excreting it commands a rather magnificent grace.

We should know that everyone has been singled out with certain graces. However, some humans may share it with him, such as the intellect. Every one, pleased with the Almighty, thinks that he is most sensible being. Likewise, every one sees others' defects, which he detests, and considers himself free from them. Therefore, he should be grateful to the Almighty for giving him good manners.

Furthermore, each person knows his self best. He recognizes its latent qualities, its imperfections and merits. If he becomes uncovered among people, he will be ashamed thereof. Hence, one should be grateful to the Almighty. We may consider a rather wider example. Each person has been gifted with certain graces in his figure, manners, qualities, household, offspring, accommodation, friends, relatives and his neighbors. If deprived therefrom and given to someone else, he would not be satisfied. For instance, Allah has made him a believer not an unbeliever, a human being not an animal, healthy not sick, normal not deformed and so on and so forth. Thus, if one deems to have his life substituted with another's, he should know that he has certain graces, which others do not have, and he would be deprived from them. This is clearly by a *Hadith* reported by Abu Hurayrah (may Allah be pleased with him). The Prophet (peace and blessing of Allah be upon him) said,

> *"If anyone of you looked at a person who was made superior to him in property and (in good) appearance, then he should also look at the one who is inferior to him, and to whom he has been made superior."*
>
> (Reported by Al-Bukhari)

Hence, considering one's status and searching for those graces he has been gifted with, one finds out that Allah has granted him endless blesses, especially *Iman*, the Qur'an, the *Sunnah*, knowledge and leisure time, health and safety. The Prophet (peace and blessings of Allah be upon him) said,

> *"Whoever begins his day enjoying safety, being healthy and possesses his daily food, has held sway over the whole world with its contents."*
>
> (Reported by At-Tirmidhi)

Now we can ask, how can ungrateful negligent hearts be awakened? In fact, hearts having insight contemplate over the clues of the Almighty's graces. But the negligent ones can only be treated by their consideration of persons inferior to them. Early Muslims used to visit hospitals to notice varieties of afflictions. Then they would think of their being healthy. They would watch criminals punished, killed, having their hands cut off or tortured and thank the Almighty for their safety. They visited graveyards knowing that the dead wish to return to life to make up for their shortcomings and increase their good deeds. Thus they thank Allah for having the chance to do so. Hence, they would do their utmost to spend the rest of their life obeying the Almighty.

We should also know that ingratitude abolishes graces. Al-Fudayl said, "Keep gratitude, for every missing grace returns with gratitude."

Inter-Relation of Patience and Gratitude

One may argue, you have stated that Allah has appointed a grace in each creature. This indicates that, in origin, there is no adversity. Thus, what is the significance of patience?! On the other hand, if adversity is there, how can we be grateful for it? How can patience and gratitude come together, since patience implies affliction whereas gratitude necessitates a bless while they are contradictory!

In fact, you should know that both adversity and prosperity are there? Patience is not required in every adversity, such as disbelief. Though an adversity, enduring it patiently is meaningless. The same applies to all kinds of disobedience. However. An unbeliever does not sense his affliction, like an ill person who does not feel his pain due to swooning. An obedient man recognizes his sins, so he should shun them. In that way, every avoidable affliction does not require patience. He is rather asked to drive out his pain. Patience comes when agonies are inevitable. Hence, patience may cover a partial misfortune. It may be a sign of grace in some aspect. Therefore, one should maintain patience and be grateful. Wealth, for example may be a detriment to its owner, leading to his death because of it [such as in robbery]. One's health may also lead him to his end. In that way, each grace can turn into an adversity. One may also be afflicted and blessed at the same time.

For example, man does not know when he will die. This is a great grace, since knowing it, his life would be disturbed. The same applies to man's ignoring people's feelings towards him. Had he known them, his life would become filled with envy, hatred and revenge. The same applies to one's unawareness of others' faults; otherwise, he would have loathed them. This also applies to concealing the Last Day, Laylat Al-Qadr, and the Hour of granting supplications on Friday. All these are graces, since concealing them instigates exerting efforts. In fact, we wonder if this is the case of ignorance, what about knowledge!

We have already stated that the Almighty has an underlying grace in every thing; even pains may be a grace as to its sufferer and a source of discomfort to others. This applies to torture of disbelievers in the Hellfire. For the inhabitants of Paradise, it is a grace. If disobedient persons did not receive their due punishment, obedient ones would not taste the sweetness of rewards. In fact, remembering their counterparts' torment, the residents of Paradise become greatly delighted.

People are not pleased with light of the sun, though they are in dire need for it. The sun is even more important than plants and vegetation, since all humans enjoy its heat. In that way, affliction can also be a grace for the person himself or someone else. Therefore, one should maintain patience and gratitude. One may be pleased with a certain aspect of something and displeased with another aspect of the same thing. Thus, the former entails gratitude whereas the latter patience.

You should know that each adversity such as poverty,

disease, fear ...etc has four aspects requiring a sensible person to be pleased therewith, namely,

1- Being afflicted, you should perceive that his misfortune could be less severe than other ones. In that way, you should be grateful to the Almighty since He has not afflicted you with a severer tribulation.

2- Your religion should remain intact, without any deficiency. `Umar Ibn Al-Khattab remarked, "Receiving an adversity, the Almighty grants me four blesses, namely, my religion remains intact, I am spared severer one, I always get contented therewith and yearn for its reward." Someone told Sahl Ibn `Abdullah, "A thief has entered my house and stolen my possessions." Sahl asked him to be grateful to the Almighty saying, "What would you do if devil infiltrated your heart undermining your faith?" You should even be grateful to him who chooses to alleviate your punishment though you deserve it if full."

3- Punishments are originally postponed to the Hereafter. However, worldly sufferings alleviate them. Hardships met in the Hereafter are persistent. If not, they cannot be relieved. Receiving punishment in this world, one becomes not liable for it on the Last Day. The Prophet (peace and blessings of Allah be upon him) said,

> *"There is nothing (in the form of trouble) that comes to a believer even if it is the pricking of a thorn that there is decreed for him by Allah good or his sins are obliterated."*
> (Reported by Muslim)

4- Such an adversity is recorded in the Mother of the Book and it is inevitable. Being afflicted therewith and freed from anxiety therefore, it is a great grace.

5- Rewards appointed for adversities excel them, since they pave the way to the Last Day; just like preventing a young boy from playing. If left alone to play, he would not achieve any knowledge nor good manners, thus rendering his life a miserable one. Likewise, wealth, children, relatives and one's own friends can lead to one's destruction. Atheists will wish that they were insane; without depending on their minds as to the Almighty's religion. Hence, whenever any thing of the like betakes a man, it is for his religious integrity. Therefore, every one should think good of the Almighty and try to sound the benefits underlying wisdom. Divine wisdom is quite an all-embracing covering all aspects of human life. Allah alone knows where interests of His servants are fulfilled. Receiving their rewards for adversity, they will be grateful to Him, like a young boy thanking his parents and teachers when he reaches maturity when he tastes the fruits of their education. An Adversity is a means whereby the Almighty refines us. He is even more Merciful and Kind than parents. The Prophet (peace and blessings of Allah be upon him) said,

"The Almighty never decrees any thing for a Muslim unless it is good for him."
(Reported by Ahmad)

The gravest sin is indulgence in these worldly affairs. The best way to salvation is to decline it with one's heart. Receiving favorable graces without suffering causes one's heart to rely on this world. When overtaken with incessant adversities, the heat becomes troubled with it and never secures its delusions. Thus, it becomes his confinement. Like a prisoner, he seeks to be rescued therefrom. However, pain is necessary, just as taking bitter medicine; where one suffers a little to be recovered. One may argue that texts explaining the virtue of patience signify that adversity in this world is better than prosperity; hence, should we ask the Almighty to be afflicted?

In fact, this is ungrounded. Anas Ibn Malik (may Allah be pleased with him) reports,

> *"Allah's Messenger (may peace be upon him) visited a person from amongst the Muslims in order to inquire (about his health) who had grown feeble like the chicken. Allah's Messenger (may peace be upon him) said, Did you supplicate for anything or beg of Him about that? He said: Yes. I used to utter (these words): Impose punishment upon me earlier in this world, what Thou art going to impose upon me in the Hereafter. Thereupon Allah's Messenger (may peace be upon him) said, Hallowed be Allah, you have neither the power nor forbearance to take upon yourself (the burden of His Punishment). Why did you not say this, O Allah, grant us good in the world and good in the Hereafter, and save us from the torment of Fire. He (the Holy Prophet) made this supplication (for him) and he was all right."*
> (Reported by Muslim)

Anas Ibn Malik (may Allah be pleased with him) also narrates,

> *"Allah's Messenger (peace and blessings of Allah be upon him) was once asked, "What is the best supplication?" He replied, "It is to seek forgiveness and well-being both in this world and the Hereafter." The same man reached the Prophet (peace and blessing of Allah be upon him) on the other day and asked him, "What is the best*

supplication?" He answered, "It is to seek forgiveness and well-being both in this world and the Hereafter." Then he asked, "What is the best supplication?" He replied, "It is to seek forgiveness and well-being both in this world and the Hereafter. When given them, you have become successful."
(Reported by Ibn Majah)

Allah's Messenger (peace and blessings of Allah be upon him) said,

"You should seek refuge in Allah from falling into the hand of calamity and from the mockery of (triumphant) enemies and from the hardship of misery and from the evil of discharge (of a debt)."
(Reported by Muslim)

Mutraf said, "It is better for me to be healthy and grateful than to be afflicted and keep patience."

Which Has Priority: Patience or Gratitude

People have held different views as to which commands priority: patience or gratitude. In brief, both patience and gratitude command respective levels. The least level of patience is to give up complain, then comes pleasure, then comes gratitude.

On the other hand, gratitude has various levels. Man's prudence due to the Almighty's successive blesses on him is gratitude. Acknowledging that we undeservedly receive all graces from the Almighty signifies gratitude. The same applies to recognizing that thanking Allah for His blesses is also gratitude. This also applies to keeping modesty in prosperity and thanking people. The Prophet (peace and blessings of Allah be upon him) said,

> "*He who does not thank the people is ungrateful to Allah.*"
>
> (Reported by Abu Dawud)

Man's praise and good manners as to his benefactor is also gratitude. The same applies to receiving graces with pleasure. Patience and gratitude also cover a wide variety deeds and utterances according to numerous levels. Thus, how can commend any of them priority over the other? However, when gratitude is related to spending wealth in Allah's cause, it is given priority, since it also implies patience and covers man's pleasure with the Almighty's grace. It also denotes man's enduring giving it to the poor rather than enjoying it in permissible things.

However, if gratitude signifies man's reluctance to spend it illegally but rather to enjoy it lawfully, patience commands priority. The patient poor is better than the greed rich spending it in permissible things. The poor man has resisted himself and happily endured the affliction. This norm applies to all cases where patience is given priority over gratitude.

In that way, each of them has its status in certain cases. A patient poor person may be better than a grateful wealthy. On the other hand, a grateful wealthy may be better than a patient poor, depending on heir respective situations and attitudes.

III. Hope and Fear

Like wings, hope and fear support those drawn to commendable states with the Almighty. Like rides, they carry people along the way to the Hereafter. Therefore, their essence, virtue and tenets should be elaborated. We will consider them in two parts.

First: Hope

Hope is a state of seekers of divine bounty and nearness to the Almighty. The Arabic word "*Maqaam*" (state) is named as such so long as it is consistent. On the other hand, "*Haal*" (condition) it is a transient situation. For example, yellowness covers two aspects namely, stable yellowness such as that of gold, and uneven one such as that of shyness. Among these two comes a third group such as that of disease. The second status of one's heart is labeled unstable since it distracts the heart.

One should know whatever man undergoes, be it detestable or lovable is either at present or was in the past. As for the former, it signifies ecstasy, sensitivity and awareness; whereas the latter refers to memory. Considering something in the future, it is called anticipation. We expect something good; it is hope. If it is bad, it is fear.

In that way, we may define hope as man's delight prediction of a lovable thing. However, such a thing should have a certain cause. If it does not have at all, it becomes *Tamanny* (wishful thinking), since man's expectation is not justified. Hope and fear cover such matters as are not decisive. One does no say, I hope the sun will rise and I fear it may set. Both aspects are certain. One can rather hope that rain may fall and dread that it may not. Sensible people have recognized that this world is like a farm for the Hereafter. One's heart resembles its field where *Iman* is sown. One purges his field through his acts of obedience. An indulgent heart is like swamp where no seeds grow.

Then comes the Last Day where every one harvests his own field. In fact, *Iman* gives seeds to all fields. *Iman* is scarcely effective within a malicious heart and bad manners. Thus, one's hope for forgiveness should be compared to that of a farmer. Finding a good soil, sawing it with good seeds, nurturing it with water in due times and purging it from all impurities, then waiting for the Almighty's grace dispelling thunder and lightening away till the crop fulfills its term, all this is hope.

On the other hand, cultivating a swamp where no water arrives and neglecting it, then waiting for the harvest, this signifies foolishness and insolence rather than hope. Cultivating a good soil, where no water falls and waiting for rain, this is wishfulness. Thus, hope signifies waiting for a lovable thing whose means is available, and still remain those involuntary ones, which come under divine providence through obedience. Hence, sawing the seeds of *Iman*, nurturing it with obedience, purifying one's heart and seeking the Almighty's assistance for till death, all this stands for commendable hope instigating consistent obedience. Otherwise, it is sheer foolishness and self-conceit. Allah says in the Qur'an,

> ❨*After them succeeded an (evil) generation: they inherited the book, but they chose (for themselves) the vanities of this world, saying (for excuse): (everything) will be forgiven us. (even so), if similar vanities came their way, they would (again) seize them. Was not the Covenant of the book taken from them, that they would not ascribe to Allah anything but the truth? And they study what is in the book.*

But best for the righteous in the home in the Hereafter. Will you not understand?

(Al-A`raf: 169)

Allah has also condemned those saying,

Nor do I deem that the Hour (of Judgment) will (ever) come: even if I am brought back to my Lord, I shall surely find (there) something better in exchange

(Al-Kahf: 36)

In the same vein, Ma`ruf Al-Karkhi (may Allah be merciful to him) remarked, hoping for the mercy of the one whom you disobey signifies disappointment and foolishness. Therefore, the almighty says,

Those who believed and those who suffered exile and fought (and strove and struggled) in the path of Allah, they have the hope of the mercy of Allah: and Allah is Oft-Forgiving, Most Merciful.

(Al-Baqarah: 218)

This verse means, those who deserve to pin hopes. However, hope is not confined to them, since others may entertain hopes.

You should know that "hope" is praiseworthy, since it stimulates one to exert efforts. On other hand despair blameworthy, since it entails idleness. Hence, finding a field out to be a swamp, water to be far-fetched and seeds are decayed one should give tending it and spare all his efforts.

As for fear, it never contradicts hope; it rather enhances it. Hopes entail doing your utmost and constantly adhering to obedience. It results in one's delight with incessant nearness to the Almighty and gracefully supplicating him. Yearning for any worldly thing, one adopts the same with mortal kings and important dignitaries. Hence, they are even worthier to be observed with the Almighty? if not observed, one rightly becomes deprived of that state of hope. Unless you experience the above-mentioned criteria, you are deluded.

Virtue of Hope

Abu Hurayrah narrated that the Prophet (peace and blessings of Allah be upon him) said,

> *"Allah thus stated, I live in the thought of My servant as he thinks of Me and with him as he calls Me."*
>
> (Reported by Muslim)

In another *Hadith*, the Almighty states,

> *"So let him think of Me the way he likes."*
>
> (Reported by Ahmad)

Jabir Ibn 'Abdullah also reports that the Prophet (peace and blessings of Allah be upon him) said,

> *"None of you should court death but only hoping good from Allah."*
>
> (Reported by Muslim)

The Almighty inspired Dawud (peace and blessings of Allah be upon him) saying, you should love Me and those who love Me. You should make my servants love Me. Dawud wondered, Lord, how can I make them love You? He replied, remember Me in good terms and reiterate My favors and prodigies. Mujahid (may Allah be merciful to him) highlighted, "When a person is commanded to thrown in Hellfire on the Last Day, and he says, "Lord, I did not think as such of You." Then Allah asks him, "What did you think of Me?" "That You will forgive me." He says. Hence, Allah says, "Let him go to Paradise!"

Treatment of Hope and its Means

Tow kinds of people need the treatment of hope, namely, a desperate person who has given up worship and an extremely frightened man so much that he harms himself. As for the former, he should be treated with fear. Hope undermines him. Honey is curative to a person stricken with cold rather than heat. Therefore, admonishing people, one should do so kindly searching for their illnesses and treating them accordingly. In our modern age, means hope should not be applied to people, but rather fear and dread. However, the virtue of means leading to hope to reconcile people's hearts and treat the sick. *Imam* `Ali highlighted, "A scholar should not make people desperate from the Almighty's Mercy nor make them secure his wrath." Thus, means of range from admonition to reminder.

As for admonition, it stands for to considering the Almighty's various graces already dealt with. Recognizing Allah's blesses on people and His wisdom in human nature, one becomes assured that the Almighty never seeks to perish them? He is Merciful both in this world and the Hereafter.

As far as reminder is concerned, one should be mindful of Allah's words in the Qur'an such as,

{*Say, O my Servants who have transgressed against their souls. Despair not of the Mercy of Allah; for Allah forgives all sins: for He is Oft-Forgiving, Most Merciful.*}

(Az-Zumar: 53)

❴*The angels celebrate the Praises of their Lord, and pray for forgiveness for (all) beings on earth: behold! Verily Allah is He, the Oft-Forgiving, Most Merciful.*❵

(Ash-Shura: 4)

Highlighting that He has prepared Hellfire for disbelievers and frightens His friends thereby, the Almighty says,

❴*They shall have Layers of Fire above them, and Layers (of Fire) below them: with this does Allah warn off His Servants: O My Servants then fear you Me.*❵

(Az-Zumar: 16)

❴*Fear the fire, which is prepared for those who reject Faith.*❵

(Al `Imran: 131)

❴*Therefore do I warn you of a Fire blazing fiercely; None shall reach it but those most unfortunate ones; Who give the lie to Truth and turn their backs.*❵

(Al-Layl: 4-16)

❴*Verily thy Lord is full of forgiveness for mankind for their wrongdoing. And verily thy Lord is (also) strict in punishment.*❵

(Ar-Ra`d: 6)

On the other hand, Abu Sa`id Al-Khudri (may Allah be pleased with him) reports that he heard Allah's Messenger (peace and blessings of Allah be upon him) saying,

"*Satan told his Lord, by Your Magnificence and Sublimity I will incessantly mislead them so long as they are alive. Then, the Almighty said, by My*

Magnificence and Sublimity I will incessantly forgive them so long as they seek my Forgiveness."
(Reported by Ahmad)

Abu Hurayrah (may Allah be pleased with him) narrates that the Prophet (peace and blessings of Allah be upon him said,

"By Him in Whose Hand is my life, if you were not to commit sin, Allah would sweep you out of existence and He would replace (you by) those people who would commit sin and seek forgiveness from Allah, and He would have pardoned them."
(Reported by Muslim)

`A'ishah (may Allah be pleased with her) reports that the Prophet (peace and blessings of Allah be upon him said,

"The good deeds of any person will not make him enter Paradise." (i.e., None can enter Paradise through his good deeds.) They (the Prophet's companions) said, 'Not even you, O Allah's Apostle?' He said, "Not even myself, unless Allah bestows His favor and mercy on me." So be moderate in your religious deeds and do the deeds that are within your ability: and none of you should wish for death, for if he is a good doer, he may increase his good deeds, and if he is an evil doer, he may repent to Allah."
(Reported by Al-Bukhari)

Likewise, Abu Sa`id Al Khudri reports that the Prophet (peace and blessings of Allah be upon him said,

"Allah will say, 'O Adam!. Adam will reply, 'Labbaik and Sa`daik' (I respond to Your Calls, I

am obedient to Your orders), 'wal Khair fi Yadaik' (and all the good is in Your Hands)!' Then Allah will say (to Adam), Bring out the people of the Fire.' Adam will say, "What (how many) are the people of the Fire?" Allah will say, "Out of every thousand (take out) nine-hundred and ninety-nine (persons)." At that time children will become hoary-headed and every pregnant female will drop her load (have an abortion) and you will see the people as if they were drunk, yet not drunk; But Allah's punishment will be very severe."

That news distressed the companions of the Prophet too much, and they said, "O Allah's Apostle! Who amongst us will be that man (the lucky one out of one-thousand who will be saved from the Fire)?" He said, "Have the good news that one-thousand will be from Gog and Magog, and the one (to be saved will be) from you." The Prophet, (peace and blessings of Allah be upon him) added, "By Him in Whose Hand my soul is, I Hope that you (Muslims) will be one third of the people of Paradise." On that, we glorified and praised Allah and said, "Allahu Akbar." The Prophet (peace and blessings of Allah be upon him) then said, "By Him in Whose Hand my soul is, I hope that you will be one half of the people of Paradise, as your (Muslims) example in comparison to the other people (non-Muslims), is like that of a white hair on the skin of a black ox, or a round hairless spot on the foreleg of a donkey."

(Reported by Al-Bukhari)

Here, the Prophet (peace and blessings of Allah be upon him) started his admonition with threats then, when the

Companions got disturbed thereby, he assured them. Inclining to whims, hearts should be distressed. When overwhelmed with worry, they should be secured to maintain the balance. Ibn Mas`ud (may Allah be pleased with him) said, "The Almighty will forgive people on the Day of Judgement in a way unthinkable to all humans." Once a Magian asked for Abraham's hospitality (peace and blessings of Allah be upon him), but he declined provided that he should become a Muslim. Then the Almighty inspired him, "I sustain him for ninety years while he disbelieves in Me." Whereupon Abraham (peace and blessings of Allah be upon him) searched for the man and informed him. He wondered of the Divine Mercy and became a Muslim.

These are the means whereby the desperate and the intimidated are inspirited. On the other hand, both the fool and insolent should not be addressed likewise. They should rather be acquainted with fear and its means. Such a treatment is proven effective with most people, like a wild slave who is reformed by the stick.

Second: Fear and its Levels

Fear signifies one's inward anguish and anxiety due to an expected catastrophe. For example, doing something wrong to a creation king, falling in his hand, one fears from punishment, while forgiveness is plausible. His hidden distress depends on his knowledge of those means leading to his punishment, the status of his crime and its impact on the king himself. The level of one's fear is determined by its means. Fear may also be instigated by the status of its source, his sublimity and magnificence. We know that the Almighty may annihilate the whole universe. No one can ever prevent Him from doing so. This is clearly expressed by the Prophet (peace and blessings of Allah be upon him) saying,

> *"By Allah, I am the most conscious of Allah among you and I fear Him most among you."*
> (Reported by Al-Bukhari & Muslim)

The Almighty says in the Qur'an,

❴*Those truly fear Allah, among His Servants, who have knowledge: for Allah is Exalted in Might Oft-Forgiving.*❵

(Fatir: 28)

Perfect knowledge results in fear, which, in its turns, touches one's heart and becomes reflected on his physique through being faint and shedding tears. It may even bring one's life to an end. It may undermine one's mental faculty. As far as its effect on one's organs is concerned, they should give up sinning and stick to obedience redressing the past and getting equipped for the future. A wise man said, fear prompts endeavors. Another one said, fear does not mean shedding tears, it rather signifies giving up what one can do. Fear curbs one's lusts and desires and troubles delights; thus, like poisoned honey, enjoyable sins become detestable.

Therefore, fear melts lusts away, admonishes organs and crushes and subdues the heart. Furthermore, fear shatters pride and arrogance away. Accordingly one becomes overtaken with anxiety and worried about his end. He becomes overwhelmed with his own affairs, considering his deeds and reforming himself. He even considers his words, gazes, breaths and contemplations. He acts like a prey fallen at the hands of a wild lion. He does not know whether it will ignore him, thus he will escape, or it will attack him. He is solely preoccupied with his own situation.

Hence, the intensity of man's fear depends on his knowledge

of the Almighty's Sublimity and His Attributes. It also counts on his knowledge of his character, its defects and detriments. The least level of fear is depicted in man's deeds; shunning prohibitions. Avoiding dubious matters signifies piety.

Fear: the Almighty's Menace

You should know that "Fear" represents the Almighty's menace on earth whereby He drives people to seek knowledge and exert efforts so that they should be drawn near to Him. Fear has three aspects namely, moderate, extreme and deficient. The first is commendable. It resembles the stick to an animal. However, neither excessive hitting nor laxity is recommended, such as shedding tears on listening to the Qur'an, but returning to negligence on its absence. This form of fear is ineffective, like striking a gigantic animal with a very tiny stick. It is never hurts, nor is it driven to the desired end. This norm applies to the masses, except the knowledgeable people who are mindful of the Almighty and His prodigies. How scarce they are! In fact, those imposters are quiet far from fearing the Almighty.

As for extreme fear, it excels moderate limits and leads to despair. It is abominable, since it hinders practical progress and kills its victim. In fact, a praiseworthy aspect of each matter is that leading to its favored objective. Thus, every thing exceeding or rather failing to achieve it is blameworthy. Fear results in warning, piety, consideration, striving, remembering the Almighty and obeying Him along with all other means drawing man nearer to Him. It also necessitates enjoying good health and intellectual integrity. If it undermines any of these essentials, it is abominable. One may wonder, what about someone dying due to fear?

Actually, dying as such, he achieves a state untenable if he died naturally. However, living and being elevated to higher standards of knowledge would have been better for him. The best form of happiness is to have a long life filled with divine obedience. Thus, every thing undermining one's life, health and mind leads to utter loss and bereavement.

Kinds of Fear

Fear commands various states. Some fear from death before repenting. Others fear from being mislead by blesses. A third group fears from distraction or ending his life badly. The highest level is to consider this world fearfully, since it paves the way for the Hereafter. The Almighty elevates whomever He deems and degrades whomever He wants with out any means. In fact, He is not questioned for His Actions. He says,

> "It is all right with Me, those enter Paradise and those the Hellfire."
>
> (Reported by Ahmad)

Furthermore, some dread agonies of death, being questioned in their grave by *Munkar and Nakir*, being brought before the Almighty and being interrogated for his deeds, passing over the *Sirat*, being thrown in Hellfire, being deprived from Paradise or rather being prevented from beholding the Almighty. The last one commands the first priority, then comes the rest.

Virtue of Fear and Hope: Which is Superior?

The virtue of a certain thing is determined by its fulfillment of happiness; it is our return to the Almighty and enjoying nearness to Him. Thus, all means leading to this end commands a virtue. The Almighty says in the Qur'an,

> ⟨But for such as fear the time when they will stand before (the Judgment Seat of) their Lord, there will

be two Gardens.⟩

(Ar-Rahman: 46)

⟨*Their reward is with Allah: Gardens of Eternity, beneath which rivers flow; they will dwell therein forever; Allah well pleased with them, and they with Him: all this for such as fear their Lord and Cherisher.*⟩

(Al-Bayyinah: 8)

Likewise, the Prophet (peace and blessing of Allah be upon him) said,

"When one's skin trembles out of fear from the Almighty, his sins drops therefrom like dry leaves dropping from a tree."

(Reported by Al-Bayhaqi)

Also, the Prophet (peace and blessing of Allah be upon him) said,

"Almighty Allah says, "By My Magnificence and Sublimity, I will never bring two fears nor two safeties together for My servant. If he does not fear Me in this world, I will make him fear Me in the Hereafter, and the vice versa."

(Reported by Al-Bayhaqi)

Ibn `Abbas (may Allah be pleased with them both) also reported that Allah's Prophet ((peace and blessing of Allah be upon him) said,

"Two eyes will never be tortured with Fire; the first shed tears out of fearing the Almighty, and the second spent the night guarding in Allah's cause."

(Reported by At-Tirmidhi)

You should know that asking "which is the best, hope or fear?" is like asking, which is best, bread or water? In fact, bread is better for a hungry person, whereas water is better for a thirsty one. Both hope and fear are remedies whereby hearts are treated. Thus, their superiority depends on the illness itself. If the heart strongly secure the Almighty's schemes, fear commands privilege. Otherwise, if it overtaken with despair and disappointment, hope is the cure.

On the other hand, considering the instance of fear and hope, we conclude that hope is more meritorious, since it sought from the Almighty's Mercy and fear from His Wrath. For a righteous person, both fear and hope are equal.

Some early Muslim once said, "If all people are invited to enter Paradise but for a single man, I fear that I may be this man. On the other hand, if all people are driven into the Hellfire except a single man, I hope I am this man." A righteous believer should act likewise.

One may wonder: how can hope and fear be equal within the believer's heart, while his hope should be superior due to his piety? In fact, a believer is not sure that his deeds are accepted. He resembles a farmer sawing new seeds in a virgin field. The seeds are *Iman*. The heart is the field. It is not ascertained whether it is pure or malicious. Here storms and thunder stands for the agonies of death. `Umar Ibn Al-Khattab (may Allah be pleased with him) was asked by Hudhaifah (may Allah be pleased with him), "Am I a hypocrite?" He was afraid of confusion and delusion. In that way, commendable fear instigates exerting efforts and disturbs the heart away from this world.

On one's death, hope commands superiority, since fear leads to endeavors that are out of sight in this case. Hope here strengthens one's heart and fosters the Almighty's love within it. Each one should leave this world loving the Almighty, his return to Him and thinking well of Him. On his death, Sulayman At-Taymi highlighted, "Tell me the divine dispensations, so that I should return to the Almighty thinking well of Him."

The Treatment Leading to Fear

This is attained through two ways, one of which is superior to the other. For example, a boy sits in a house where a lion or a snake enters. He may not be afraid of them. He may even approach the snake to play with it. However, if his father happens to be with him and escapes for fear of them. The boy follows his father. His fear is not grounded, he only emulates his father who know why he escapes. Thus, fearing the Almighty has two states, namely,

1- Fearing His punishment. This state is entertained by all people, and is fulfilled by one's faith in Hellfire and Paradise as a chastisement or recompense respectively. This state is undermined by man's feeble faith and strong negligence. This latter is shattered by continuous remembrance and contemplation over being tortured in the Hereafter. It is further nurtured by considering those entertaining fear, listening to their tales and keeping their company.

2- Fearing the Almighty. This is the state of the knowledgeable. Allah says in the Qur'an,

> ❲But Allah caution you (to remember) Himself. And Allah is full of kindness to those that serve Him.❳
> (Al `Imran: 30)

The Almighty's Attributes entails glorifying and fearing Him. Dhun-Nun said, "One's fear from Fire one his death is only a drop in a vast ocean. All people share this fear, but through emulation; like a young boy dreading the snake following his father. This state of fear is vulnerable. This norm applies to all beliefs obtained through emulation, unless they are enhanced by considering their recurrent tenets and fulfilling their requirements of obedience and shunning disobedience. Being elevated to knowing the Almighty, one consequently fears Him. Thus, he needs no treatment to foster fear in his heart. Otherwise, one should treat himself through contemplating over the states and utterances of those fearing the Almighty. Nevertheless, he should not hesitate to follow their example, for they are either the Prophets (peace and blessings of Allah be upon them), knowledgeable scholars or friends of the Almighty.

In this respect, `A'ishah, the mother of the believers, (may Allah be pleased with her) narrated,

> *"The Prophet (peace and blessings of Allah be upon him) was called to lead the funeral prayer of a child of the Ansar. I said: Allah's Messenger, there is happiness for this child who is a bird from the birds of Paradise for it committed no sin nor has he reached the age when one can commit sin. He said: `A'ishah, per adventure, it may be otherwise, because Allah created for Paradise those who are fit for it while they were yet in their father's loins and created for Hell those who are to go to Hell. He created them for Hell while they were yet in their father's loins."*
>
> (Reported by Muslim)

We may also meditate over this verse which obviously deals

with hope, but indirectly imparts extreme fear; Allah says,

❨*But, without doubt, I forgive again and again, those who repent, believe, and do right; who, in fine, are ready to receive true guidance.*❩

(Taha: 82)

Here, forgiveness is based on four stipulations, which are quiet testing. Likewise, the Almighty highlights fear saying,

❨*By (the Token of) time (through the Ages), verily Man is in loss.*❩

(Al-`Asr: 1-2)

After these verses, the Almighty has enumerated four reasons whereby salvation from loss is secured, namely,

❨*Except such as have Faith, and do righteous deeds, and (join together) in the mutual teaching of Truth, and of Patience and Constancy.*❩

(Al-`Asr: 3)

The Almighty further says,

❨*If We had so willed we could certainly have brought every soul its true guidance: but the World from Me will come true, I will fill Hell with Jinns and men all together.*❩

(As-Sajdah: 13)

It is self-evident that if matters were to be resumed, people's ambitions and artifices would have been endless. Thus, the past cannot be changed, so we have to give in. but for the Almighty's Mercy on His servants filling their hearts with hope in Him alone, they would have been perished due to fear.

Abu Ad-Dardaa' (may Allah be pleased with him) said, "None becomes confident in his faith but he will be deprived therefrom." When Sufyan Ath-Thawri (may Allah be merciful to him) was on his death bed, he shed tears. Some one asked, "I think you have many sins, Abu `Abdullah." He toke some dust in his hand and said, "Verily, my sins are less worthy than this. But I fear being deprived from faith before I die." Sahl (may Allah be merciful to him) used to say, "An aspirant fears from disobedience, whereas a divine friend dreads disbelief." It is also reported that once a Prophet complained of having neither food nor clothes to the Almighty. Hence, the Almighty inspired him, "Are you not pleased with my saving your heart from disbelief so you ask for worldly gaieties?" Thence, he put dust on his head saying, "I am pleased. O Lord, protect me against disbelief."

Having a bad end in one's life has its own means such as peddling an innovation, hypocrisy, pride, etc. Therefore, all Early Muslims warded off hypocrisy. Some of them even said, "I do not know anything more delightful for me that being free from hypocrisy." However, they did not refer to unbelief, but rather dissemblance. This is clearly elaborated by the Prophet's (peace and blessings of Allah be upon him) saying,

> *"Three are the signs of a hypocrite: when he spoke he told a lie, when he made a promise he acted treacherously against it, when he was trusted he betrayed."*
>
> (Reported by Muslim)

This horrible end of one's life has two levels. The first of them is the most heinous, i.e. having one's heart overwhelmed with suspicion or denial of *Iman* on his death anguish; thus resulting in eternal chastisement. The second level is to be displeased with the Destiny, to inveigh against it, to distribute his property unjustly or die insisting on a certain sin. Satan is not more tempting to a human than on his death. The Prophet (peace and blessings of Allah be upon him) used to supplicate,

> "O Lord, I seek refuge in You from Satan's temptations on my death."
>
> (Reported by Abu Dawud)

Elaborating these words, Al-Khattabi views that they mean being possessed by devil then, thus misleading one and prevent one from repentance, reforming an offence or rather fill him with despair and make him hate death.

Practically speaking, those means leading to a bad end of life cannot be cited in detail. However, they can be dealt with in brief. As for dying in a state of denial and suspicion, it brought about by innovation, that is to say having an unbefitting belief in the Almighty, His Attributes and Actions due to sheer emulation or corrupt premises. Having recognized the truth on his death, his beliefs turn into falsehood. However, following the example of Early Muslims in this regard, even with no detailed consideration, one become secure from this lapse.

As for ending one's life badly due to disobedience, it comes through the weakness of one's *Iman* that results in indulgence. It in turn undermines *Iman*; thus weakening love for Allah. Suffering the agonies of death, his *Iman* further wanes due to his feeling of demise. Thus, feeling that the Almighty's love is more stronger that loving worldly comfort, one becomes saved. Dying while loving the Almighty, one returns to Him like an obedient slave to his mater. Accordingly, he is received properly and happily, not to mention generously.

When one dies displeased with Allah's Decrees or insisting in disobeying Him, he returns to Him like a wild slave who deserves punishment. Hence, yearning for salvation, one should give means of loss and ruin. Sahl Ibn Sa`d reports that the Prophet (peace and blessings of Allah be upon him) said,

> *"A person performs deeds like the deeds of the people of Paradise apparently before people and he would be amongst the dwellers of Hell and a person acts apparently like the people of Hell, but (in fact) he would be among the dwellers of Paradise."*
>
> (Reported by Muslim)

When one's spirit is raised to Heaves after his death, the angels wonder, "How has he managed to escape devilish temptations? This being the case, you should be mindful of those means leading thereto and ward off them. You should never postpone your repentance, since life is too short. In fact, a breath may be inhaled and exhaled with your spirit out. Your life determines the status of your death, and your death your resurrection.

Fear of the Angels (peace be upon them)

Dealing with this subject, the Almighty says,

❴*They all reverently fear their Lord, high above them, and they do all that they are commanded.*❵
(An-Nahl: 50)

The Prophet (peace and blessings of be upon him) also said,

> *" The Almighty has Angels who tremble due to His Fear."*
>
> (Reported by Al-Baihaki)

Yazid Al-Qurashi also highlights that the Almighty has angels stationed around the Throne. They tears are shed like rivers till the Last Day. They shake and shiver due to fearing the Almighty. Allah addresses them, "What for you are fearing while you are by Me?" They reply, "O Lord, if people of the earth had known of Your Magnificence and Sublimity what we know, they would have never relished food or drink, they would have never slept and they would have set out for deserts moaning like cows.

Muhammad Ibn Al-Munkider said, "When Hell was created, the Angels were strongly disturbed." It is also reported that when Satan committed his sin, both Gabriel and Michael wept. When questioned about their weeping by the Almighty, they said, "O Lord, we are not sure of Your schemes." Allah remarked, "Stick to this state."

Fear of the Prophets (peace and blessings of Allah be upon them)

Wahb said that Adam (peace and blessings of Allah be upon him) wept for being ousted from Paradise for three hundred years. Wahib Ibn Al-Ward said, "When the Almighty reproached Noah (peace and blessings of Allah be upon him) saying,

> {So ask not of me that of which you has no knowledge I give thee counsel, lest you act like the ignorant.}

(Hud: 46)

He also wept for about three hundred years. Abu Ad-Darda' (may Allah be pleased with him) said, "When Abraham performed Prayers, his chest produced groaned for fear of the Almighty."

Fear of Prophet Muhammad (peace and blessings of Allah be upon him)

`A'ishah (may Allah be pleased with her) narrated,

> *"I never saw Allah's Messenger laughing loudly enough to enable me to see his uvula, but he used to smile only. And whenever he saw clouds or winds, signs of deep concern would appear on his face. I said, "O Allah's Apostle! When people see clouds they usually feel happy, hoping that it would rain, while I see that when you see clouds, one could notice signs of dissatisfaction on your face." He said, "O `A'ishah! What is the guarantee for me that there will be no punishment in it, since some people were punished with a wind? Verily, some people saw (received) the punishment, but (while seeing the cloud) they said, 'This cloud will give us rain.'"*

(Reported by Al-Bukhari)

`Abdullah Ibn Ash-Shakhir reported that,

> *"Whenever the Prophet (peace and blessings of Allah be upon him) performed the Prayers, he growled like a boiler."*

(Reported by At-Tirmidhi)

Fear of the Prophet's Companions (may Allah be pleased with them)

We have already stated that Abu Bakr used to hold his tongue and say, "This has thrown me into all evils." He also said, "I wish I were a tree to be cut and devoured." The same words have been also reported from Talhah, Abud-Dardaa', and

Abu Dharr (may Allah be pleased with them). Listening to the Qur'an, `Umar (may Allah be pleased with him) would become ill for long days and the Companions (may Allah be pleased with them) would visit him. He once took a particle of dust and remarked, "I wish I were this particle. I wish I were nothing. I wish I were not born." `Uthman (may Allah be pleased with him) said, "I wish I would not be resurrected after I die." Abu `Ubaidah (may Allah be pleased with him) said, "I wish I were a ram and sacrificed by my family." `Umran Ibn Hasin (may Allah be pleased with him) remarked, I wish I were ashes stormed by wind."

Furthermore, Hudhayfah (may Allah be pleased with him) said, "I wish I had someone undertaking my financial affairs, then I would be confined within my home." Tears dug their way on Ibn `Abbas' checks. `A'ishah (may Allah be pleased with her) said, "I wish I had been a thing forgotten and out of sight." `Ali (may Allah be pleased with him) said, "Looking at the Prophet's Companions, I see them peerless. They are disheveled. Sorrow overtakes their eyes. They spend the night worshipping the Almighty, reciting the Qur'an. In the morning, they remember Allah like trees shaken by the wind. Their clothes became wet by their tears.

Fear of the Successors

Hirim Ibn Hayyan said, I wish I were a tree eaten by a camel then excreted rather than being held for accountability on the Last Day." `Ali Ibn Al-Husain (may Allah be pleased with them) became pale whenever he performed ablution. When asked, what is the matter? He replied, "Do you before Whom [Allah] I am going to stand! Muhammad Ibn Wasi` used to spend the whole night shedding tears. When `Umar Ibn `Abd Al-`Aziz (may Allah be pleased with him) remembered death, he would be alarmed like birds. His tears would fall on his beard; causing his household to weep. His daughter Fatimah told him, "Why did you weep?" He said, "I remembered the people's departure after their accountability before their Lord, either to Paradise or to the Hellfire. Then he cried and lost his consciousness.

When Al-Mansur visited Jerusalem, he called on a monk by whom `Umar Ibn `Abd Al-`Aziz (may Allah be pleased with him) used to stay. He asked him about the most remarkable thing he found in `Umar. The monk said that `Umar visited him once and decide to sleep on the roof of his house. It was tiled with marble. I noticed some drops of water falling form the gutter. I went upstairs to find out what happened. I found `Umar prostrating and his tears run through the gutter. `Isa Al-Yashkari narrates that he visited a man from Al-Bahrein in his solitude. Remembering the Hereafter and death, that man sighed till he gave up his ghost. Masma` reported that he attended a circle for `Abd Al-Wahid Ibn Zaid where four persons among the attendants died due to his admonition. Yazid Ibn Murshid used to cry saying, "By Allah, if my Lord had threatened to confine me in the bath, I should have never stopped weeping. Then, how about His threat to confine me in Hellfire if I disobey Him?" As-Sirri remarked that he daily looked at his nose for fear of his face becoming black.

This being the case of the Angels, Prophets, scholars and divine friends, what about ours. We even deserve to entertain fear more than them. Fear is not reflected in sins. It is rather depicted by inward purity and perfect knowledge. We feel safe due to our sheer ignorance. A pure heart is moved by a slight threat. Whereas the hard one is not affected by voluminous admonitions. An Early Muslim said that he asked a monk to advise him. He replied, "If you can act like a man overtaken by wild animals, thus he fears if he dwindles, they will devour him. Therefore, he is frightened. If you can do so, you should do. Then he asked him for more advice. He said, "Little water is sufficient for a thirsty person." This is in fact a word in season, since man is overtaken by a variety of wild feelings such as envy, anger, hatred, dissemblance, pride, etc. They all wear him out if he ignores them. However, they are veiled in this world. Being disclosed in his grave, they become snakes and scorpions stinging him. Thus, it is better for you to overcome them in your life.

IV. Asceticism and Poverty

One should know that love for worldly comfort is the source of all sins, while detesting them leads to obedience. We will deal here with detesting this world and renouncing it, since this attitude is the origin of salvation. Fors aking it may be due to poverty or asceticism. Each one commands a certain degree of happiness and assistance for obtaining salvation. We will deal with both of them, their levels and categories in the following lines.

First: Poverty

Poverty signifies being in need for a certain thing. Thus, all creatures are poor since they all require enhanced existence. This is achieved by the Almighty's grace. In fact, aspects of man's poverty are boundless. Only to give an example, we mention wealth. This aspect command s five instances, namely,

1- Though man is a poor, he will fearfully turn away from wealth detesting it, since it may harm him. This is asceticism.

2- He may neither be displeased nor delighted with wealth. Thus, this is satisfaction.

3- He may love wealth rather t han being poor, but he does not exert efforts to earn it. If it reaches him pre chance, he delightfully takes it. Otherwise, he is not preoccupied with gaining it. This is called contentment.

4- He may not endeavor to obtain it due to his inability, while he aspires for it. Finding some means to secure it, he will adopt it at once. This is greed covetousness.

5- He may be forced to earn it due to hunger and so on and so forth. This is necessity.

This first instance, i.e. asceticism, commands superiority over the rest. However, there is even a more superior state than asceticism. It is to have the same attitude in case of poverty and rich; i.e. when given wealth, one is not delighted therewith and is not distressed if no gifted it. `A'ishah (may Allah be pleased with her) was once given two purses of money. She distributed all it among the poor. Then, her slave girl told her, "Should you not have spared a *dirham* to buy breakfast?" She replied, "I should have done if you had reminded me."

In that way, such a person will never be distracted even if he possesses the whole universe, since for him wealth is saved in the Almighty's stores. This is sufficiency. Ahmad Ibn Al-Hawari said to Abi Sulayman Ad-Darani, " Malik Ibn Dinar told Al-Mughirah, 'Go to my house and resto re your charity, for Satan tempts me that a thief has stolen it.'" Abu Sulayman remarked, "This is an inferior form of asceticism, since he should not have taken it." Renouncing worldly pleasure by the weak is a sign of perfection. As for Prophets (peace a nd blessings of Allah be upon them) both poverty and richness are particularly equal.

Merits of Poverty and the Poor

The Qur'an contains countless verses dealing with this subject. For example, the Almighty praises the poor saying,

> ❴*(Charity is) for those in need who, in Allah's cause are restricted (from travel), and cannot move about in the land, seeking (for trade or work).*❵
> (Al-Baqarah:173)

((Some part is due) to the indigent Muhajirs, those who were expelled from their homes and their property, while seeking Grace from Allah and (His) Good Pleasure, and aiding Allah and His Messenger: such are indeed the sincere ones)

(Al-Hashr: 8)

On the other hand, the Prophet (peace and blessings of Allah be upon him) said,

"I stood at the door of Paradise and I found that the overwhelming majority of those who entered therein was that of poor persons and the wealthy persons were detained to get into that. The denizens of Hell were commanded to get into Hell, and I stood upon the door of Fire and the majority amongst them who entered there was that of women."

(Reported by Al-Bukhari)

Abu Hurayrah (may Allah be pleased with him) reported Allah's Messenger (peace and blessing of Allah be upon him) as saying,

"O Allah, make for the family of Muhammad the provision which is a bare subsistence."

(Reported by Muslim)

`A'ishah (may Allah be pleased with her) reported,

"Never had the family of Muhammad (peace and blessings of Allah be upon him) eaten to the fill since their, arrival in Medina with the bread of wheat for three successive nights until his (Holy Prophet's) death."

(Reported by Muslim)

`Umar Ibn Al-Khattab (may Allah be pleased with him) further narrated,

> *"I saw that your Prophet (peace and blessings of Allah be upon him) (at times) could not find even an inferior quality of the dates with which he could fill his belly."*
>
> (Reported by Muslim)

Abu Hurayrah also reports that the Prophet (peace and blessing of Allah be upon him) said,

> *"The poor believers will be admitted into Paradise five hundred years before the rich ones."*
>
> (Reported by At-Tirmidhi)

Prophet Musa (peace and blessing of Allah be upon him) was once addressed, "When you see poverty coming, you should say, 'Welcome to the symbol of the righteous.' But when you behold richness, you should say, 'You are a pu nishable sin.'" Abu Ad-Drada' (may Allah be pleased with him) remarked that a person having two Dirhams will spend a longer time in accountability than him who has one *dirham*. Sufiyan Ath-Thawri used to seat the poor nearer to him." Ibrahim Ibn Adham was once given then thousand *dirhams*, but he declined taking them saying, "Do you want to erase my name from the list of the poor? Nay, I will not." The Prophet (peace and blessings of Allah be upon him) is also reported to have said,

> *"He is successful who has accepted Islam, who has been provided with sufficient for his want and been made contented by Allah with what He has given him."*
>
> (Reported by Muslim)

As far as superiority of poverty and wealth is concerned, *Shr`i* texts obviously indicate the poverty is su perior. However, we should deal with this issue in more details. Superiority is sought in case of a contented patient poor compared to a grateful rich who spends in charitable actions. The contented poor is superior to the greed rich one. On the other hand , the rich who gives charity is better that the greed poor. If he spends his wealth on permissible things, then the poor is superior to him. The determining factor in this regard is the end itself. This world is not condemned in its own right, but rather b ecause it hinders becoming nearer to the Almighty. Likewise, poverty is not sought for it own sake, but because it frees man from this hindrance. Countless wealth men have not been prevented by their property from rendering the Almighty's due, such as the Prophet Solomon (peace and blessings of Allah be upon him), `Utman Ibn `Affan and `Abdur-Rahman Ibn `Awf (may Allah be pleased with both of them).

On the other hand, innumerable poor men have been hindered from the main objective, i.e., worshipping the Almighty due to their being preoccupied with this world. Love for this world never coexists with love for the Almighty. A lover is constantly mindful of his beloved, both in separation and communion; though the latter is more effective. This world is the beloved of the negligent. It is sought by the deprived, and enslaves those possessing it.

Thus, the poor is aloof from this peril, since few are those who maintain righteousness in prosperity. You should also partition between lovers is quite severe. Hence, lo ving this world, one detests returning to the Almighty. Therefore, you should the everlasting friend, the Almighty Alone.

Manners of the Poor

A poor person should be contented with his state. He should rather be pleased and delighted therewith. He should r ely on the Almighty. Otherwise, if he complains of his poverty to humans rather than the Almighty, his poverty will be a sort of punishment. He should rather maintain continence and modesty. The Almighty says in the Qur'an,

{*The ignorant man thinks, because of their modesty, that they are free from want.*}

(Al-Baqarah: 273)

A poor person should not treat the wealthy humbly due to his richness. He should never seek to keep his company. He should not slacken in his worship. He should spend his surplus as a charity. The Prophet (peace and blessings of Allah be upon him) was once asked about the best charity, he said,

"*It is that is given by the poor.*"

(Reported by Ahmad)

Manners of Accepting a Gift

When given something without asking, a poor person should consider three things, namely, the property given, the giver's purpose and his own purpose behind taking it.

1- The property given should be evidently lawful. If it is doubted, he should not take it. We have elaborated this issue under (The Lawful and the Prohibite d) the giver may seek by his gift to foster affiliation and friendship. This is a gift that can be accepted.

2- If the giver yearns for reward by his gift, i.e. giving it as *Zakah* or charity, the recipient should consider himself, whether he is entitled to take it or not. If unable to determine, he should decline taking it due to suspicion. If it is a charity given to him due to his piety, he should think about his hidden affairs. Finding out that he commits a sin which prevents the giver from giving him if he knows, he should not also take it.

3- The giver may seek by his gift ostentation, pride and dissemblance, hence; the recipient should decline it due to the corrupt purpose of its giver. If otherwise he accepts it, he will be enhancing his mischief. The recipient should also consider his purpose in taking it, whether he need it or not. If not, he should not take it. If he needs it, and it is free from suspicion, he should take it. `Umar ibn Al-Khattab (may Allah be pleased with him) narrates that the Prophet (peace and blessing of Allah be upon him) said,

> *"Take it. If you are given something from this property, without asking for it or having greed for it take it; and if not given, do not run for it."*
> (Reported by Al-Bukhari)

Khalid Ibn `Adi Al-Juhani (may Allah be pleased with him) reports that the Prophet (peace and blessings of Allah be upon him) said,

> *"If any one of you is given something by his brother without asking or coveting for it, he should take it; since it is subsistence sent to him by Allah."*
> (Reported by Ahmad)

Prohibition of Begging and Manners of Asking

You should know that there are many *Hadiths* condemning asking the people and other one permitting it. As for the latter, the Prophet is reported to have said,

> *"A beggar should be given anything even if it be a burnt hoof."*
>
> (Reported by At-Tirmidhi)

As far as condemnation is concerned, Abdullah Ibn Umar (may Allah be pleased with him) narrates that the Prophet (peace and blessings of Allah be upon him) said,

> *"A man keeps on asking others for something till he comes on the Day of Resurrection without any piece of flesh on his face."*
>
> (Reported by Al-Bukhari)

Hakim Ibn Hizam (may Allah be pleased with him) narrated the Prophet (peace and blessings of Allah be upon him) said,

> *"The upper hand is better than the lower hand (i.e., he who gives in charity is better than him who takes it). One should start giving first to his dependents."*
>
> (Reported by Al-Bukhari)

Ibn Mas'ud (may Allah be pleased with him) also reported that the Prophet (peace and blessings of Allah be upon him) said,

> *"He who asks people while he has sufficient means will come on the Day of Judgment having his asking like scars on his face."*
>
> (Reported by Ibn Majah)

Against this background, we conclude that begging is originally forbidden, since it has three aspects, i.e. complain, humility which is unfitting for a believer and hurting the one asked. However, it can be provisionally permitted under necessity alone, such asking for food due to extreme hunger that is likely to kill him.

Regarding the one in need for an important thing, such as wearing only one rope in winter; so he suffers cold, but to an extent lesser than necessity, he may ask for another rope though it is preferred that he should not. The same applies to a traveler who is hardly able to walk. He can ask for the fare, although he should walk. Likewise, having bread but nothing to eat with, he may ask for it. A man asking should express his gratitude to the Almighty overtly. He should first ask his parents, brothers, relatives and those who will not despise him. He may also ask a generous person who spends his wealth in charity. If he knows that someone gives him out of modesty, he should not take; but he should rather return what he took.

A poor person should ask only for what s atisfies his need. If he finds some one whom he can ask every day, he should be satisfied with his daily food. If he fears that he may not find any one giving him, he may ask more than this. In general, he is not permitted to ask for more than what satisfi es him for a whole year. This is clearly expressed by the Prophet (peace and blessing of Allah be upon him) in a *Hadith* where he estimated richness as having fifty *dirhams*. It suffices a moderate person for a whole year.

States of Those Who Ask

Bishr Al-Hafi (may Allah be merciful to him) classified the poor into three categories, namely, a poor person who does not ask the people. Even if he is given something, he never takes it. This is a spiritual being. A poor person who does not ask but takes when given a thing. And a poor person who asks. His truthfulness mitigates his asking.

Sheikh Jamalud-Deen (may Allah be merciful to him) said, "the sound view is that if the poor can manage his affairs without asking, he is not permitted to ask. But if he can hardl y handle them, it needs some consideration. If his state is unbearable, he can ask though giving it up is meritorious." Sufiyan Ath-Thawri (may Allah have mercy on him) said, "Who suffers hunger and declines asking for food until he dies will enter the Hell."

Second: Asceticism, its Virtue and States

You should know that asceticism is an honorable state adopted by travelers along the divine path. It signifies renouncing something for another better one. The forsaken object should possess some aspects of att raction; otherwise, it cannot be called asceticism. A perfect ascetic is he who renounces all worldly pleasures and love the Almighty Alone. Forsaking this world while yearning for Paradise, one is called an ascetic, but of inferior state to the former.

Asceticism does not mean abandoning wealth, spending it generously and reconciling hearts. It rather stands for turning away from this world due to one's knowledge of its inferiority to the Hereafter.

Recognizing that this world is like ice, and the Hereafte r like pearl, one becomes strongly ready to substitute the former for the latter. In this context, Allah says,

> ⦃*Say, short is the enjoyment of this world; the Hereafter is the best for those who do right: never will you be dealt with unjustly in the very least.*⦄
> (An-Nisa': 77)

He, Most High, also says,

❨*What is with you must vanish: what is with Allah will endure. And we will certainly bestow, on those who patiently persevere, their reward according to the best of their actions.*❩

(An-Nahl: 96)

The Almighty lays out the virtue of asceticism saying,

❨*Nor strain your eyes in longing for the things we have given for enjoyment to parties Of them, the splendor Of the life of this world, through which we test them: But the provision of the Lord is better and more enduring.*❩

(Taha:131)

The Prophet (peace and blessings of Allah be upon him) said,

"He who becomes fully preoccupied with this world, his unity will be dissolved, he will be doomed to poverty and he will not achieve of it except what Allah has designed for him. He who is completely interested in the Hereafter, his distress will be shattered, his unity will be enhanced, his heart will be filled with content and this world be driven to him."

(Reported by Ibn Majah)

Al-Hasan said, "All humans will be resurrected naked except the ascetics. Some people have honored this world, so it enslaved them. Thus, you should disdain it where it becomes amiable." Al-Fudayl likened mischief to a house whose key is love for this world. On the other hand, he equated goodness to a house whose key is asceticism. Some Early Muslims said, renouncing this world relieves one's heart and body. But longing for it duplicates worry and anxiety.

States of Asceticism

Some turn away from this world while they desire it. They do their utmost to do so. These are seekers of asceticism.

The second state refers to renouncing it willingly and easily. However, considering his asceticism, he may be pleased therewith thinking that he has abandoned a noble thing for a greater one. This state is also deficient.

The third and foremost state is agreeable asceticism. It covers even one's state itself; seeing that he has not renounced anything. For him, this world stands for nothing. Thus, he forsakes a filth rag for a pearl. The former is this world whereas the latter is the Hereafter.

You should know that turning away from this world resembles being prevented from reaching a king because of dog standing on his door. The he distracts it by a piece of bread and advances along. Then he is drawn near to the kin g. Do you think that he has done a favor to the king by casting that piece of bread to the dog? This dog is Satan stationed on the way of becoming near to the Almighty. Satan prevents people from advancing along this path though its gate is open. It has no chamberlain. The world is that piece of bread. One throws it to the dog to secure nearness to the King. Even if one lives for thousand years, whatever he achieves in this world is naught compared to the Hereafter. Mortality is of no value before immortality. Pleasures of this world are quite distressing.

As far as the end of asceticism is concerned, it has three categories, namely,

1- To be saved from torture, accountability and anxieties of the Hereafter. This asceticism is entertained by those fearing the Almighty.

2- To receive rewards and enter Paradise. This is practiced by those who renounce this world longing for the life to come.

3- To set oneself free from ails and worries, and to enjoy nearness to the Almighty Alone. This is observed by the righteous friends of Allah. Being near to the Almighty compared to entering Paradise is similar to swaying the whole universe compared to jesting with a tiny bird.

Virtue of Asceticism as to Essentials of Life

Worldly life has seven essentials, namely; food, clothing, accommodation, its furniture, marriage, water and influence.

As for food, the ascetic seeks therefrom to drive hunger away according to his physical needs rather than enjoying eating. The Prophet (peace and blessings of Allah be upon him) is reported to have said,

> *"The Almighty has servant who does not lead a life of ease."*
>
> (Reported by Ahmad)

`Urwa (may Allah be pleased with him) narrated,

> *"`A'ishah (may Allah be pleased with her) said to me, "O my nephew! We used to see the crescent, and then the crescent and then the crescent in this way we saw three crescents in two months and no fire (for cooking) used to be made in the houses of Allah's Prophet (peace and blessings of Allah be upon him). I said, "O my aunt! Then what use to*

> *sustain you?"* `A'ishah (may Allah be pleased with her) said, "The two black things: dates and water."*
> (Reported by Al-Bukhari)

Most ascetics detested eating, even some of them abhorred it. However, Sufiyan Ath-Thawri used to take roasted meat on his journeys. In brief, an ascetic is satisfied with the food necessary for his health. He does not seek enjoyment thereby. However, human bodies are not the same. Some bodies fail to endure harsh life, thus; some people my have some lawful food whereby they sustain their physiques. This by no means annuls their asceticism. As-Sabti used to work every Saturday and maintain himself therefrom. Dawud At-Ta'i inherited twenty *dirhams* which he spent in twenty years.

Coming to clothing, an ascetic is satisfied with such attire as protect him from heat and cold. He can also be dressed well to avoid being famous for asceticism. Early Muslims used to wear coarse clothes, therefore; ascetics have become known for it. Abu Burdah (may Allah be pleased with him) narrated,

> *"`A'ishah (may Allah be pleased with her) brought out to us a Kisa (a square black piece of woolen cloth.) and an Izar (a sheet cloth garment covering the lower half of the body), and said, "The Prophet (peace and blessing of Allah be upon him) died while wearing these two."*
> (Reported by Al-Bukhari)

Al-Hasan highlighted that `Umar Ibn Al-Khattab (may Allah be pleased with him) delivered the Friday sermon while his rope had twelve patches.

We now deal with accommodation. An ascetic has three levels in this regard. The foremost one is to be cont ented with corners in mosques. Second, he may have a private place such as a shanty. The least one is to have a room built for him. Raising its ceiling and yearning for more, he has renounced asceticism itself. The Prophet's rooms (may Allah be pleased with him) were never built till his demise. Al-Hasan remarked that he would reach the ceiling of the Prophet's room (peace and blessings of Allah be upon him) with his hand. The Prophet (peace and blessings of Allah be upon him) said,

> *"A Muslim is rewarded (in the Hereafter) for whatever he spends except for something that he spends on building."*
>
> (Reported by Al-Bukhari)

Ibrahim An-Nakh`i said, "Having a modest building incurs neither rewards nor punishment."

The fourth essential of life is furniture of one's home. An ascetic should employ house gadgets in all their possible usages. Having redundant gadgets precludes asceticism. He should be fully aware of the Prophet's life (peace and blessings of Allah be upon him). `Umar Ibn Al-Khattab (may Allah be pleased with him) narrated,

> *"I visited Allah's Messenger (peace and blessings of Allah be upon him), and he was lying on a mat. I sat down and he drew up his lower garment over him and he had nothing (else) over him, and that the mat had left its marks on his sides. I looked with my eyes in the storeroom of Allah's Messenger (peace and blessings of Allah be upon him). I found only a handful of barley equal to one Sa` and an equal quantity of the leaves of Mimosa Flava placed in the nook of the cell, and a semi-tanned leather bag*

hanging (in one side), and I was moved to tears."
(Reported by Muslim)

`Umar (may Allah be pleased with him) added,

"On seeing the marks of the mat imprinted on his side, I wept. He said.' 'Why are you weeping?' I replied, "O Allah's Apostle! Caesar and Khosrau are leading the life (i.e., Luxurious life) while you, Allah's Messenger though you are, is living in destitute". The Prophet then replied. 'Won't you be satisfied that they enjoy this world and we the Hereafter?'"
(Reported by Al-Bukhari)

`Ali Ibn Abu Talib (may Allah be pleased with him) says, "I married Fatimah (may Allah be pleased with her) while I was having a hide to lie on at night and provide fodder on it for our camel on the day. She alone served me. Some one once visited Abu Dharr (may Allah be pleased with him). Roaming the house with his eyes, he said, "O Abu Dharr, I see your house empty of furniture." Abu Dharr replied, "We have another house where we store the best furniture (i.e. the Hereafter). The man said, "But you need some gadgets so long as you are alive." Abu Dharr remarked, "But the Owner of that house will expel us soon (i.e. we will die and leave everything behind)."

The fifth essential is marriage. In fact, asceticism has nothing to do with marriage altogether. They Almighty has endeared marriage to the Prophet (peace and blessings of Allah be upon him) though `Ali (may Allah be pleased with him) was the most ascetic among the Companions (may Allah be pleased with them), he had four wives. Abu Sulayman Ad-Darani highlighted, "Whatever distracts you from the Almighty's Remembrance, be it a family, wealth or children, is condemned."

Practically speaking, if one fears sinning due to his lust, he should marry. However, scholars have held different views as to the one who does not fear sinning. On the other hand, people get married for a variety of purposes. Some long for offspring, while they can maintain a family. Getting married, they will not be distracted thereby, nor will their religion be undermined; they will rather be enhanced. In that case, marriage is strongly recommended. Thus, those who claim asceticism by renouncing marriage are mere pretenders. Early Muslims sought for the religious woman rather than the beautiful one. The latter trouble one's heart and commands more expenditure.

The sixth essential is wealth. An ascetic is satisfied with what fulfills the purpose. Some righteous persons were traders for the sake of content. Hammad Ibn Salamah used to leave his shop after earning two *dirhams*. Sa`id Ibn Al-Musayyib sold oil and left four hundred *dirhams* for his family. When asked about it, he said, "I preserve thereby my honor and religion."

The seventh essential is influence. Every one should enjoy some sort of influence even as to his servant. Being devoted to asceticism, influence finds its way into the ascetic's heart. Thus, he should ward of its evil.

Generally, those essentials do not come under worldly gaieties. Many Early Muslims were given lawful properties, but they declined them lest their religion should be undermined.

Milestones of Asceticism

Renouncing wealth, you may take some one after an ascetic. In fact, it is quite easy for any one loving to be labeled as such to turn away from wealth. Many monks have confined themselves in monasteries subsisting on trivial food. Only their yearning for being praised enhanced them. Asceticism should cover wealth and fame in order to be perfect. Ibn Al-Mubarak remarked, "Asceticism means concealing being an ascetic." This depends on three factors, namely,

1- One should be delighted with gains nor distressed with losses. Highlighting the sign abandoning wealth, the Almighty says,

> ﴿*In order that you may not despair over matters that pass you by, nor exult over favors bestowed upon you. For Allah loves, not any vainglorious boaster.*﴾
> (Al-Hadid: 23)

2- Both praise of him and criticizing should be of equal value to him.

3- He should only be heedful of the Almighty and taste the sweetness of obedience within his heart.

Love of this world and love of the Almighty are like water and air in a certain pot. They never coexist. An ascetic was once asked, "Whereto has asceticism lead you?" "To the friendship of the Almighty," he replied. Yahiya Ibn Mu`adh remarked, "This world is a bride. Its suitor becomes its maid. But asceticism blackens its face, cuts its hair and tears its dress. An ascetic is preoccupied with Divine Remembrance.

We have elaborated the essence of asceticism and its related rules. Since it is not fulfilled properly unless it is supported with reliance on the Almighty, we will consider it in the following lines if Allah so wills.

V. Oneness of Allah and Trust in Him

Virtue of Putting One's Trust in the Almighty

The Almighty says in the Qur'an,

❨*In Allah should the faithful (ever) put their trust.*❩
(Al `Imran: 122)

He also says,

❨*If any one puts his trust in Allah, sufficient is (Allah) for him.*❩
(At-Talaq: 3)

Ibn `Abbas (may Allah be pleased with them both) narrated that the Prophet (peace and blessings of Allah be upon him) said,

> *"Seventy thousand people of my Ummah would be admitted into Paradise without rendering any account. They (the companions) said: Who would be of those (fortunate persons)? He (the Prophet) said, 'They are those persons who neither practice charm, nor ask others to practice it, nor do they take omens, and repose their trust in their Lord."*
> (Reported by Muslim)

`Umar Ibn Al-Khattab (may Allah be pleased with him) also reports that he heard the Prophet (peace and blessings of Allah be upon him) as saying,

> *"If you put your trust in Allah properly, He will provide for you like birds; going with empty bellies in*

the morning and returning satiated in the evening."
(Reported by At-Tirmidhi)

Trust in the Almighty is based on His Oneness, which in turn commands three states,

A- To believe in one's heart, in addition to declaring with his tongue, that there is no God but Allah and that He has no partner. He is the King of the world. All Praise is due to Him. He is the Omnipotent. Holding this belief without a proof is the state of the common people.

B- To consider various creations; seeing them made by the One and Only. This state is entertained by those drawn near to the Almighty.

C- To see the Almighty as the Sole Active Agent in the whole universe. Thus, one fears none but Him Alone. He trusts none but Him Alone. The whole world runs after His Command. Thus, one will not depend on worldly means, but rather on the Source of these means. For example, being on board, he does not consider the wind for driving the ship forward. He is rather aware of Allah Who sends such a wind. Thinking of the wind deems like thinking of the ink and the paper whereby an amnesty decree is signed by a graceful king. Thus, such a person would ignorantly thank the pen and the paper for his salvation rather than the king himself.

States of Trust in Allah, its Criteria and Deeds

The Arabic word '*Tawakkul*' signifies entrusting some one with something and relying on him in this regard. Thus, '*Tawakkul*' stands for an inward dependence on the trustee. You should never trust in any one unless h e fulfills three factors, namely, kindness, strength and guidance. This being the case, you should think of trusting the Almighty. Knowing that He is the Omnipotent, the All Merciful, the All Knowing, then trust Him Alone with your heart. You should disregard all other than Him. Failing to ascertain this within your soul, there are two reasons for it. Your faith in any of these Attributes may be wavering.

On the other hand, your heart may be undermined by cowardice and overwhelming propensities. One's heart can be deluded by whims and keep adherence to them. These can also affect it without undermining his faith.

If a sensible person were asked to stay with a dead one in one grave or even one bed, he would naturally detest this very idea. However, the same person spends most of his life with inanimate things, but he does not abhor them. This is due to cowardice of one's heart. Scarce are those who do not suffer this deficiency. In fact, this feeling may become a chronic illness, so much that one would fear sleeping alone. Thus, trust is only tenable with strength of one's heart and faith. Ascertaining the essence of trust in the Almighty, you should know that this state has three states as follows,

A- Trusting the Almighty with His full Sovereignty over the universe, as already elaborated.

B- This state is even stronger than the former. With the Almighty, one acts like a child with his mother. He knows none other than her. She is the sole refuge before him. He depends solely on her. When overtaken by anything, she is the first of whom he thinks and the first name he utters. Being constantly aware of the Almighty, trusting Him Alone, one will love Him like the child to his mother.

C- The third state is even the strongest. He gives in to the Almighty like a dead person at the hand of the undertaker. The sole difference is that he is alive. These three states are ascertained amongst people, though they are scarcely incessant.

Actions of those Putting Their Trust in Allah

Some may wrongfully think that trusting Allah means gi ving up working and managing one's life. This is legally forbidden. The *Shari`ah* has commended those trusting the Almighty. Such a trust is clearly reflected in man's endeavors to achieve his objectives. These endeavors my seek to secure an absent benefit such as earning subsistence, or rather enhancing an existent one such as saving. They may also seek to defend an expected harm, such as repelling an enemy, or to remove a present one such as treating an illness. All man's actions fall within these four categories.

A- Securing benefits. There are three levels for the means leading thereto, namely,

   i) Definite means, such as those means divinely ordained to result constantly in certain ends. For example, having food but one does not take it with his hand claiming that he relies on Allah. This is sheer insanity. It has nothing to do with reliance on the Almighty. Presuming that the Almighty would satiate you without food, that He would cause food to reach your mouth and that He would appoint an angel to chew the food for you then carry it to your stomach, you should have ignored the Almighty tenets in the universe. The same applies to yearning for plants without cultivation and children without fertilization. Trust here signifies knowledge and an inward attitude.

As for knowledge, you should know that the Almighty has created food, your hands, the means producing food and the ability to move. You should also know that He alone provides you with food and water. On the other hand, you should inwardly rely on the Almight y, rather than your hands or food. Your hands may be paralyzed. Your food may be devoured by a stronger person.

ii) Means are not decisively incessant. They are rather often recurrent. For example, leaving for wild deserts without food or water, such a person seemingly to try the Almighty. Admittedly, this is an abominable act. The Prophet (peace and blessings of Allah be upon him) prepared himself well with food, water, a guide, etc. when he sought to migrate.

iii) Undertaking means that he obviously doubts their leading to their ends such as considering the minutest details of earning livelihood. If his objective and deeds are lawful, he falls within reliance on the Almighty. But he may join the greedy if he seeks for the remnants. Giving up merchandizing has nothing to do with trust in the Almighty. `Umar Ibn Al-Khattab (may Allah be pleased with him) likened a man who trusts Allah to a farmer cultivating a field and then relies on Allah.

B- Means enhancing an existent benefit such as saving. In fact, finding lawful food whose earning would distract him, he may save it, especially if he has dependants. `Umar Ibn Al-Khattab (may Allah be pleased with him) narrated,

"The Prophet (peace and blessings of be upon him) used to sell the dates of the garden of Bani An-

Nadir and store for his family so much food as would cover their needs for a whole year."
(Reported by Al-Bukhari)

One may argue that the Prophet (peace and blessings of Allah be upon him) ordered Bilal (may Allah be pleased with him) no to save as reported by Abu Dawud. In fact, Bilal's guests were all poor. If he had saved, they would have suffered hunger. Furthermore, Bilal's state necessitated that he should not save anything.

C- Embarking on those means of defense. Putting one's trust in the Almighty does not mean giving in to harms. Thus, man should get himself prepared with all necessary equipment. In this regard, the Almighty says in the Qur'an,

{*Let them pray with thee, taking all precautions, and bearing arms.*}
(An-Nisa': 102)

Likewise, a man asked the Prophet (peace and blessings of Allah be upon him) what he should do as to his she-camel. He replied,

"Fast bind, fast find."
(Reported by At-Tirmidhi)

However, you should trust in the origin of all causes, the Almighty, and be pleased with His Decrees. If you p resume that precaution guard against Divine Decree, or rather complain of an adversity, you will away from trusting in the Almighty. You should know that 'Destiny' is a physician. If you are given or even deprived of something, you should know that it is f or your interests.

In that way, if you do not think of the Almighty the way you do as to a skilled kind physician, you are not relying on the Almighty. Once a man complained to a scholar of high robbery. He replied, if you not more distressed about this be ing done by a Muslim than losing your wealth, then you are interested in the *'Ummah's* affairs.

D- Seeking to remove an adversity such as treating an illness. In fact, means of repelling injury has three categories, namely,

i) Inevitable means, such as quenching thirst with water and hunger with food. Renouncing this kind has nothing to do with trust in the Almighty.

ii) Presumptive means, such as taking a certain medicine to cure a disease. This type does not contradict relying on the Almighty. The Prophet (peace and blessing of Allah be upon him) has taken medicines and commanded taking them as reported by At-Tirmidhi and Abu Dawud. On the other hand, Abu Bakr (may Allah be pleased with him) was once asked to be examined by a doctor, but he said, "He [Allah] has examined me and said, I do whatever I want." However, treatment is recommended. Actually, Abu Bakr (may Allah be pleased with him) gave up taking medicine as soon as he felt recovery. Treatments are ordained by the Almighty.

iii) Imaginary means, such as cauterizing. This repudiates trust in Allah. The Prophet (peace and blessing of Allah be upon him) has described those relying on the Almighty saying,

"They are those persons who neither cauterize nor ask others to practice it, nor do they take omens, and repose their trust in their Lord."
(Reported by Al-Bukhari)

A patient's complain expels him out of trust in the Almighty. Early Muslims even disliked moaning since it may denote complain. *Imam* Ahmad was once asked, "How are you? He answered, "I am fine." The man sai d, "Did you suffer from fever yesterday?" He replied, I say I am fine. Do not bother me with what I detest. Al-Fudayl said, I yearn for an illness with no visitors. However, this does not preclude describing the nature of an ailment to the physician. Some Early Muslims did so highlighting that he describes the Almighty's Omnipotence therein. It may also be reported to a disciple to strengthen him; while considering it a praiseworthy grace. The Prophet (peace and blessings of Allah be upon him) said,

> *"I suffer illness as much as two men among you would suffer."*
>
> (Reported by Al-Bukhari)

VI. Love and Pleasure with Allah

One should know that love for the Almighty is the highest state. It yields its fruits of longing for and pleasure with Him. Rightly before it comes some other states paving the way such as repentance, patience and asceticism.

It unanimously agreed that love for Allah and His Messenger (peace and blessings of Allah be upon him) is compulsory. The Almighty says in the Qur'an,

> ﴿*Soon will Allah produce a people whom He will love as they will love Him.*﴾
>
> (Al-Ma'idah: 54)

He also says,

> ﴿*But those of Faith are overflowing in their love for Allah.*﴾
>
> (Al-Baqarah: 165)

On the other hand, Anas Ibn Malik (may Allah be pleased with him) narrated,

> "A Bedouin came to the Prophet (peace and blessings of Allah be upon him) said, "O Allah's Apostle! When will The Hour be established?" The Prophet (peace and blessings of Allah be upon him) said, "Wailaka (Woe to you), What have you prepared for it?" The Bedouin said, "I have not prepared anything for it, except that I love Allah and His Prophet." The Prophet (peace and blessings of Allah be upon him) said, "You will be with those whom you love." We (the companions of the Prophet) said, "And will we too be so? The

Prophet (peace and blessings of Allah be upon him) said, "Yes." So we became very glad on that day."
(Reported by Al-Bukhari)

It is also reported that the Azrael (the angel of death) visited Ibrahim (peace and blessings of Allah be upon him) to take his soul. Ibrahim wondered, "Do a friend take the soul of His friend? Then the Almighty inspired him, "Do a lover hate returning to his beloved? So Ibrahim said, "O Angel of death, take out my soul!" Al-Hasan said, "Knowledge of the Almighty results in His love, and *vice versa.*"

Likewise, love for the Prophet (peace and blessings of Allah be upon him) results from one's love for Allah. Messengers of the beloved are also received with due love. Even their deeds command our love too. The sole source of love is, in fact, the Almighty. This is due to some reasons, as follows,

1- All human beings naturally love themselves, their integrity and eternity; they detest the vice versa. Knowing the Almighty, one recognizes that his existence, eternity and integrity come from the Almighty. He is his creator. Thus, Al-Hasan said, "Knowing your Lord, you will love Him. Whereas knowing this world, you will renounce it."

2- Humans naturally love benefactors who support and assist them in all cases. Thus, knowing that Allah is the Sole Benefactor surrounding man with boundless favors, he will certainly love Him Alone. The Almighty says in the Qur'an,

{*If you would count up the favors of Allah, never would you be able to number them: for Allah is Oft-Forgiving, Most Merciful.*}

(An-Nahl: 18)

We have already elaborated this point under "Gratitude". However, benevolence is metaphorically ascribed to humans. The Almighty is the virtual source of goodness. For example, suppose that someone granted you all his property, giving you all authority to do whatever you want. You wrongfully think that he has done a favor for you. In fact, such a favor is completed by his property, his authority over it and his desire to spend it. You should wonder, who has gracefully created this man, his property, his will and his desire? Who has endeared you to him, and attracted his attention to you thinking that his goodness both in this life and the Hereafter lies with you? Considering these factors, you will find out that he is a mere storekeeper commanded by a king to give so and so a certain gift. Thus, a storekeeper is not a benefactor, since he is obliged to do so. If he is left to himself, he will never do so. The same applies to all benevolent persons. If left alone, they will never spend anything. Hence, your love should be confined to the Almighty alone, since benevolence only comes by His Command.

3- Benefactors are naturally loved even if their benevolence does not reach you. For example, hearing of a knowledgeable, just, devout and a kind king in a remote country, you love him. This aspect of love is attached to benevolence itself, not to mention having a share of it. These criteria necessitate love for the Almighty alone, since He is the original and sole source of benevolence.

Likewise, attributes of knowledge, power and infallibility incur love for their owners. In that way, one's love for the righteous persons is due to their knowledge of the Almighty, His Angels, His Books and His Messengers (peace and blessings of Allah be upon them), as well as their ability to reform themselves and ward off vices. This is the reason behind our love for the Prophets (peace and blessings of Allah be upon them). Comparing these qualities to the Almighty's Attributes, they become naught.

As far as knowledge is concerned, one should know that Allah is the source of knowledge in the universe, in the past, at present and in the future. Declaring the status of human knowledge, He says,

> ❴*Of knowledge it is only a little that is communicated to you, (O men).*❵
>
> (Al-'Isra': 85)

All the residents of heavens and the earth can never sound the hidden treasures in the creation of even a tiny gnat. They attain some aspects of knowledge only through his permission. Thus, the Almighty's grace of Knowledge bounds human in an endless way.

The Almighty is also Omnipotent. Comparing the power of all creatures to the Almighty's, you find out that the most powerful among humans is unable to benefit himself to rather save himself the from troubles of life. He cannot maintain his life when death comes. He can not even protect himself against blindness, dumbness, deafness or illness. He cannot subdue any creature on earth. His power is not spontaneous. The Almighty he inspirited it within him and provided him with all the necessary equipment therefor. If the Almighty sends a small gnat to a great king, it will bring his life to an end. The Almighty's Grace is clearly expressed in case of Prophet Dawud (peace and blessings of Allah be upon him).

> ❴*Verily we established his power on earth, and we gave him the ways and the means to all ends.*❵
>
> (Al-Kahf: 84)

In that all his kingdom and sovereignty were established for him by Allah. All people's lives lie in His Power. He may perish them if He so wills, without undermining His Kingdom. Even if He doubles creature for a thousand times, He will not be worried about them. He is the sole Omnipotence, Magnificence, Sovereign and King. Thus, none else deserves your love. He has no partner and no equal. He is the sole Self sufficient, Who does whatever He wants. He judges the way he deems. His Decrees are decisive. His knowledge encompasses the whole universe.

Knowledge of Allah is the Supreme Delight

One should know that delights are determined by man's perception. Man has been favored with a variety of instincts giving different delights. These instincts have been created to fulfill certain objectives. For example, man eats to maintain his life. He is granted eyes to see and ears to hear. The heart, in its turn, accommodates divine guidance. It bears various names such as the mind, insight, the light of faith and certitude. This instinct has been designed to recognize the truth. It naturally yearns for knowledge, which is its delight.

It is evident that knowledge is commendable, whereas ignorance is abominable. This is due the pleasure produced by knowledge. It is the best attribute one can possess and the sign of perfection. Therefore, one is pleased when he is praised for his intelligence and erudite knowledge. However, knowledge commands various branches, some of which is superior to others. For example, knowledge of certain crafts like dressmaking or cultivation is not of the same value as politics. Thus, the value of knowledge is determined by its object. The same applies to the delight derived therefrom. Hence, knowledge of the Most high, the Most Magnificent and the Most Perfect results in the supreme delight. In fact, none else enjoys any status above that of the Almighty. He is far and above.

Furthermore, one should know that the delight of knowledge is superior to all other delights felt by the rest of senses. Thematic purports tend to be more perfect than tangible pleasures. If one is made to choose between the delight of eating meat and that of authority and subduing enemies, if he is overtaken by his carnal desire having weak resolution, he will opt for food. But if he enjoys sound judgment, he will choose authority, enduring hunger patiently.

Opting for authority signifies that he is more delighted with it than with food. Likewise, knowledge of the Almighty is the even more supreme than that of authority. Those who have experienced both delights ascertain this. Undoubtedly, such persons would prefer devotion, contemplation and divine remembrance rather than authority due to their knowledge that everything is mortal. He will be greatly thoughtful of the Almighty's Attributes, Actions and the way He disciplines the universe. They all are free from worries and anxieties. They are spacious enough to accommodate all seekers. Knowledge of them is amount to being in Paradise enjoying its fruits and drinking from its rivers. They are eternal. Even one's death does put them to an end, since it does not undermine the residence of knowledge, i.e. the spirit. It rather moves it to another world, that is the life to come.

Those possessing knowledge of the Almighty command various levels, which are tasted only through experience. In that way, you should have become aware of the fact that knowledge of the Almighty is the supreme delight. Therefore, Abu Sulayman Ad-Darani (may Allah be merciful to him) said, "The Almighty has servants who are not distracted by fear from Hell, nor hope in Paradise. How can they be deluded by this world?"

Once Ma'ruf was asked about the reason that lead him to worship. He declined to answer. The man wondered, "Is it death?" But he exclaimed, "What is death! The man continued, "Is it remembering the grave?" He replied, "What is the grave?" The man furthered, "Is it your fear from Hell and hope in Paradise?" Ma'ruf said, "What is all this about? If you love the King who controls all these things and enjoy knowledge of Him, He will save you from all these agonies."

Ahmad ibn Al-Fath said, "I saw Al-Bishr ibn Al-Harith in a dream then I asked him, 'What has Ma'ruf Al-Karkhi done?' He nodded with his head and said, we have been separated from him. Ma'ruf has not worshipped the Almighty yearning for His Paradise nor fearing from His Hell. He has rather worshipped Him out of love. Thus, the Almighty has elevated him and disclosed Himself to him." Hence, when one loves the Almighty, his heart becomes fully preoccupied therewith, disregarding Hell and paradise, since he has attained the supreme pleasure.

You should also know that the delight of beholding the Almighty in the Hereafter is even greater than knowledge of Him in this world. The Almighty has willed that so long as one's soul is shrouded with physical impediments and desires, it cannot perceive the Almighty, just like lashes to the eye. When this veil is raised by death, the soul still maintains some impurities from this worldly life. Entering Paradise, souls become quite pure. Hence, the Almighty discloses Himself to souls according to their knowledge of Him in this world. Thus, ignoring the Almighty in worldly life deprives man from beholding Him in the Hereafter. No worldly loss is made up for in the Hereafter. This is clearly expressed by the Almighty saying,

{What is the life of this world but amusement and

play? But verily the Home in the Hereafter, that is life indeed, if they but knew.

(Al-`Ankabut: 64)

The status of life in the Hereafter is determined by one's knowledge in this world. Therefore, the Prophet (peace and blessings of Allah be upon him) said,

"The best one amongst people is he who enjoys long life and does good deeds."

(Reported by Ahmad)

One's knowledge is increased and enhanced with one's long life. It grants you ample time for further contemplation and remembrance. Thus, we have elaborated the significance of love for the Almighty, the delight of knowledge and beholding the Almighty and its being the supreme pleasure.

Means of Enhancing Love for the Almighty

The most pleased one in the Hereafter will be the one who enjoys the greatest knowledge of the Almighty. The Hereafter signifies return to Allah and being delighted therewith. How pleased a lover is when he returns to his beloved after long separation, when he beholds him with neither worry nor anxiety. However, this pleasure is determined by the status of one's love. The more the love is, the delighted he becomes. Each believer originally loves the Almighty, since he is closely attached to the Source of knowledge, i.e. the Almighty. However, the strength of love is not entertained by many. This is rather fulfilled by two means, namely,

The first means is renouncing worldly gaieties and purging one's heart from all sorts of love other than for Allah. Love for this world weakens one's love for the Almighty. The more one's heart is preoccupied with this world, the more it becomes negligent of the Almighty. Like water and air in a certain pot, love for this world and love for the Almighty can never coexist. The sole way out is to turn away from this world adopting fear, hope and patience in addition to the above-mentioned states.

The second means is knowledge of the Almighty. Knowledge initiates love. This kind of knowledge is only attained through abandoning this world, through contemplation and divine remembrance. It is also tenable through constant endeavor and consideration of Allah's Decrees on earth. You should also think of the universe and all its moving and stationary constellations. You should also meditate over the heaven and the angels dwelling there. Think of the creation of humans from dust along with other animals. Compare man's value to the earth. Take the gnat as an example, how Allah has created it like a huge elephant and supported it with two wings? How has He created its stomach and other physiological systems? How can it fly? How can it absorb blood with its trunk? Consider bees taking their nectar from flowers warding off impure ones. Consider their obedience to their master so much that it kills every bee eating impure nectars. Meditate over how do they choose the hexagonal to be their home. This shape is the widest among all geometrical shapes. Angles of a square building are never congruent. If they build their house like a circle, some of their fellows will remain out. Circular shapes never fit tightly together. Thus, the hexagonal fulfills the purpose in the best way. Consider how the Almighty has inspired them and guided them. All such considerations result in love for the Almighty.

Disparity among People in Love for Allah

All people originally love the Almighty. But their love varies according to their knowledge. Some only know those Divine Attributes reaching their ears. However, a knowledgeable person considers the minutes of creation in order to sound the underlying wisdom; thus recognizing the Almighty's Magnificence within his heart. This further enhances his love for Allah. This way of meditation drives man to an endless ocean the Almighty's marvels.

However, people fail to grasp the essence of knowledge of the Almighty. Practically, every production refers to a certain producer who enjoys specific qualities reflected in his article. Even if these qualities are not felt with the five senses, the Almighty's Existence, His Omnipotence, His Knowledge, etc. are ascertained by all aspects of creatures, by they stones, plants, animals, heavens, lands and seas. Even our own bodies, souls, states, hearts and all our various situations and movements prove the Almighty's Existence. All creations in the universe testify that they have a Creator who undertakes all their affairs according to His Knowledge, Wisdom, Meekness, Magnificence, Sublimity and All-Living. Each atom in the massive universe utters with an eloquent tongue, "We have not initiated our own selves but we have a creator." In fact, like bats that cannot see in daylight, our minds fail to comprehend the divine Being. Due to its faint eyesight, the bat sees only at night. He fails to see in daylight due to its brightness. The same applies to our minds as to the divine Being.

Practically, man feels all his surroundings since his early childhood, long before having an integral mental power. Then his mind grows slowly, wh ile he is preoccupied with it and its perception of such things. Getting accustomed to these things, man fails to sense their impact on his heart. On the other hand, seeing a marvelous animal, plant or anything of the like, you find him at once exclaiming, Glory be to the Almighty, how wonderful! He actually feels himself, his organs, all familiar animals, while they al testify that the Almighty is the Creator, but he does not sense their testimony due to his long familiarity with them. Faithfully speaking, if a blind person reaches maturity in his blindness. Then he restores his eyesight. Then he looks at the sky, the earth, the plants and the animals all at once, we will fear that he may be dazzled due to his excessive astonishment with these prodigies and their declaration of their creator. Such reasons as well as man's indulgence have hindered man's advance towards the Divine Knowledge and Guidance.

Significance of Longing for the Almighty

We have already dealt with love for the Almighty and its proofs. This love yields longing for the Almighty.

One should know that longing for something is possible only when some of its aspects are ascertained. Undetectable thins are neglected. Perception in this regard is completed by Beholding Him in the Hereafter.

The Almighty's Attributes are limitless. Every one becomes conversant with some of them only. Friends of the Almighty are aware of their existence and ascription to Allah. He also recognizes that the hidden treasures are even greater than the manifest ones. Thus, he constantly longs for more knowledge. His first state of longing ends in the Hereafter with beholding the Almighty. A lover's longing is never settled in this world. Ibrahim ibn Adham said, "O Lord, if You have comforted any loving heart in this world before returning to You, please comfort my heart, since I am extremely worried." Then the Almighty addressed him in a dream saying, "Do not you feel shy from asking Me to comfort your heart before returning to Me?" Ibrahim replied, O Lord, Your Love has overwhelmed me so much that I did not know what I was saying." Such a kind of longing gets soothed in the Hereafter. Other endless forms of longing are gratified the way He ordains. Both grace and delight increase incessantly till man gets totally preoccupied with them.

Likewise, the Prophet (peace and blessings of Allah be upon him) has taught a man some supplication and ordered him to keep reiterating it every day saying,

> *"O Lord, I ask You pleasure with Your Decree; prosperity after death; the delight of beholding You and a longing for You."*
>
> (Reported by An-Nasa'i)

The Almighty says in the Torah, "The righteous have longed for Me for a long time." Once the Almighty addressed a close servant, "I have servants who love Me and I love them. They long for Me and I for Me. They remember Me and I remember them. If you adopt their path, I will love you too. If you forsake their way, I will abhor you." He said, "O Lord, describe them!" Allah said, "Like a shepherd, they work all the day. Like birds, they yearn for sunset to rest. When night befalls them, beds get made, and lovers become alone with their beloved, they spend their night praying, prostrating, reciting My Words, and currying My favors. They cry and weep, moan and complain, prostrate and kneel down before Me. I behold and listen to their suffering due to My love."

The Almighty's Love for a Servant and its Signs

The Qur'an is full of verses that clearly denote the Almighty's love for His servants. For example, Allah says,

> ❨*For Allah loves those who turn to him constantly and he loves those who keep themselves pure and clean.*❩
>
> (Al-Baqarah: 222)

He also says,

> {Truly Allah loves those who fight in His Cause in battle array, as if they were a solid cemented structure.}
>
> (As-Saff: 4)

The Almighty has stated that He does not torture those whom He loves replying to the Jews and the Christians who pretended to be sons of Allah, and his beloved,

> {Say: why then does he punish you for your sins?}
>
> (Al-Ma'idah: 18)

This love necessitates forgiving sins, as the Almighty says,

> {Say, "If you do love Allah, follow me; Allah will love you and forgive you your sins; for Allah is Oft-Forgiving, Most Merciful.}
>
> (Al 'Imran: 31)

On the other hand, the Prophet (peace and blessings of Allah be upon him) said,

> "Allah said, 'I will declare war against him who shows hostility to a pious worshipper of Mine. And the most beloved things with which My servant comes nearer to Me, is what I have enjoined upon him; and My servant keeps on coming closer to Me through performing Nawafil (praying or doing extra deeds besides what is obligatory) till I love him."
>
> (Reported by Al-Bukhari)

Affliction is a sign of love of the Almighty for His servant. The Prophet (peace and blessings of Allah be upon him) said,

"When the Almighty loves a servant, He afflicts him."

(Reported by At-Tirmidhi)

When the Almighty love a servant, He causes his affairs to be goodly manageable. He fosters the best discipline in this servant. He inscribes *Iman* in his heart and enlightens his mind. Thus, the servant endeavors to be closer to the Almighty, and wards off those actions that incur His wrath. Then, Allah makes his life convenient with no humility. When this love increases, the servant becomes preoccupied with the Almighty alone.

As far as the servant's love is concerned, you should know that many persons claim their love of Allah. You should not be deluded by satanic temptations and wishful thinking. Evidence and signs should enhance love for the Almighty. One's love to return to the Almighty in Paradise. Lovers long for beholding their beloved. In fact, this does not contradict one's abhorrence to death. A believer may detest death while we return to Allah after we die. Some Early Muslims loved death whereas others disliked it due to their feeble love or their more love for this world. They may also disliked death due to their sins that they hoped to repent therefrom. Some of them considered themselves just embarking on that state of love. So they hate death before being prepared for returning to the Almighty, like a lover who is informed of his beloved's return; he postpones seeing him till he gets properly prepared. This state does not contradict perfection of one's love. This is further signified by constant endeavors and earnest preparedness.

Furthermore, he gives priority to what the Almighty loves in all aspects of his life. Thus, he should shun whims, laziness and stick to obedience getting nearer to Him through voluntary rites. Loving the Almighty, one should not disobey Him. However, disobedience does not repudiate love in origin. It rather undermines its perfection. For example, we love being healthy, but some of us eat unhealthy food. This is due to the fact that man's knowledge maybe defected while desires are enhanced. Therefore, one fails to fulfill his duties. This is supported by a *Hadith* narrated by `Umar ibn Al-Khattab (may Allah be pleased with him). He reports that An-Nu`aiman was brought drunkard before the Prophet (peace and blessings of Allah be upon him), so he was given forty lashes. Then a man from among the attendants cursed him, but the Prophet (peace and blessings of Allah be upon him) remarked,

"You should not curse him for he loves Allah and His Prophet."
(Reported by Al-Bukhari)

In that way, his disobedience did not preclude his original love for Allah and his Messenger (peace and blessings of Allah be upon him).

Loving the Almighty, one should be always busy with Divine Remembrance. His heart should be adorned with meditation. Love initiates remembering the beloved and all things attached to him. Thus, you should love the Almighty, the Qur'an, and His Prophet (peace and blessings of Allah be upon him). Allah, Most High, says,

❴*Say, 'If you do love Allah, follow me; Allah will love you and forgive you your sins; for Allah is Oft-Forgiving, Most Merciful.*❵
(Al `Imran: 31)

An early Muslim said, "I tasted the sweetness of reciting His Words. Thus, I constantly read the Qur'an. After a while, I stopped its recitation. Then, I was addressed in a dream, "Pretending my love, how then you forsake My Book! Have you not sensed My meek blame."

One should also like solitude with the Almighty, supplicating him and reciting His Book. *Tahajjud* Prayer is another outstanding sign of man's love for Allah. One should employ the quietness of night and renunciation o f worldly affairs. The least state of love is to be delighted with being alone with your beloved and converse with him secretly. Once a man worshipped the Almighty in a groove. He noticed a bird nesting in a tree and singing. That man viewed, "If I move my mosque by that tree so that I get soothed by the bird's singing. He moved his mosque there. Thence, the Almighty inspired this nation's Prophet (peace and blessings of Allah be upon him), "Tell so and so, are you comforted with the bird. Verily, I will relegate you to a status which you can not redeem with your deeds."

In that way, love is reflected in one's closeness to the Almighty. The highest delight is in being alone with him. This being the case, this delight and nearness become one's joy. One becomes preoccupied with obedience regretting what he has lost.

In this regard, Malik Al-Banani (may Allah have mercy on him) said, "I endured performing Prayers for twenty years and I enjoyed it for twenty years." Al Junayd said, "Love is denoted by your constant vigilance." When one's perseverance is driven by his love, his heart never wanes." Lovers endeavor earnestly to please their beloved. Therefore, one discards laziness, wealth and everything for his beloved's sake. A lover treats his fellow lovers kindly, and his enemies harshly. The Almighty says,

(Muhammad is the Messenger of Allah; and those who are with him are strong against Unbelievers,

(but) compassionate amongst each other.
(Al-Fath: 29)

Lovers for the Almighty are never restrained to enact the good. These are the milestones of love for Allah. Fulfilling them, one secures pleasure in the Hereafter. One is also delighted on the Last Day in proportion to his love, joining those drawn close to the Almighty; as He says,

{Truly the Righteous will be in Bliss: On Thrones (of Dignity) will they command a sight (of all things): Thou wilt recognize in their Faces the beaming brightness of Bliss. Their thirst will be slaked with Pure Wine sealed: The seal thereof will be musk: and for this let those aspire, who have aspirations: With it will be (given) a mixture of Tasnim: A spring, from (the waters) whereof drink those Nearest to Allah.}
(Al-Mutaffifin: 22-28)

The Almighty also says,

{Then shall anyone who has done an atom's weight of good, see it! And anyone who has done an atom's weight of evil, shall see it.}
(Az-Zalzalah: 7-8)

Furthermore, one's love should be shaded with fear, reverence and glorification. Fear never contradicts love. Those unique lovers entertain some special aspects of fear. They star t with fear from being deserted, then being separated, then comes their fear from expulsion.

Another sign of love is hiding it, avoiding its propagation and concealing one's ecstasy due to veneration of the beloved.

Love is hidden treasure that should be kept within the lover's heart. However, if it is unintentionally reflected, you are excused for it.

Pleasure with the Almighty's Decree

You should know that being overwhelmed with closeness to the Almighty, one is only delighted with solitude. One's heart is rather distressed by any thing hindering solitude. `Abd Al-Wahid ibn Zayd said, "'I told a monk, you are delighted with closeness to the Almighty.' he replied, 'If you taste its sweetness, you will abhor even your soul.' He asked, 'When does this take place?' He answered, 'When intimacy is not disturbed.' Ibn Zayd wondered, 'When does this happen?' He said, 'When you become preoccupied only with obedience.'" One may wonder: How can this be identified! In fact, it is when one feels estranged when he lives amongst people.

One should know that when closeness perpetuates, it yield intimacy and informality. This might be unfeasible, since it may signify boldness. However, if it observed by an ignorant, he is fraught to fall in disbelief. Abu Hafs was once met by a dazzled man. He asked, what is the matter? He said, I have lost my sole donkey. Then Abu Hafs adjured to the Almighty saying, "By Your Glory, I will not move before You restore this man's donkey!" Hence, the donkey turned up. Barkh Al-`Abid once searched for water. Then he supplicated, "You are All Generous, so send us rain at once."

As for being pleased with the Almighty's decree, it commands a very supreme state. It comes from love. It nature is indiscernible. It is purely divine.

Highlighting the virtue of pleasure, the Prophet (peace and blessing of Allah be upon him) said,

> *"When the Almighty deems good to a servant, He makes him pleased with His Decree"*
> (Reported by ibn Abi Ad-Dunya)

The Almighty Allah inspired Dawud, "You will not return to Me with anything more pleasing to Me and more obliterating to your sins than being pleased with My Decree." `Ali ibn Abu Talib (may Allah pleased with him) once met `Adi ibn Hatim (may Allah pleased with him). Seeing him distressed, `Ali asked, "Why are you distressed?" `Adi remarked, "Why not! My son has been killed. My eye has been gouged." `Ali (may Allah pleased with him) replied, "If you are pleased with the Almighty's Decree, you are rewarded for it. Otherwise, you are condemned, and it befalls you."

Abu Ad-Darda' (may Allah be pleased with him) once visited a man on his deathbed. He heard him praising the Almighty. So, he remarked, "You have done rightly. When the Almighty decrees something, he loves His servant to be pleased therewith." Ibn Mas`ud (may Allah be pleased with him) said, "Out of His Justice, the Almighty has twinned delight and happiness with pleasure and certitude. He has also joined sorrow and distress with suspicion and disgust." `Alqamah (may Allah be pleased with him) commented on the verse which reads,

> ❴*No kind of calamity can occur, except by the leave of Allah: and if any one believes in Allah, (Allah) guides his heart (aright): for Allah knows all things.*❵
> (At-Taghabun: 18)

He said that it refers to an adversity befalling a man while he knows that it is purely divine. So he get contented and pleased with it. Abu Mu`awyah Al-Aswad also explained that verse reading,

❧ *Whoever works righteousness, man or woman, and has Faith, verily, to him will we give a new Life, a life that is good and pure.* ❧

(An-Nahl: 97)

He highlighted that it signifies both pleasure and content. It is also reported that a Prophet (peace and blessings of Allah be upon him) complained of poverty and hunger to the Almighty for ten years. Then the Almighty inspired him, "How long have you been complaining? I have decreed your life on My Book before creating the Heavens and the earth, and even long before creating this world. Do you wish Me to alter My Decree for your sake? Do you wish Me to give priority to your will over Mine? Verily, if you do not give up such thoughts, you will be ousted from Prophethood."

We read in the Psalms of Dawud (peace and blessings of Allah be upon him), "Do you know who is the fastest on the Straight Path in the Hereafter? It is those who are pleased with My Decree and hymn My Remembrance." Dawud (peace and blessings of Allah be upon him) asked the Almighty saying, "O Lord! Who is the most detestable servant?" Allah said, "It is a servant who has sought My Counsel. Giving it to him, he is not pleased therewith." `Umar Ibn `Abd Al-`Aziz (may Allah be pleased with him) said, "I am only pleased with the Almighty's Decrees." He was also once asked, "What do you love?" He replied, "I love what the Almighty decrees." Al-Hasan said, "Being pleased with one's destiny, one finds sufficiency therein and the Almighty blesses it. Otherwise, one suffers insufficiency and the Almighty forsakes him." `Abd Al-Wahid Ibn Zayd said, "Pleasure with the Almighty's Decree is His vast door, the Garden of this world and the repose of worshippers." Someone said, "None commands the highest states on the Hereafter than those pleased with the Almighty. Thus pleasure initiates the highest degrees."

Pleasure Covers What Conflicts Man's Desire

Man can also be pleased even in case s which contradict his own desires. For example, man may suffer an agony and be pleased therewith, yearning for its increase though he naturally detests it. In fact, one is pleased with a very bitter medicine willingly though it is painful. One also travel s merchandising though he suffers the ails of the journey. Being inflicted while possessing certitude, one expects the Almighty's rewards. Thus, he becomes pleased with his adversity and praises the Almighty for it. He may also be overwhelmed by Divine Lov e so much that he does not feel the pain. A fighter may be hurt in a battlefield but he does not feel the pain since his heart is preoccupied with a certain end.

Al-Junayd said, "I asked Saryya, does a lover feel the pain of affliction?" He answered in the negative. Many afflicted persons used to say, "Even if we are cut apart, our love for Him (Allah) will certainly increase." Someone narrated that his neighbor had a slave girl whom he loved. One day, she became ill. Then he prepared some food for her. Whi le he was stirring the food with the spoon, she groaned. So the spoon fell off and he continued stirring the food with his hand till his finger dropped off while he was unaware. This is further enhanced by the story of those women who cut their hands when they saw the Prophet Yusuf (peace and blessing of Allah be upon him). They did not feel the pain of cutting their hands. In fact, this is quite possible from three aspects,

1- The believer knows that the Almighty manages his affairs better than him. The Prophet (peace and blessings of Allah be upon him) said,

> *"Whatever the Almighty decrees for a Believer is for his goodness."*
>
> (Reported by ibn `Adi)

Makhul narrated that he heard ibn `Umar (may Allah be pleased with them) saying, "A man seeks the Almighty counsel, so He guides him. Then, he becomes displeased with it. However, considering the end, he finds it better for him." Masruq said that there was a Bedouin in a desert. He had a dog, a donkey and a cock. He carried water on the donkey. The cock used to awaken him and his family. The dog guarded them. Then a fox devoured the cock. Seeing his family distressed, he remarked that it should be good. Then, a wolf cut the donkey's belly open. Thus, his family got worried but he quieted them. Then, the dog died, so they were disturbed. But he consoled them likewise. One day, they found out that all their neighbors had been captured due to the noise heard in their homes. Therefore, they thanked Allah.

Sa`id ibn Al-Musayyib said that one day Luqman addressed his son saying, "Son, you should know that whatever befalls you, be it good or bad, it is for your goodness. His son replied, "I will not take it for granted unless I experience it." Then Luqman said, "The Almighty has sent a new Prophet; let us visit him. He will explain it for you." So his son went with him. Each of them rode a donkey. They took with them the necessary provision. On their way, they came to an endless desert. Then the heat of the sun became intense so much that they drank all the water they had. Their donkeys became fatigue; so they dismounted and walked. Then Luqman beheld smoke and a dark thing on the horizon. He thought the smoke a sign of habitation and the darkness trees. While they were walking, his son strode on a bone. So his leg was severely injured. Luqman hastened to his son. He took the bone out with his teeth. He tore his turban and bandaged his son's leg. Seeing his son in such a state, he shed tears, which fell on his son's cheeks. So he got up. He saw his father weeping. He said, "Father, do you cry and say that it is good for me. How come? We have run out of food and water. We are alone in this place." Luqman answered, "Son, I weep since I wish to save your life with all what I have. I am a father to you! However, you wonder how can it be good for you? You should have been spared a severer tribulation than this." Suddenly Luqman noticed that both the smoke and darkness were no longer there. He was somewhat confused. Then he concluded: The Almighty should have caused something thereby. Being totally contemplating, he beheld a man standing on a horse addressing him, "Are you Luqman? He answered in the affirmative. He asked, "What has your son said? Luqman wondered, "Who are you? I hear your words but I do not see your face." He said, "I am Gabriel. None can see me but an elevated angel or a messenger. What has your son said?" He replied, "Did you not know?" Gabriel replied in the negative. He furthered, "The angels entrusted with your protection have informed me. The Almighty has commanded that this city and all its inhabitants be destroyed. The angels told me that you were leaving for the same city. So I asked my Lord to hinder you. He did so through your son's sufferings. But for this, you should have been destroyed." Then Gabriel rubbed the boy's leg, so he got recovered at once. Then, their bag was filled with water and their donkeys were rehabilitated. Then, Gabriel took them all fast to their home.

2- You should be pleased with the pain, due to its expected rewards as we have already elaborated.

3- You should also be pleased with pain for its own sake, rather than anything else. Thus, one finds his utmost delight in pleasing his beloved even if his life was endangered. It was said, "If my suffering pleases You, I never feel its pain." We have already stated that when love possesses a servant, he never feels any pain. A dumb person never tastes the sweet voices. Losing one's heart, one should consequently deny this delight of love that resides in the heart.

Supplication Does not Contradict Pleasure

One should know that supplication never undermines one's pleasure. The same applies to detesting disobedience and its doers. Seeking to reform it does not impair pleasure. As for supplication, we are worshipping the Almighty thereby. The Almighty has praised some of His servants saying,

{*They used to call on us with love And reverence, and humble themselves before us.*}

(Al-Anbiya': 90)

In this regard, we have received countless supplications from the Prophet (peace and blessings of Allah be upon him) and the righteous after him.

On the other hand, we should condemn disobedience and never be pleased with it. This, in fact, reflects our devout obedience to the Almighty. The same applies to hating the disbelievers, the sinful and reproving them. The Qur'an contains innumerable references to this norm. But someone may wonder, many *Ahadith* command pleasure with the Almighty's Decree. If disobedience takes place without the Almighty's Decree, it is quite unthinkable. So they should happen by His Decree, thus; detesting them signifies hating the Almighty's Decree. So how can they both be reconciled?

In fact, such intricate matters are only sounded by those grounded in knowledge. Some people fail to understand them, so they prefer silence considering a state of pleasure with the Almighty's Decree. They rather label it as 'good manner'. However, this is sheer ignorance. Practically, both love and hatred are contradictory if they cover one and the same issue.

On the other hand, if you love some aspects of a certain thing and hate other ones, they are not at odds. For example, you may have an enemy who is at the same time hostile to other enemies of yours. Then he dies. Thus, you are pleased with his death for his being an enemy to you. But you are also annoyed since you enemies have lost a feud. The same applies to disobedience. It has two aspects. The first is purely divine, i.e. its being decreed by Him; so you get pleased with it in that way of total surrender to the Almighty. The second is purely human, i.e. its being willingly committed by; thus incurring the Almighty's wrath.

This should, however, be demonstrated. Someone may seek to appoint a criterion to measure those who love him and those who hate him. He may say, "I will hurt so and so severely so much that he will have to swear at me. Thence, I will hate him and consider him an enemy. All those who love him are also my enemies. But those who hate him will be my friends. Then he fulfills his plan and he succeeds in achieving his end. Every true lover should say, "I love your decree upon this person. It is your own judgment. However, his swear against you is sheer aggression. He should rather have kept patience." The same applies to desires and lusts within man and detesting him for his disobedience.

Thus, every servant loving the Almighty should hate what He hates and consider an enemy those who declare hostility against Him.

In that way, all those *Ahadith* dealing with love for Allah and treating them harshly, we are at the same time pleased with the Almighty's Decree. This is derived from the hidden treasure of Destiny. Both goodness and evil are determined by the Almighty, though the latter is detested and the former is loved.

As for love for the Almighty, He inspired Dawud (peace and blessings of Allah be upon him), "If those turning away from Me knew how I long for them, how love them and yearn for their obedience, they would be torn apart due to their love and longing for Me. O Dawud, this is My Will as to those persons; then how about those obeying Me! O Dawud, when a servant forsakes Me, he becomes in a dire need for Me. When he returns, I love him most."

A devout woman used to say, "I am fed up with this life. Even if death was sold, I would buy it longing for the Almighty and my return to Him." She was asked, "Are you sure you are doing good?" She replied, "No, but I love Him and think good of Him; so will He torture Me?"

VII. Intention, Sincerity, and Truthfulness

You should know that actions are not accepted by Allah except when they are dedicated to Him, Most High.

Deeds without sincere intentions signify dissemblance. Sincerity without practice is futile. The Almighty says in the Qur'an,

⟨*And We shall turn to whatever deeds they did (in this life), and We shall make such deeds as floating dust scattered about.*⟩

(Al-Furqan: 23)

We wonder: how can one's intention be valid though he does not even know the essence of intention itself! How can he be sincere though he ignores the purport of sincerity? How can he be truthful while he understands it not? Thus, we should first comprehend what intention means, then rectify it with deeds after assimilating the significance of truthfulness and sincerity whereby salvation is secure.

Intention: Concept and Virtue

The Almighty says,

⟨*Send not away those who call on their Lord morning and evening, seeking his face.*⟩

(Al-An`am: 52)

"Seeking" here refers to their intention. `Umar ibn Al-Khattab (may Allah be pleased with him) narrated that he heard Allah's Messenger saying,

"*The reward of deeds depends on the intentions, so

whoever emigrated for the worldly benefits or to marry a woman, his emigration was for that for which he emigrated, but whoever emigrated for the Sake of Allah and His Messenger, his emigration is for Allah and His Messenger."

(Reported by Al-Bukhari)

Abu Musa (may Allah be pleased with him) narrated,

"A man came to the Prophet (peace and blessings of Allah be upon him) and asked, 'O Allah's Messenger! What kind of fighting is in Allah's cause? (I ask this), for some of us fight because of being enraged and angry and some for the sake of his pride and haughtiness.' The Prophet raised his head (as the questioner was standing) and said, 'He who fights so that Allah's Word (Islam) should be superior, then he fights in Allah's cause.'"

(Reported by Al-Bukhari)

On the authority of Jabir (may Allah be pleased with him) who said,

"We were with the Prophet (peace and blessings of Allah be upon him) on an expedition. He said, 'There are some people in Madinah. They are with you whenever you cover a distance or cross a valley. They have been detained by illness."

(Reported by Muslim)

Ibn `Abbas (may Allah be pleased with them both) also narrated that the Prophet (peace and blessing of Allah be upon him) said,

> "If somebody intends to do a good deed and he does not do it, then Allah will write for him a full good deed."
>
> (Reported by Al-Bukhari)

Abu Kabshah Al-Anmari (may Allah be pleased with him) reported that the Prophet (peace and blessings of Allah be upon him) said,

> "The parable of those this Ummah is that of four people. The first is given wealth and knowledge, so he spends his wealth in Allah's cause. The second is gifted with knowledge only; so he says, 'If I have had wealth like that person, I would spend it likewise.' Then the Prophet (peace and blessings of Allah be upon him) comments that they will have equal rewards. The third man is granted wealth, which he wrongfully spends. The fourth person is deprived from both wealth and knowledge and he opines, 'If I had like him, I would do likewise.' Thus; the will have equal punishment."
>
> (Reported by At-Tirmidhi)

Abu `Imran Al-Juni said, "The angels ascend to heavens carrying deeds with them. The Almighty addresses them, 'Discard this tablet.' Then the angles exclaim, 'O Lord, he has done good and we have recorded it for him.' The Almighty says, 'He does not seek My Face thereby.'" Al-Juni also said, "The Almighty commands His angels t o double some one's deed." They wonder, "O Lord, he has done nothing." The Almighty replies, "He has intended to do it."

`Umar (may Allah be pleased with him) said, "The best deeds is to fulfill what the Almighty has made obligatory, to avoid what He has p rohibited, and to have a truthful intention."

Some one asked a righteous person, "Guide me to a deed for the Almighty's sake." He answered, "You should intend to do good; thus toy will be rewarded according to your intention." The Prophet (peace and blessings of Allah be upon him) said,

"If someone usually performs prayers on night, but he once fell asleep, he will be rewarded for his Prayers while his sleeping is a gift from Allah."
(Reported by Abu Dawud)

Deeds are classified into three categories, namely

1- Disobedience: Its status is not affected by man's intention. For example, building a mosque by illegal property intending good is null and void. In fact, seeking to do good through mischief incurs another wrong. Good deeds are determined by the *Shai`ah*, so mischief can never be good.

You should know that rulers who establish mosques and schools by forbidden property resemble insidious scholars who teach knowledge to the impious and whimsical persons. If they learn, they drive people away from the Almighty's Path. They become solely preoccupied with worldly gaieties and lusts. This mischief is brought about by their scholars' corrupt intentions and vile objectives such as learning stories for worldly comforts. Teaching them enhances mischief. Obedience can be annulled by vile intentions. Yet, good intentions can never change mischief to be good.

2- Obedience: It is closely attached to intentions in their original validity and double rewards. One intends to worship the Almighty Alone. If he seeks dissemblance thereby, he is sinful. As for receiving double rewards, it comes from consecutive good intentions. A single act of obedience may hide a variety of good intentions. Thus, one is rewarded accordingly. For example, sitting in a mosque is an act of obedience. He may seek thereby manifold good ends for which he receives many rewards. This norm applies to all other good deeds which comprise various good intentions

3- The permissible acts: Every permitted thing may contain various good intentions, which elevates one to the highest degrees. Thus, neglecting such acts, one suffers immense losses. One should not accordingly overlook any slight thing, since he is held accountable for it on the Last day. For example, one may apply perfume following the Prophet's *Sunnah* (peace and blessing of Allah be upon him).

Ash-Shfi`i remarked, "He who smells good, gets his mind enhanced." Some early Muslim said, "I love having an intention in every thing, even in drinking, eating, sleeping, and answering the call of nature." When one seeks by eating to strengthen his body for worship, and by marriage to be chaste, please his wife, and have a child worshipping Allah, he will be rewarded for all these acts. So, you should never disdain any thing in your life. You should consider your action s before being held accountable for them.

Furthermore, you should perceive that intention signifies one's inclination to interests, either in the future or at present. Some ignorant persons may wrongfully say, "I eat for Allah's sake, or I read for Allah's sake." Presuming as such an intention. Intention lies within the heart and is gifted by the Almighty. It is not a matter of choice. Thus, it may be absent in certain cases. However, it is always entertained by the righteous people.

In fact, people in view of their intentions are of three types as follows,

Some of them obey the Almighty due to fear from Him. Others worship Him due to their hope in Him. The third type is the most supreme, i.e., to worship the Almighty due to His Sublimity and Glory. Lovers of this world never sense this state. This type of people never neglects remembering the Almighty and contemplating over His prodigies. It is reported that the Almighty addressed Ahmad ibn Khadrawyh in a dream saying, "All people are asking My favors but Ab u Yazid asks for Me." People have various objectives behind their intentions. Getting overwhelmed with it, one hardly lives without it. Having a good intention in a permissible thing and a virtue, he should start with the former and the latter will reach him soon. For example, one may intend to eat and sleep to refresh his body for obedience. But he does not intend to pray or fast at that time. Then eating and sleeping command priority. Even if he gets tired from worship due to his persistence, he may refresh himself for a while to restore his vigor.

`Ali (may Allah be pleased with him) said, "You should refresh your hearts and seek for wisdom, since they get bored like your bodies." Some said, "Revitalize your hearts so that they should assimilate Divine Remembrance." Such delicate matters are only observed by keeping in company with scholars. A skilled fighter, for instance, may run before his enemy to trap him. In fact, advancing along the path towards the Almighty teems with battles with our enemy, i.e., Satan, and treatments with our heart. The sensible person winds up the keen temptations indiscernible to the weak. They should in turn entrust those who are more grounded with disclosing these secrets.

Sincerity: Essence, Virtue, and States

The Qour'an contains ample references to Sincerity. For example, the Almighty says,

> ⟨*And they have been commanded no more than this: to worship Allah, offering Him sincere devotion, being True (in Faith).*⟩
>
> (Al-Bayyinah: 5)

He also says,

> ⟨*Verily, to Allah sincere devotion is due?*⟩
>
> (Az-Zumar: 3)

The Prophet's *Sunnah* (peace and blessings of Allah be upon him) also highlights the virtue of sincerity. The Prophet (peace and blessings of Allah be upon him) was reported to have said to Mu`adh,

> "*Be sincere in your religion, then little work will be sufficient for you.*"
>
> (Reported by Al-Hakim)

But this *Hadith's* chain of narrators is interrupted. However, Al-Hasan said: There was a tree that some people worshipped. A man then said: I will uproot this tree. When he reached it, Satan, transfigured in a man, met him and said: What do want to do? He said: I want to cut this tree that people worship instead of the Almighty. Satan said: So long as you do not worship it, leave it alone. He said: I will cut it. Satan said: Should not I guide to something better? The man asked: What is that? Satan said: It is to have two *Dinars* by your pillow every morning. The man asked: Who will give them to me? Satan replied: I will. So the man returned. When he got up in the morning, he found two *Dinars* by his pillow. On the next day, he did not find anything. So he furiously hastened to cut the tree. Then Satan appeared to him asking: What do you want? He said: I want to cut this tree for the Almighty's sake? Satan said: You are a liar and will not be able to cut it. But the man reached the tree and tried to uproot it. Thence, Satan attacked him and knocked him down so much that he was about to kill him. Then Satan remarked: Do you know who am I? I am Satan. You at first time was sincere so I could not defea t you, but now you seek to cut it because of the two *Dinars* with which I beguiled you.

Ma`ruf Al-Karkhi used to say, "O soul, keep sincerity and be purified." Abu Sulayman said, "He is successful who has even a single sincere step seeking the Almighty Alon e."

Once, a man used to wear female clothes and get mixed with women. In one of his mixing, a pearl was stolen form one of the women. So they decided to privately search every one present. All women were searched but for that man and another woman. He prayed sincerely for the Almighty if he does not reveal his reality, he would never do it again. Hence, they found the pearl with the other woman and said: Set her (the man dressed like a woman) free, we have found the pearl.

The Essence of Sincerity

Practically, every thing can be impaired by another thing. But when it is purged and purified, it is termed 'sincere'. Sincerity contradicts unfaithfulness. Thus, every insincere person is also unfaithful. But unfaithfulness commands various degrees. Sincerity to t he Almighty's oneness is in conflict with polytheism. Unfaithfulness is either obvious or hidden. The same applies to sincerity. We have elaborated the levels of dissemblance. We are dealing now with means of becoming nearer to the Almighty, Most High. Som etimes, this objective may be mixed with another, be it dissemblance or worldly gaieties. For example, one may set a slave free to get rid of his bad manners or escape maintaining him. One may perform *Hajj* to convalesce or avoid an expected damage. One may fight to be more skilled in battlefield affairs. One may pray at night to drive sleep away and guard his property or family. One may also seek knowledge to be rich and so on and so forth. When one's main objective is getting closer to the Almighty, but another end is annexed to it; thus making the deed more convenient, he is not regarded sincere. How scarce are those cases where such instances are precluded! In that way, it was said: If man enjoys in his whole life sincerity with his Lord even for a while, he wins salvation. This is due to the virtue of sincerity and the difficulty of purging one's heart. The sincere person is only driven by being near to the Almighty, Most High.

Sahl was once asked, "What is the most difficult thing for one's soul?" He said, "It is sincerity, for it will have no share in it."

You should know that sincerity is disturbed by a variety of impurities; some of which are discernible whereas the others are quite hidden. In fact, some sorts of dissemblance are so much concealed that they cannot be ascertained. The main norm is man's feeling when he embarks on a certain deed. If he adopts different attitude in different situations in one and the same case, he is insincere. None is saved from satanic temptation but through the Almighty's support. It is clearly stated that two *Rak`at* performed by a knowledgeable person is better that seventy *Rak`at* by an ignoramus. The former meditates over the detriments of one's deeds, whereas the latter is satisfied with the outer form of his worship

The Value of Insincere Deeds

In fact, those acts of dissemblance are unacceptable and punishable just as sincere ones are accredited and rewarded.

These two divisions are quite clear. However, insincere deeds are those mixed with dissemblance and seeking worldly gaieties. However, the strength of incentives should be considered. If the religious objective stands on an equal footing with the psychological one, the man's deed is turned void, in the sense that he is neither rewarded nor punished for it. But if the motivation of dissemblance is superior, he is held punishable for it. However, his punishment is rather inferior to pure dissemblance. If his religious motive has the upper hand, he will be rewarded in proportion to it. The Almighty Allah says,

⟨*Allah is never unjust in the least degree; if there is any good (done), He doubles it, and gives from His own presence a great reward.*⟩

(Al-Nisa': 40)

This is clearly substantiated by the *Ummah's* consensus on the point that if some one repairs for *Hajj* in a trade, he is rewarded for his *Hajj*, though it is joined with a worldly comfort provided that he is mainly motivated by performing *Hajj*. The same applies to a fighter who seeks both fighting in Allah's cause and the spoils of war so long as he is originally driven by the former. However, they both do not enjoy the same reward of pure *Hajj* and fighting.

Truthfulness: its Essence and Virtue

`Abdullah ibn Masud (may Allah be pleased with him) narrated that the Prophet (peace and blessings of Allah be upon him) as saying,

"*Truthfulness leads to righteousness, and righteousness leads to Paradise. And, a man keeps on telling the truth until he becomes a truthful person. Falsehood leads to Al-Fajur (i.e.,*

wickedness, evil-doing), and Al-Fujur leads to the (Hell) Fire, and a man may keep on telling lies until he is written before Allah as a liar."
(Reported by Al-Bukhari and Muslim)

Bishr Al-Hafi said, "Being truthful to the Almighty, one prefers solitude." The term truthfulness covers various aspects, namely,

1- Telling the truth: Every one should be careful of his words, telling only the truth. Verbal honesty is the most common form truthfulness. You should also avoid adopting figurative language, since it is akin to lying. However, if driven by necessity, one may resort to allegorical speech. Ka`b ibn Malik (may Allah be pleased with him) narrated,

> *"Whenever Allah's Prophet (peace and blessings of Allah be upon him) intended to lead a Ghazwa, he would use an equivocation from which one would understand that he was going to a different destination."*
> (Reported by Al-Bukhari)

Um Kulthum bint `Uqba (may Allah be pleased with her) narrated that she heard Allah's Prophet (peace and blessings of Allah be upon him) saying,

> *"He who makes peace between the people by inventing good information or saying good things, is not a liar."*
> (Reported by Al-Bukhari)

However, one should observe veracity in his supplication to the Almighty such as I have directed my face to Him Who has created the Heavens and the Earth. Otherwise, if his heart is preoccupied with this world rather than the Almighty, he is a liar.

2- Having a truthful intention: This depends on sincerity. If one's act is imbued with securing a worldly comfort, one's intention is not truthful. Even its owner may be a liar. This is supported by the following *Hadith* of the Prophet (peace and blessings of Allah be upon him):

> *"The first of men (whose case) will be decided on the Day of Judgment... Then will be brought forward a man who acquired knowledge and imparted it (to others) and recited the Qur'an. He will be brought and Allah will make him recount His blessings and he will recount them (and admit having enjoyed them in his lifetime). Then will Allah ask: What did you do (to requite these blessings)? He will say: I acquired knowledge and disseminated it and recited the Qur'an seeking Your pleasure. Allah will say: You have told a lie. You acquired knowledge so that you might be called a scholar, and you recited the Qur'an so that it might be said: He is a Qari' (reciter of the Qur'an) and such has been said. Then orders will be passed against him and he shall be dragged with his face downward and cast into the Fire."*
>
> (Reported by Muslim)

This refers to that man's corrupt intention, rather than his recitation. The same applies to the othe r two.

3- Truthful promise and fulfilling it: The former can be exemplified by a person saying, "If Allah grants me wealth, I will spend it all in charity." This vow may be truthful or indecisive. Fulfilling one's promise is reflected in his adherence to his promise. The Almighty Allah says,

❲*Among the Believers are men who have been true to their Covenant with Allah, of them some have completed their vow.*❳

(Al-Ahzab: 23)

In another Qur'anic verse, He, Most High, says,

❲*Amongst them are men who made a Covenant with Allah, that if He bestowed on them of His bounty, they would give (largely) in charity, and be truly amongst those who are righteous. But when He did bestow of his Bounty, they became covetous, and turned back (from their Covenant), averse (from its fulfillment). So He hath put as a consequence hypocrisy into their hearts, (to last) till the day whereon they shall meet Him; because they broke their Covenant with Allah, and because they lied (again and again).*❳

(At-Tawbah: 75-77)

4- **Truthful deeds**: This means that both man's inward and outward states should not vary. In fact, one's deeds should reflect what he actually entertains in his heart. Mutraf said, "When man's inward and outward realities become identical, the Almighty says: This is My true servant .

5- **Truthful adherence to the states of religion**: This is the highest level, such as being truthful in one's fear, hope, asceticism, pleasure, love, and trust in the Almighty. All such states have a starting point and certain ends and essence. Only the truthful attain their reality. When a thing is perfect, its owner is labeled a truthful. The Almighty says,

❲*It is not righteousness that you turn your faces towards East or West; but it is righteousness - to*

believe in Allah and the Last Day, and the Angels, and the Book, and the Messengers; to spend of your substance, out of love for Him, for your kin, for orphans, for the needy, for the wayfarer, for those who ask, and for the ransom of slaves; to be steadfast in Prayer, and practice regular charity; to fulfill the contracts which you have made; and to be firm and patient, in pain (or suffering) and adversity, and throughout all periods of panic. Such are the people of truth, fearing the Almighty.
(Al-Baqarah: 177)

Allah, Most High, also says,

(Only those are Believers who have believed in Allah and His Messenger, and have never since doubted, but have striven with their belongings and their persons in the Cause of Allah: such are the sincere ones.)
(Al-Hujurat: 15)

We may give an example of fear. In fact, eve ry one fears the Almighty, but this fear does not amount to a full degree. Fearing from a ruler, one trembles lest an abominable thing takes place. On the other hand, he dreads Fire, but he does nothing to ward off it. Therefore, `Amir ibn Qays said, "I wonder how those longing for Paradise and how those fearing from Fire enjoy sleeping." These states have endless limits disabling seekers to attain them. However, each one reaches the end according to his being strong or weak. When the Almighty knows that His servant is truthful, He purges him. Truthfulness in such states is practically rare. One may be truthful in some states. This is signified by hiding tribulations and obedience. It also incurs concealing them from fellow humans.

VIII. Self-scrutiny

The Almighty, Most High, says,

﴾*On the day when every soul will be confronted with all the good it has done, it will wish there where a great distance between it and its evil. But Allah cautions you (to remember) Himself.*﴿

(Al `Imran: 3)

He, Most High, also says,

﴾*We shall set up scales of justice for the Day of Judgment, so that not a soul will be dealt with unjustly in the least. And if there be (no more than) the weight of a mustard seed, We will bring it (to account): and enough are we to take account.*﴿

(Al-Anbiya': 47)

The Almighty further states,

﴾*And the Book (of deeds) will be placed (before you); and thou wilt see the sinful in great terror because of what is (recorded) therein; they will say, Ah woe to us what a book is this it leaves out nothing small or great, but takes account thereof they will find all that they did, placed before them: and not one will thy Lord treat with injustice.*﴿

(Al-Kahf: 49)

Moreover, He says,

﴾*On that Day will men proceed in companies sorted out, to be shown the Deeds that they (had done). Then shall anyone who has done an atom's weight of good, see it! And anyone who has done an atom's weight of evil, shall see it.*}

(Az-Zalzalah: 6-8)

All these verse highlight the value of self-scrutiny in the Hereafter. In fact, sensible peop le have discovered that the sole way to salvation is to examine themselves and truthfully censor them. Investigating your self in this world paves the way for convenient accountability in the Hereafter. Neglecting it results in consecutive losses. They hav e recognized that their salvation is based on obedience. The Almighty has commanded them to maintain patience saying,

{*O you who believe persevere in patience and constancy; vie in such perseverance; strengthen each other; and fear Allah; that you may prosper.*}

(Al `Imran: 200)

Thus, they have full control over themselves through adopting a specific agreement, censorship, accountability, punishment, perseverance and reprimand. In that way, they command six states in this regard. However, accountability follows agreement. In case of lose, reprimand and punishment come. We will deal with such states in a somewhat detailed way.

First: Agreement

Partners in trade cooperate to secure profits. They agree on certain conditions and censor each other. They are also h eld responsible before one another. The same applies to a person with his mind. They need to cooperate and agree on specific stipulations guiding him to the straight path. Furthermore, one's mind should constantly consider one's activities to secure his fidelity and prosperity. After that, he is held responsible for his conditions and is required to fulfill them. Such a trade yields Paradise. Liability in this regard is truly greater than its worldly counterpart. Thus, all believers should not overlook examining themselves and have full control over all their affairs. Each moment in life is a precious pearl. Performing the *Fajr* Prayer, one should free himself a while to have an arrangement with his soul, such as saying, "My life is my goods. If I lose my capital, both trade and profits are out of sight. The Almighty has given me an extension of one day. If He had taken my soul, I would have wished to return to this world to make up for what I have lost. O soul, you should act as if you were sent back to this world after your expiry. Thus, you should not waste that day. Know that a day has twenty-four hours only whereby a servant has twenty-four stores. Opening one of them, he finds it full of light due to his good deeds, so he becomes delighted therewith. Opening another one, he finds it teeming with darkness and stench smell due to his disobedience in that hour. So he becomes worried, troubled and intimidated. Then a third store is opened. He finds it empty. It significs that hour when he sleeps or does any permissible thing. He regrets its being empty. He endures the same sufferings of a trader who can gain profits but he disdains them." In that way, he sees all the stores of his life. So one should urge his soul to exert its utmost to fill these stores with obedience rather than leaving them empty or filled with wrong doings.

Some one remarked: Even if a wrong-doer is exempted, he has lost the reward of good-doing. This is man's counsel to his soul. After that he should also advise his seven organs, his eyes, ears, tongue, belly, genitals, hands and his legs. They all should be subservient to his soul serving it to achieve profits in this trade.

As for one's eye, he should lower his gaze. He should be

only preoccupied with his own affairs, confining them to what they have created for. He should consider the universe. He should detect good deeds and apply them. He should recite the Qur'an, read the Prophet's *Sunnah* (peace and blessings of Allah be upon him) as well as books of wisdom to benefit therefrom. This methodology should be applied to all organs according to their missions respectively. We have already mentioned evils of the tongue, so one should occupy it with remembrance of Allah, Most High, imparting knowledge, guiding people to the Almighty, making peace between people, etc.

Coming to one's belly, one should avoid voracity and doubtful food. He should be satisfied with the necessary amount. He should agree with his soul on the principle that if it violates this norm, he will punish it with deprivation. This system should rather be adopted in regard to all other organs.

Such arrangements should be taken every day until he gets accustomed to them. However, every day enjoys new incidents, which command a certain status. This is frequent in worldly affairs such as trade, authority, etc. Thus, one should stipulate uprightness in all aspects of his life. The Prophet (peace and blessings of Allah be upon him) said,

> *"A sagacious person is he who subdues his self and considers his life after death. But the unwise one obeys his lusts and holds to wishful thinking."*
> (Reported by At-Tirmidhi)

`Umar ibn Al-Khattab (may Allah be pleased with him) said, "Hold your selves responsible for your deeds before you are accounted for them (on the Day of Judgment). Consider your acts before they measured against you and get prepared to the Day of Judgement." The he recited,

❨*That Day shall you be brought to Judgment: not an act of yours that you hide will be hidden.*❩

(Al-Haqqah: 18)

Second: Censorship

Fulfilling the above-mentioned norm, then observation and censorship come. The Prophet (peace and blessings of Allah be upon him) was once asked about *Ihsan*, he said,

> "To worship Allah as if you see Him, for if you cannot see Him, you must consider that He is looking at you."
>
> (Reported by Al-Bukhari)

Ash-Shibly once visited Abu Al-Husayn An-Nuri while he was motionless. He wondered, "Who has granted you this silence and observation?" He replied, "I have learnt them from our eagles. When they sought a prey, they remained motionless." Man should observe himself likewise and censor his activities long before doing them and after. He should ask himself if they are driven by sincerity to the Almighty. If this is the case, he should fulfill them. Otherwise, he should give up them at once.

Al-Hasan remarked, "May Allah be merciful to a man who considers his intention. If it is divine, he fulfills it. Otherwise, he gives it up." This sort of observation covers obedience, i.e., maintaining sincerity. As for disobedience, he should repent, regret doing it, and shun it. Censorship in permissible things signifies good manners and gratitude. Every one enjoys graces and faces tribulations. He should be grateful to the former and endure the latter patiently.

Wahb ibn Munabbih said, "A sensible person should be

preoccupied with four hours. He soliloquizes with his Lord in the first hour. Then, he censors himself in the second. Then, he mixes with his brothers informing his of his defects in the third. Finally, he is alone with his self and its desires, consid ing the lawful and the prohibited therein. This last hour enhances him through the previous ones. However, he should rather be busy remembering the Almighty and contemplating over his prodigies."

Third: Accountability after Work

The Almighty, Most High, says,

{*O you who believe! Fear Allah, and let every soul look to what (provision) he has sent forth for the morrow. Yea, fear Allah: for Allah is well acquainted with (all) that you do.*}

(Al-Hashr: 18)

This Qur'anic verse refers to considering one's a cts after they are done. Therefore, `Umar ibn Al -Khattab (may Allah be pleased with him) said, "Hold your selves responsible for your deeds before you are accounted for them." Al -Hasan said, "A believer is the superintendent of his self, holding responsibility." In fact, believers are tied fast by the Qur'an securing their lives. Like a captive, the believer seeks to set himself free from this world. He never entrust anything. He returns to the Almighty. He knows that he is accountable for what he hears, sees, and speaks as well as all his deeds.

Every one should afford himself an opportunity to reconsider his deeds, like traders. Accountability signifies considering your capital, the profits and losses to ascertain decrease or increase in your merchandise. The capital here stands for religious obligations, profits for voluntary obedience, and loss for disobedience. Committing a sin, one should think of it prudently to make up for it. Tawbah ibn As Summah used to check his deeds. One day he found out that he was sixty years old. He counted their days (about 21500 days). So he cried, "Woe to me. The angel has recorded 21500 sins. Each day has ten thousand sins." Then he died at once. Then his attendants heard someone saying, "He has jumped into Paradise!" Thus, we should hold our selves accountable for our deeds, breaths, and even our thoughts. If any one were to through a stone for each sin, he would fill a vast house. They all are recorded. The Almighty says,

⟨*Allah has reckoned its (value), though they may have forgotten it.*⟩

(Al-Mujadalah: 6)

Fourth: Punishment

Seeing that he has slackened or committed a sin, a believer should not overlook this. Otherwise, he will find sinning convenient for him and become unable to control himself. He should rather punish himself. `Umar ibn Al-Khattab (may Allah be pleased with him) once visited his grove. When he returned, he found that people had performed the `Asr Prayer. So he said, "I went to my grove and returned after people observed the `Asr Prayer. I give my garden in charity to the poor." Al-Layth remarked that `Umar missed the first congregation of that Prayer. We have already stated that missing the Sunset Prayer, he set two slaves free after observing it. Tamim Ad-Darri (may Allah be pleased with him) missed his night Prayer due to falling asleep. So he spent a while praying all the night. Hassan ibn Sinan passed by a room and wondered, "When was this room built?" Then he reprimanded himself saying, "You ask about what is not of your concern." Then he punished himself by fasting a whole year.

However, other forms of unlawful punishment should not be adopted. For example, an Israelite once touched a woman, so he put his hand in fire until it was paralyzed. Another man advanced towards a woman but he contemplated, " What do you want to do?" Desiring to return, he addressed his leg, you will not return with me. So he had it cut off. A third one gouged his eye when he glanced at a woman. All such things are decisively prohibited in our *Sari`ah* though they were permitted in their law.

Fifth: Perseverance

Committing a sin, one should punish himself as we have already elaborated. Seeing that he lags behind as to doing virtuous deeds, he should overload himself with more activities. `Umar ibn Al-Khattab (may Allah be pleased with him) once missed the congregational Prayer, so he spent that night praying. If one's soul disobeys him, he should let it endure perseveringly. Ibn Al-Mubarak, said, "Souls of the righteous obeyed them in goodness conveniently, but our souls need perseverance." He should seek support in the righteous persons' narrations and their virtues. He should also keep in company with whomever he finds of them and follow his example.

Some one said, "When my resolution weakened, I used to look at Muhammad ibn Wasi` and consider his diligence for a whole week." `Amir ibn Qays used to pray a thousand *Rak`at* a day. Al-Asawd ibn Yazid used to fast until he extremely faints. When Masruq performed *Hajj*, he never slept so much that he fell asleep while prostrating. Dawud At-Ta' used to eat small piece of beard and recite fifty verses between each piece. Karz ibn Wabrah used to recite the whole Qur'an three times a day. Early Muslims used to pray the *Fajr* by the ablution of the `Isha' Prayer. Muhammad Al-Hariri spent a whole year without sleeping or even leaning on a wall. When questioned by Abu Bakr Al-Kittani about it, he replied, I endured it through innate truthfulness.

Sixth: Reprimand

Abu Bakr (may Allah be pleased with him) said, "Who despises his soul for Allah's sake, He will save him from His wrath." Anas (may Allah be pleased with him) said that he heard `Umar ibn Al-Khattab (may Allah be pleased with him) when he entered a garden saying, "Unless you fear Allah, He will torture you, ibn Al-Khattab." Al-Bukhturi ibn Harithah said, "I visited `Abid. I found him kindling a blazing fire and reproving himself so much that he died at once."

You should know that your own soul is your ruthless enemy. It urges man to do wrong. You are commanded to reprove it, leading it with chains of submission to the Almighty's obedience. If neglected, it becomes wild and intractable. You will never be able to hold control over it again. If you keep reprimanding it, it is likely to be reformed. So, you should never overlook reprimanding it. One way of achieving this is to express its ignorance saying, "O soul, how ignorant you are! You pretend intelligence and acumen, but you are totally stupid and foolish. Do you not know that you either enter Paradise or Hellfire? How then can you be indifferent? You may be snatched any day. Do you not know that things change very soon and death is very close? It has no time, nor has it a specific age. It may be in each breath you inhale or exhale. Even if not, you may die suddenly in your deathbed. Thus, why are you not prepared for it? O soul your boldness to commit sin presuming that the Almighty does not see you signifies your unfaithfulness! If you know that He sees you, you are extremely foolish! If you are prevented from obedience by desires, then you should yearn for the eternal pure ones. What do you think of an ill mind prevented from water for three days to restore its health, and then it would be permitted to a ceaseless drink? What should it do? Should it be patient to enjoy good health the rest of life or rather fulfill its temporary desire and keep ailing forever? In that way, your life is naught compared to pleasure in the Hereafter."

One should further address it, saying, "In fact, I wonder which lasts more: the pain of warding off lust patiently or torture in the Hellfire? Failing to endure pain in this life, how can you bear torture in the Hereafter? Are you busy longing for influence? Would not you lose it when become sixty years old? Would you then renounce this world due to its disgrace? Do you substitute your nearness to the Almighty for keeping in company with the fool? You have lost a lot. Only a little remains. You should employ these short days for happiness on the longer ones in the Hereafter. Prepare your answers for the test. Try to leave this world like free men rather than those expelled therefrom. Having day and night, one perishes even if he never moved. Be mindful of this admonition. If ineffective, you should lament your state. Shed tears, since it is a sign of mercy."

IX. Contemplation

The Almighty has commanded contemplation and consideration in numerous verses of the Glorious Qur'an. Commending those who contemplate, He says,

❨*Men who celebrate the praises of Allah, standing, sitting, and lying down on their sides, and contemplate the (wonders of) creation in the heavens and the earth, (with the thought); our Lord not for naught has Thou created (all) this glory to thee give us salvation from the penalty of the fire.*❩

(Al `Imran: 191)

He also says,

❨*Verily in these things there are Signs for those who consider.*❩

(Al-Ra`d: 3)

Abu Ad-Darda' (may Allah be pleased with him) said, "To contemplate for a while is better than praying the whole night." Wahb ibn Munabbih said, "Long contemplation results in understanding, which in turn yields knowledge that is reflected in practice." Bishr Al-Hafi remarked, "If people meditate over the Almighty's Glory, they will never disobey Him." Al-Firiabi commented on the Qur'anic verse that reads,

❨*Those who behave arrogantly on the earth in defiance of right them will I turn away from my Signs; even if they see all the Signs, they will not believe in them.*❩

(Al-A`raf: 146)

"It means that Allah will prevent such person's heart from

mediating over His Signs." Dawud At-Ta'i sat on a roof at a moony night reflecting over the heavens and the earth. Then he fell in his neighbor's house, so he hastened to rescue him. He ran undressed and having the sword in his hand. Seeing him as such, his neighbor asked, "What is that?" Dawud replied, "I did not notice it."

Yusuf ibn Asbat said, "This world is not created to enjoy its good appearance; it is rather designed to enjoy the Hereafter through it." Sufiyan urinated blood due to excessive reflection. Abu Bakr Al-Kattani said, "Entertaining fear on retaining awareness, renouncing worldly gaieties and trembling due to fear from severance outweigh worship of all jinn and men."

Aspects of Contemplation and its Fruits

Contemplation covers religious matters and worldly ones. We are rather concerned with the former. In this respect, man should consider four aspects, namely, obedience, disobedience, means of salvation, and destructive flaws. One should never disregard his soul, his qualities parting him from the Almighty and those drawing him nearer to Allah. Every one should have a daily report where he records his adherence to these four aspects. As for those qualities causing destruction, he should be mindful of ten ones, namely, niggardliness, greed, pride, ostentation, envy, intense anger, excessive desire for food, extreme sexual appetite, love for property, and love for influence.

Likewise, he should also be aware of ten means of salvation, namely, regretting committing sins, enduring affliction patiently, pleasure with the Almighty's Decree, gratitude, keeping a balance between fear and hope, renouncing this world, sincerity, good manners, love and reverence for the Almighty.

Thus, evading an abominable quality, he marks it in his report, disregards it and expresses his gratitude to Allah. He should know that such a thing has taken place by the Almighty's leave. Then, he should consider the rest and does likewise until he gets freed from them all. Moreover, he should impel himself to adopt the means of salvation in the same way. Securing an attribute, he also marks it and become preoccupied with the rest. This is observed by earnest worshippers.

However, most upright persons record in their daily reports obvious disobedience such as doubtful matters, backbiting, hypocrisy, self-conceit, excessive allegiance to rulers, implacable enmity, and the neglect of commanding the good and forbidding the evil. Unless one's heart is purged from such impurities, it cannot be filled with obedience. Thus, the upright ones should reflect over these defects. May Allah reform our hearts and guide us to his pleasure.

Meditation over "the Almighty's Being" Is Forbidden

We have already mentioned the Prophet's (peace and blessings of Allah be upon him) saying,

> "*Meditate over the Almighty's prodigies, but never reflect over His Being.*"
> (Reported by Abud-Dunya)

Human minds cannot grasp His Being. He is indescribable. The Almighty clearly states this fact saying,

> ❴There is nothing whatever like unto Him, and He is the All Hearing and All Seeing.❵
> (Ash-Shura: 11)

The Qur'an contains numerous references to meditation over the Almighty's signs. For example, Allah says,

{*Behold in the creation of the heavens and the earth, and the alternation of night and day, there are indeed Signs for men of understanding.*}
(Al `Imran: 190)

{*Say: behold all that is in the heavens and on earth.*}
(Yunus: 101)

Among the Almighty's signs is the creation of man. So one should reflect over his creation. His creation reflects the Almighty's Glory. Allah has commanded man to meditate over himself saying,

{*As also in your own selves: will you not then see?*}
(Adh-Dhariyat: 21)

We have already elaborated some aspects of man's creation under "Gratitude". Furthermore, among His signs are the jewels, minerals, gold, silver, oil, sulfur, etc. Among these portents are also the vast sees and oceans surrounding the earth and its continents. The whole land is like a small island compared to the sees. They, in turn, contain more outstanding marvels than those we notice on earth. We may take the pearl as an example. Consider how it is fo rmed within a shell under water. Think also how corals grow in rocks under water. We may move to ships and how the Almighty has caused them to maintain their balance on the surface of water and how they are driven on water by the wind. In fact, water itsel f is an amazing prodigy. It is the source of life on earth. Being thirsty, one is ready to spare everything he has to drink. Drinking water but being unable to excrete it, he will do the same to have it excreted. Thus, every one should be mindful of this g reat bless.

In the same vein, we should also think of air. It is indiscernible with the naked eye. Nevertheless, it is terribly intense. Consider the weather, its clouds, rains, hurricanes, lightening, thunder, etc. We should also reflect over birds flying in the sky like see creatures swimming in water. We should also meditate over the heavens, its spaciousness, planets, the sun, and the moon. All its bodies are designed for a certain wisdom determined by the Almighty. We should think of the day and night; how they are interlocked, how the sun circles, and how the seasons are brought about.

In fact, scientists have discovered that the sun is about one hundred and sixty times more than the earth. The smallest planet is eight times bigger than the earth. Then , what about the other innumerable planets. It is also amazing that on entering a good decorated house, one likes it and never forgets it. Likewise, we look at this massive structure, its ground, its ceiling, its marvels, and decorations, but our hearts ar e never moved thereby. We do not even think of our own structure. We have become preoccupied with our lusts, thus we are like a tiny ant. Seeking food in a palace, it meets another ant in its hole. Thus, it wonders over its beautiful cell and forgets all about the palace. We do the same. Our scope of knowledge and consideration is similar to that ant.

These are some examples where contemplation is exercised. In fact, sciences fail to wholly decide the depth of some creatures. However, the more prodigies you reach of these creatures, the more you become acquainted with the Almighty's Glory. So you should meditate over what we have already cited under "Gratitude". Considering such objects as being made by the Almighty, one gains more knowledge about His Magnificence and Sublimity. Otherwise, one falls in distress and worry. May the Almighty guard us against ignorant persons and means of destruction!

Finally, reflecting over the Angels and Jinn is of no avail, since we do not behold them; so we should confine ou r selves with visible objects.

X. Remembering Death and Life after It

Every one preoccupied with this world and its gaieties has a negligent heart. He is never mindful of death. Even if he remembers it, he abhors it. In fact, people are of three types, namely, an indulgent, a fresh repentant, or an aware cognizant.

The indulgent man never thinks of death. If he remembers it, he does so only to lament his life and disdain it. Such a type is drawn farther from the Almighty.

As for the repentant, he often thinks of death to entertain fear, so his repentance is completed. He may hate death lest it should overtake him before effecting his repentance or being properly prepared. In that way, his detest is justified, so he does not fall under the Prophet's (peace and blessings of Allah be upon him) saying,

> "*He who hates the meeting with Allah, Allah hates the meeting with him too.*"
> (Reported by Al-Bukhari)

Such a person hates returning to the Almighty due to his shortcomings and defects. He resembles a man who adjourns seeing a beloved until he gets properly prepared. This is marked by his constant readiness and awareness. Otherwise, he joins the first kind.

Coming to the aware cognizant, he is always heedful of death since it means meeting the beloved One. He never forgets this. Such a type of people mostly accelerates death to get rid of disobedient persons and enjoy the company of the Almighty. Some one said, "May a pain lead to the beloved." The repentant one is excused for his detest to death, while the cognizant's love for death is justified. However, there is a more supreme state; it is to trust totally in the Almighty. Thus, he loves what Allah loves and detests what He hates. Due to this utmost love and faithfulness to Allah, one has given up all things to Him and got pleased therewith.

Nevertheless, remembering death commands greater rewards, since indulgent people may renounce this world due to their remembrance of death.

Virtue of Remembering Death

Abu Hurayrah (may Allah be pleased with him) narrated that the Prophet (peace and blessings of Allah be upon him) said,

> *"You should frequently remember what renders delights turbid; that is death."*
>
> (Reported by At-Tirmidhi)

Anas (may Allah be pleased with him) reported,

> *"A man was highly praised before the Prophet (peace and blessings of Allah be upon him). So he said, 'How did he remember death?' They replied that they never heard him mentioning it. Thus, he remarked, 'Accordingly, he does not deserve your praise.'"*
>
> (Reported by Abud-Dunya)

Ibn `Umar narrated,

> *"The Prophet (peace and blessings of Allah be upon him) was once asked, 'Who is the most sagacious of people?' He answered, 'It is he who remembers*

death most and get properly prepared for it.'"
(Reported by ibn Majah)

Al-Hasan Al-Basri said, "Death has exposed this world, leaving no delight for sensible people therein." As a result of constant remembrance of death, this world become very trivial in one's eyes. He even easily renounces it. When ibn `Umar (may Allah be pleased with them both) remembered death, he trembled like birds. He used to convene with jurists every night talking about death and the Hereafter. Then, they shed tears as if they were in a funeral. Hamid Al-Qaysari said, "Though we know that death is certain, we have not prepared ourselves for it. Though we know that Paradise is definite, we have not worked for it. Though we know that Hell is sure, we have not feared it. So why are you delighted? What are you waiting for? Death is the first visitor from the Almighty, bringing good or evil tidings. Brothers, get goodly closer to your Lord." Shumayt ibn `Aglan said, "Being mindful of death, one never cares for this world's delights or hardships."

You should know that death is absolutely serious. However, people have neglected death due to their scarce remembrance of it. Even when they remember it, their hearts are forgetful. Thus, remembering death, in this way, is ineffective. The sole way out of this dilemma is to devote your heart to thinking of death. Like a traveler to a wild desert or sea, he is only preoccupied by his anxiety. The best assistance is to consider his mates and predecessors; remembering their demise and burial.

Ibn Mas`ud (may Allah be pleased with him) said, "He is delighted who is admonished by others' affliction." Abu Ad-Darda' (may Allah be pleased with him) said, "Remembering the majority who have passed away, consider that you are joining them." one should frequently visit graveyards. Securing something in this world, one should recognize that they would part. He should not p in great aspirations. `Abdullah ibn `Umar (may Allah be pleased with them both) narrated that Allah's Messenger (peace and blessings of Allah be upon him) took hold of my shoulder and said,

> *"Be in this world as if you were a stranger or a traveler." The sub-narrator added: Ibn `Umar (may Allah be pleased with them both) used to say, "If you survive until the evening, do not expect to be alive in the morning, and if you survive until the morning, do not expect to be alive in the evening, and take from your health for your sickness, and (take) from your life for your death."*
>
> (Reported by Al-Bukhari)

Al-Hasan narrated that the Prophet (peace and blessings of Allah be upon him) said to his Companions (may Allah be pleased with them),

> *"Do you all love to be admitted into Paradise?" They all answered in the affirmative. Then he (peace and blessings of Allah be upon him) added, "Then you should limit your aspirations, be fully aware of your death, and be properly bashful before the Almighty."*
>
> (Reported by Abu Ad-Dunya)

Abu Zakariya At-Taymi said: While Sulayman ibn `Abd Al-Malik was in the mosque, a stone, having something inscribed on it, was brought before him. He summoned some one to read it. It was written, 'O son of Adam, if you knew the remaining term of your life, you would give up your hopes, wish to enhance your deeds and lessen your endeavors. You will regret it only when you sin, your life comes to an end and be separated from your kindred. You will neither return to this world, nor have your good deeds inc reased. So get your self prepared for the Hereafter, where remorse and sorrow prevail.

Causes of Unlimited Aspirations

Unlimited aspirations are brought about by two vital reasons, namely,

1- Love for this world: When one gets possessed by it, its desires, and its gaieties, his heart fails to renounce it. In this way, it never thinks of death for it turns them apart. Detest for something drives one to avoid it. Man leads a life of wishful thinking, such as eternity in this world. He seeks all the means, which he wrongfully thinks to enhance his wishes. So he neglects death and its being virtually close. Even if he remembers death and his need to be prepared for it, he postpones presuming, "Days are coming, so you will repent when you become older." Even when he advances in age, he further adjourns repentance to a latter time until he breathes his last. He continues doing so until he is suddenly overtaken by death. Thence, his regret lasts. Most residents of Hell lament saying "we will". All such wishes are cause d by love for this world and negligence. The Prophet (peace and blessings of Allah be upon him) said,

"Love whatever you want for you are separated."
(Reported by Ash-Shawkani)

2- Ignorance: In this respect, man depends on his youthfulness, precluding death i n that young age. We wonder: does he not know that if the old among the dead returned to life, they would be only one -tenth? This is due to the fact death mostly afflicts the young. Man may be deluded by his health ignoring that death comes suddenly.

Even if not, one falls ill unexpectedly. Being ill, death comes closer. If one knows that death has no specific time such as winter or summer, day or night, nor does it have a specific age, he will surly get himself prepared for it.

Variation in People's Aspirations

People vary greatly in their aspirations. Some of them wish to have a very long life. Some of them have endless wishes. Others enjoy limited aspirations. Abu `Uthman Al-Hindi said, "I am a hundred and thirty years old. I have recognized that everything diminishes but for my aspirations. They have never waned." As for limited aspirations, Habib ibn Muhammad's wife said that Habib used to tell me, "If I die today, get so-and-so to bath me." She was asked if he had seen a dream of his death. She replied that he used to tell her likewise every day. Ibrahim ibn Sibt was addressed by Abu Zar`ah, "I will tell you something. I have never left the mosque since twenty years but my soul asks me to return." Some one was asked, "Do you not wash your robe?" He replied, "Death is more close that to wash it." Muhammad ibn Abu Tawbah narrated that Ma`ruf called for Prayer and asked me to lead them. Muhammad said, "Leading you in this Prayer, I will not lead you in another." Ma`ruf remarked, "Do you wish to perform another Prayer? May Allah guard us against long aspirations, since they annul good deeds."

In that way, the ascetics lead a life of short aspirations. The more limited your aspirations are, the more perfect your deeds become, for you expect death. Therefore, you get yourself properly prepared for it. Living until the evening, you should express your gratitude to the Almighty. The Prophet (peace and blessings of Allah be upon him) said,

> "There are two blessings which many people are

> *unaware of their value: (They are) Health and free time (for doing good)."*
>
> (Reported by Al-Bukhari)

Likewise, he (peace and blessings of Allah be upon him) said,

> *"Make use of five before you are overtaken by other five. Take from your youth to your senility, from your health for your sickness, from your richness to your poverty, from your free time to your busy one, and from your life for your death."*
>
> (Reported by Al-Hakim)

`Umar (may Allah be pleased with him) said, "Slowness is recommended in everything unless it has to do with the Hereafter." Al-Hasan used to say, "I wonder about people commanded to take provision and called to leave this world, but they all are unwise and negligent." Sahim said, "I waited for `Abdullah ibn `Abdullah. Finishing his Prayer, he addressed me, 'Tell me your question very quickly for I expect a visitor.' I asked, 'Whom do you expect?' He answered, 'The Angel of death.'" Abdullah used to pray about a thousand *Rak`at* a day. Early Muslims used to increase their good deeds as far as they could. Ibn `Umar (may Allah be pleased with them both) used to pray at night, then sleep for a little time and pray again. He used to do so for several times in one night. `Umayr ibn Hai' used to hymn the Almighty's praise for over a hundred thousand times a day. Abu Bakr ibn `Ayyash remarked that he has recited the whole Qur'an eighteen thousand times.

Agonies of Death

Death disturbs man's life and spoils it. If man enjoys the

best delights but he expects some one to kill him, his life and pleasures will be unsettled. In fact, A ngel of death, `Uzra'il, is expected to visit one any moment, but he is neglectful. This is due to ignorance and conceit. You should know that the agonies of death are more intense than a sword. Smitten with a sword, one may cry for help, for he still main tains his power, but a dying man becomes dumb out of his sufferings. He is so overwhelmed by anguish that all his body becomes weak and paralyzed. He even wishes being able to release a single cry to appease his affliction. His spirit is taken away from hi s body, starting with his legs till his uvula. Hence, he cannot repent any more. The Prophet (peace and blessings of Allah be upon him) said,

> *"Allah accepts a servant's repentance so long as he is not dying."*
>
> (Reported by At-Tirmidhi)

It is also reported the Angels entrusted with keeping company of a servant appear before him on his death. If he is righteous, they praise him. Otherwise, they condemn him. The Prophet (peace and blessings of Allah be upon him) said,

> *"When a believer (at the time of death) is given the glad tidings of the mercy of Allah, His Pleasure, and of Paradise, he loves to meet Allah, and Allah also loves to meet him, and when an unbeliever is given the news of the torment at the Hand of Allah, and Hardship to be imposed by Him, he dislikes to meet Allah and Allah also abhors to meet him."*
>
> (Reported by Muslim)

Early Muslims feared from ending their lives in state of sin or disobedience. We have elaborated this point under "Fear".

There are some commendable things to be observed by a dying person. First, his heart should think good of the Almighty. His tongue should pronounce the *Shahadah* (testifying that there is no god but Allah, and that Muhammad is the Messenger of Allah). Remaining motionless is a sign of mercy. It signifies that he has seen something good. We should ask him to pronounce the *Shahadah*. Abu Sa`id Al-Khudri (may Allah be pleased with him) reported that the Prophet (peace and blessings of Allah be upon him) said,

> *"Exhort to recite "There is no god but Allah" to those of you who are dying."*
> (Reported by Muslim)

This should be done kindly and gently. Jabir ibn `Adullah (may Allah be pleased with him reported that the Prophet (peace and blessings of Allah be upon him) said,

> *"None of you should die but hoping only good from Allah, the Exalted and Glorious."*
> (Reported by Muslim)

Anas ibn Malik (may Allah be pleased by him) narrated,

> *"The Prophet (peace and blessings of Allah be upon him) visited a dying person. He asked him, "What do you think of your self?" He replied, "I hope good from Allah and fear my sins." He remarked, "When a servant entertains these both in this state, Allah grants him his hope and secures his fear."*
> (Reported by At-Tirmidhi)

In fact, hope is better in this situation, since fear requires activity but it is now no more. In this state, Satan tries to saw disgust against the Almighty's Decree and intimidate man.

Thus, good hope in the Almighty is the best weapon to disperse an enemy. On his death, Sulayman At-Taymi asked his son to highlight the Almighty's dispensations so that he should return to the Him hoping good from Him.

The Prophet's Demise (peace and blessings of Allah be upon him)

You should know that the Prophet (peace and blessings of Allah be upon him) provided a good example in all aspects of his life. It is also known that no other creature is closer to the Almighty than him. However, the Almighty did not postpone his demise when he fulfilled his term on earth. He (peace and blessings of Allah be upon him) suffered the agonies of death. `A'ishah (may Allah be pleased with her) narrated,

> *"There was a leather or wood container full of water in front of Allah's Messenger (at the time of his death). He would put his hand into the water and rub his face with it, saying, "None has the right to be worshipped but Allah! No doubt, death has its agonies."*
>
> (Reported by Al-Bukhari)

Anas ibn Malik (may Allah be pleased with him) also reported,

> *"When the ailment of the Prophet (peace and blessings of Allah be upon him) got aggravated, he became unconscious whereupon Fatimah said, 'Oh, how distressed my father is!' He said, 'Your father will have no more distress after today.'"*
>
> (Reported by Al-Bukhari)

Ibn Mas`ud narrated, "We gathered in our mother

`A'ishah's room. The Prophet looked at us and said,

> 'Welcome, may Allah greet you with peace! May He guard, protect, unite, defend, support, elevate, and integrate you! Keep piety. I keep you in the trust of Allah.' Then we asked, 'When is your term?' He replied, 'It is very close now. My return is to the Almighty and the Highest Paradise.' Then we asked, 'In what cloth should we wrap you?' He said, 'In my clothes if you desire. Otherwise, it should be Yemeni or white clothes.' Then we asked, 'Who should lead your funeral Prayer?' And we cried. He said, 'May Allah be merciful to you and reward you for your Prophet! On bathing and wrapping me, put me on my bed. Then leave me alone for an hour. My funeral Prayer is first observed by my beloved friend Jibril, and then by Mika'il, Israfil, `Uzra'il, and many angels. After that, you offer my funeral Prayer in groups. You should never hurt me with praise, crying, or shouting. Men amongst my family should observe my funeral Prayer first, and then women amongst my family should observe it. Then you follow them. Mention me to my absent companions and those who follow me until the Day of Judgment. Now you witness that I have greeted with peace all adherents to Islam."

(Reported by ibn Sa`d)

Angel Jibril, Gabriel, visited the Prophet (peace and blessings of Allah be upon him) three days before his demise saying, "O Muhammad, the Almighty has sent inquiring about what He knows best. He asks, 'How do you fell?'" He answered, "Gabriel, I feel distressed and worried." Then he visited him on the second day repeating the same words. The

Prophet answered likewise. He visited him on the third day asking him the same question. The Prophet gave the same answer. Thence, the Angel of death sought permission to get in. Hence, Gabriel said, "O Ahmad, this is the Angel of death seeking permission to come in. This is the first and last time to seek permission from a human being." The prophet (peace and blessings of Allah be upon him) gave him permission. Coming in, `Uzra'il said, the Almighty has sent me and commanded me to obey you. You are either to command me to take your spirit or leave it. The Prophet (peace and blessings of Allah be upon him) wondered, "Would you do so?" He replied, "I am commanded to obey you."

Then Gabriel said, "O Ahmad, the Almighty longs for you." Whereupon, he said, "O Angel of death, fulfil your mission." Hence, Gabriel said, "Peace be with you Prophet of Allah. This is my last visit to earth. You were my end in this world."

The Prophet (peace and blessings of Allah be upon him) breathed his last while leaning on `A'ishah's chest wearing harsh woolen cloth as reported by Al-Bukhari. Anas ibn Malik (may Allah be pleased with him) reported,

> *"When the ailment of the Prophet got aggravated, he became unconscious whereupon Fatimah said, 'Oh, how distressed my father is!' He said, 'Your father will have no more distress after today.' When he expired, she said, 'O Father! Who has responded to the call of the Lord Who has invited him! O Father, whose dwelling place is the Garden of Paradise (i.e., Al-Firdaus)! O Father! We convey this news (of your death) to Gabriel.' When he was buried, Fatimah said, 'O Anas! Do you feel pleased*

to throw earth over Allah's Messenger?'"
                                        (Reported by Al-Bukhari)

The Death of Abu Bakr (may Allah be pleased with him)

Abu Mulaih narrated that when Abu Bakr (may Allah be pleased with him) was about to die, he summoned `Umar (may Allah be pleased with him). He said, "I commend you with some advice. The Almighty has a right on you at night, which He never admits on day. He also has a right on daytime which He never accepts at night. The Almighty also never admits voluntary worship unless the obligatory one is observed. Scales of Judgement are weighty by adherence to truth in this world. Otherwise, they are insubstantial. Do you not notice the Almighty has joined verses of hope with those of intimidation and the *vice versa* so that man should be consider both of them rather than undermining himself. Being mindful of this counsel, your death will be the dearest absent thing for you. Otherwise, it will be the most dete stable; though you must face it one day."

At the time of Abu Bakr's death, his daughter, `A'ishah (may Allah be pleased with her), expressed her grief when the former said to her, "You should rather say,

> ⟨*And the anguish of death will bring truth (before his eyes): This was the thing, which thou was trying to escape!*⟩
>   (Qaf: 19)

Then he remarked, these are my robes, wash them and wrap me within. The dead need nothing new anymore.

The Death of `Umar ibn Al-Khattab (may Allah be pleased with him)

Ibn `Umar (may Allah be pleased with them both) narrated that after `Umar was stabbed, he put his head on my thigh. But he asked me to put his face on the ground. I wondered what difference did it make? I thought he was annoyed but he was not. He repeated, "Put my cheek on the ground; woe to me and my mother if Allah has no mercy on me."

Al-Bukhari reported on the authority of ` Amr ibn Maimun (may Allah be pleased with him) that the latter said,

"I saw `Umar ibn Al-Khattab (when he was stabbed) saying, 'O `Abdullah ibn `Umar! Go to the mother of the believers, `A'ishah, and say: `Umar ibn Al-Khattab sends his greetings to you. And, request her to allow me to be buried with my companions.' So, Ibn `Umar conveyed the message to `A'ishah. She said, 'I had the idea of having this place for myself but today I prefer him (`Umar) to myself (and allow him to be buried there).' When `Abdullah ibn `Umar returned, `Umar asked him, 'What (news) do you have?'" He replied, "O Commander of the Believers! She has allowed you (to be buried there).' On that `Umar said, 'Nothing was more important to me than to be buried in that (sacred) place. So, when I expire, carry me there and pay my greetings to her (`A'ishah ) and say: `Umar ibn Al-Khattab asks permission; and if she gives permission, then bury me (there) and if she does not, then take me to the graveyard of the Muslims.'"

Meanwhile, a young man from Ansar came and said, "O Commander of the Believers! Be happy with Allah's glad tidings. The grade which you have in Islam is known to you, then you became the caliph and you ruled with justice and then you have been awarded martyrdom after all this." `Umar replied, "O son of my brother! Would that all that privileges will counterbalance (my shortcomings), so that I neither lose nor gain anything." Al-Bukhari also reported that 'Umar (may Allah be pleased with him) said, "If I have as much gold as the whole earth, I will spend it to be saved from Allah's punishment before I meet it." The same statement is also narrated by Imam Ahmad.

The Death of 'Uthman ibn 'Affan (may Allah be pleased with him)

Na'iah bint Al-Frafisah, 'Uthman's wife (may Allah be pleased with him) narrated, "'Uthman fasted the day before his murder. On his break of the fast, he asked for water, but they did not give him water. So he slept without breaking his fast. Before the dawn, some women brought jars filled with water. I asked them for some water and they gave me a cup. Then I awakened him saying, "This is fresh water." However, he noticed that the *Fajr* was due so that he said, "I am fasting. The Prophet (peace and blessings of Allah be upon him) has visited me tonight and gave me fresh water saying: Drink 'Uthman! Then I drank until I quenched my thirst. Then, he (peace and blessings of Allah be upon him) said: Drink more! Then I drank more and more. Then he (peace and blessings of Allah be upon him) said: People will revolt against you. If you fight them, you will defeat them. But if you leave them, you will break your fast with us in heavens.' Then they entered the house and killed him."

Al-'Ala' ibn Al-Fudayl reported from his father that when 'Uthman was murdered, people searched his house and opened his safe. They found a closed box. Opening it, they found a piece of paper written on it, "This is 'Uthman's bequest. I, 'Uthman ibn 'Affan, testify that there is no god but Allah and that Muhammad is His Messenger and servant. Paradise is true. Hell-fire is true. Resurrection after death is true. The Almighty never breaks His Promise. By this testimony, we live, die, and be resurrected by the Almighty's leave."

The Death of `Ali ibn Abi Talib (may Allah be pleased with him)

As-Sha`bi narrated, "When `Ali was stabbed, he asked: What have you done to my murderer? They replied: He is imprisoned. He said: Feed him from my foo d and give him my water to drink. If I live, I will consider his case. But if I die, you should smite him once. Then he asked Al -Hasan to bathe him saying: Do not exaggerate my wrappings since I heard the Prophet (peace and blessings of Allah be upon him) say,

> *"Do not exaggerate your death wrappings since they are quickly worn out."*
> (Reported by Abu Dawud)

He then said, "Carrying me, walk in a moderate way, neither quickly nor slowly. If it is good, you will hasten me for it. Otherwise, you will be relieved me from." It is also reported that at the night when he died, At -Tayyah reached him at Dawn informing him of *Fajr* Prayer. He was grumpily leaning. Then he informed him for the second and the third times. `Ali (may Allah be pleased with him) went and when he reached the door, ibn Muljam stabbed him.

Miscellaneous Accounts about Death

When Al-Hasan ibn `Ali (may Allah be pleased with them) was dying, he asked people to take him out to the hall. Then he said: O Lord, I trust myself in You.

On his death, Mu`ad h ibn Jabal (may Allah be pleased with

him) said: Look if the day has broken? They looked and answered in the negative. Latter on, he was informed that it was morning. Then he remarked: I seek refuge in Allah from a night whose morning leads to Hell-fire. Welcome to death, an absent visitor and a beloved returning while we are defected. O Lord, I used to fear You, but now I expect good from You. You know that I never loved this world or long stay in it. I used to observe fasting on extremely hot days, praying at long nights of winter, and joining scholars in their circles of knowledge.

Abu Muslim said, "I visited Abu Ad-Darda' on his death. He said, 'Would you get prepared for this day and for this hour?' Then he breathed his last."

Salman Al-Farisi wept on his death. Asked about this, he said, "The Prophet (peace and blessings of Allah be upon him) commanded us to have sufficient provision for the Hereafter."

Al-Mazni said that he visited Ash-Shafi`i on his deathbed. He said, "I asked him, 'how are you?' He replied, 'I am leaving this world, leaving my brothers, meeting my sins, drinking the cup of death, and returning to the Almighty. But I do not know to Hell or into Paradise my spirit will be admitted.'"

Visiting the Graveyard

Abu Ad-Darda' (may Allah be pleased with him) was once asked about his visit to graves. He said, "I visit people who remind me of my death. They never backbite me when I depart."

Maymun ibn Mahran said, "I joined `Umar ibn `Abd Al-`Aziz in his visit to graves. Beholding them, he wept and told me, 'Maymun, these are the tombs of my predecessors from Bani Umayyah. Look, as if they never shared this world's delights. Do you not see them lying being exemplary for others? They have decayed.' Then he shed tears and said, 'By Allah, I know none better that the dead who have been saved from the Almighty's torture.'"

It is recommended to visit the graveyard since the Prophet (peace and blessings of Allah be upon him) said,

> *"Visit the graves for they remind you of the Hereafter."*
>
> (Reported by Muslim)

When visiting graves, one should reach the dead by his face, recite some verses of the Qur'an, and gift their rewards for him. It is recommended to be on Friday.

When `Asim Al-Jahdri died, he was in a dream after two years. He was asked, "Have you returned?" He answered in the negative. The man asked, "Where are you?" He replied, "In a garden of Paradise with some of my friends. We meet every Friday night by Abu Bakr ibn `Abdullah Al-Mazni to receive your news." He asked, "By your bodies or spirits?" He said, "Our bodies have decayed. But our spirits meet." He asked, "Do you feel our visit?" He answered that they know this on Friday evening until sunrise on Saturday. He asked, "Why on these specific days?" He replied, "Due to the virtue of Friday." `Uthman ibn Sawad At-Tafawi said that when his mother was dying, she looked up to heavens and said, "O my Support and Relief, in Whom I trust in this world and after death; please do not forsake me nor leave me alone in my grave!" Then she died. He said, "I used to visit her grave every Friday, and pray for her. One night, I saw her in a dream. I asked her, 'How are you mother?' She answered,

'Son, death is a severe anguish. I am now in a good place until the Day of Judgment.' I asked, 'Do you want anything?' She said, 'Never interrupt your visit to us since I am delighted with your visit. In fact, all the dead here are pleased with your visit.'"

Anas ibn Mansur said that there was a man who used to observe funeral Prayer. In the evening, he would visit the graves and say (addressing the dead ones), "May Allah soothe your loneliness and admit your good deeds." He never uttered more words. Then he said, "One night, I did not visit the graves to offer the same supplication. When I was asleep, I saw many people coming towards me. I asked, 'Who are you? What do you want?' They answered, 'We are the dead who used to receive a gift from you.' I wondered, 'What is that?' They replied, 'Your supplications.' I said, 'I would offer them forever.'"

Bashshar ibn Ghalib said, "I saw Rabi`ah in a dream. I used to pray frequently for her. She said, 'Bashshar, we receive your gifts on plates of light covered with silk. I wondered, 'How is that?' She replied, 'Thus are the supplications offered by those alive for the dead. They are granted. They are put on plates of light covered with silk, then brought to their recipients who are addressed: Here is a gift for you.'"

The Nature of Death

The verses of the Glorious Qur'an and many *Ahadith* prove that death signifies departure of the spirit from the body. The spirit then lasts enduring torture or enjoying pleasure. The spirit itself feels pains of anguish and distress as well as the joys of pleasure and bliss. It maintains all its attributes even after leaving the body. However, all its physical attachments come to an end until it returns to the body once more. It is probable to be restored in the grave or rather adjourned until the Day of Judgment. The Almighty alone knows best.

In this way, death means separation of the spirit from th e physique, which ceases in its turn to be its tool. It signifies man's exit from this world, his belongings, and his fellows to another world totally different. If he has a source of joy in this world, he becomes severely distressed by death. If he is delighted by remembering the Almighty, he is immensely pleased by his closeness to Him and being dissociated from worldly gaieties since they distract him therefrom. By death, many things are revealed to man like a sleeping person who perceives things after h is awakening. The first thing revealed to him is his good deeds and sins. They all are recorded in his heart but he was unaware of them due to his indulgence. When one's life comes to an end, all hidden secrets are disclosed. Thus, he strongly regrets his sins so much that he wishes to enter Hell to be saved therefrom. All these anxieties are undergone by disobedient persons before being buried. May Allah save us! The fact that spirits never perish after death is what the Almighty says,

> ❴*Think not of those who are slain in Allah's way as dead. Nay, they live, finding their sustenance in the presence of their Lord.*❵
>
> (Al `Imran: 169)

Masruq narraeted, "We asked `Abdullah ibn Mas`ud about this verse. He said, 'We asked about the meaning of this verse from the Prophet (peace and blessings of Allah be upon him) who said,

> *'The souls of the martyrs live in the bodies of green birds who have their nests in chandeliers hung from*

the throne of the Almighty. They eat the fruits of Paradise from wherever they like and then nestle in these chandeliers.'"

(Reported by Muslim)

The Almighty also says in the Qur'an,

❨*In front of the Fire will they be brought, morning and evening: and (the Sentence will be) on the Day that judgment will be established: Cast you the People of Pharaoh into the severest Penalty!*❩

(Ghafir: 46)

This Qur'anic verse proves that disobedient persons are tortured after their death. Likewise, ibn `Umar (may Allah be pleased with them both) narrated that the Prophet (peace and blessings of Allah be upon him) said,

"When any one of you dies, he is shown his seat (in the Hereafter) morning and evening; if he is amongst the inmates of Paradise, (he is shown the seat) from amongst the inmates of Paradise and if he is one from amongst the denizens of Hell, (he is shown the seat) from amongst the denizens of Hell, and it would be said to him: That is your seat until Allah raises you on the Day of Resurrection (and sends you to your proper seat)."

(Reported by Muslim)

We have already said that a disobedient regrets his sins. As for the believer, `Abdullah ibn `Umar (may Allah be pleased with them) remarked, "The parable of a believer when his spirit is taken out of his body is that of a prisoner who is set free. He journeys through the earth safe and sound. After his death, many of the Almighty's favors and graces are disclosed to the believer in a way that resembles a prisoner in a dark frightful house who suddenly has a very wide door opened before him. It leads to a very spacious garden. It is full of various trees. Thus, he does not like returning to this world, as he hates being back in his mother's womb."

In addition, Mujahid said, "Furthermore, a believer is given the glad tidings of his child's righteousness after him to be pleased therewith."

The Grave

The Prophet (peace and blessings of Allah be upon him) said,

> *"The grave addresses the dead saying: Woe to you, son of Adam. What has seduced you? Did you not know that I am the house of darkness, loneliness, and worms."*
>
> (Reported by At-Tabarani)

Abu Sa`id (may Allah be pleased with him) narrated that one day the Prophet (peace ad blessings of Allah be upon him) entered his mosque. Finding numerous people chatting about this world, the Prophet (peace ad blessings of Allah be upon him) said,

> *"If you frequently remember what turns delights turbid, you will be distracted from your present state. Thus, remember it very often. Everyday, the grave says: I am the house of alienation, loneliness, dust, and worms. Receiving a righteous resident, the grave welcomes him and says: Being the most beloved visitor in your life, and being my resident now, you will see what I have prepared for you.*

> *Thus it becomes as vast as he can see. Then he has a door to Paradise opened before him. In contrast, receiving a sinful or a disbelieving resident, it does not welcome him. But it says: Being the most detestable visitor in your life, being my guest now, you will see what I have prepared for you. Then it withholds him so much that his ribs get juxtaposed."*
>
> (Reported by At-Tirmidhi)

Ka`b said, when the righteous person is buried, his good deeds such as Prayers, Fasting, *Hajj*, *Jihad*, and charity surround him. When the angels of torture reach him by his legs, his Prayers say: Leave him, he has prayed for the Almighty's sake. Reaching him by his head, Fasting says likewise. Then, reaching him by his body, both *Hajj* and *Jihad* say: Leave him, he has devoted himself and endured hardships for Allah's sake. Coming to him by his hands, charity says: Leave him; these hands have spent much alms that h ave been admitted by the Almighty. Thus, he is addressed: You are pleased in your life and death. Then the angels of mercy reach him preparing his grave with mats and robes from Paradise. His grave become as vast as he can see. It is enlightened by the light of Paradise.

Anas ibn Malik (may Allah be pleased with him) narrated that the Prophet (peace and blessings of Allah be upon him) said,

> *"When a human being is laid in his grave and his companions return and he even hears their foot steps, two angels come to him and make him sit and ask him: What did you use to say about this man, Muhammad? He will say: I testify that he is Allah's servant and His Messenger. Then it will be said to*

him: Look at your place in the Hell-Fire. Allah has given you a place in Paradise instead of it. The Prophet added, 'The dead person will see both his places. But a non-believer or a hypocrite will say to the angels: I do not know, but I used to say what the people used to say! It will be said to him, 'Neither did you know nor did you take the guidance (by reciting the Qur'an).' Then he will be hit with an iron hammer between his two ears, and he will cry and that cry will be heard by whatever approaches him except human beings and Jinn."

(Reported by Al-Bukhari)

A similar *Hadith* is also reported by Al-Bukhari on the authority of Asma' bint Abi Bakr (may Allah be pleased with them both). Ibn `Abbas (may Allah be pleased with them both) narrated,

"When we followed the funeral of Sa`d ibn Mu`adh (may Allah be pleased with him) and buried him, the Prophet (peace and blessings of Allah be upon him) looked at us and said, 'Everyone suffers tightening in the grave. Verily, if anyone were to escape this tightening, he would be Sa`d ibn Mu`adh.'"

(Reported by Ahmad)

`Abdullah As-San`ani aid, "I saw Yazid ibn Harun in a dream four nights after his death. I asked him what had been done to him. He answered, 'My good deeds have been admitted and my sins remitted.' I then asked, 'Then what happened?' He replied, 'What do you expect from the All Generous? He has forgiven me and admitted me into Paradise.' I asked, 'How have you achieved this?' He said, 'By attending circles of knowledge, telling the truth, praying at night, and enduring poverty patiently.' I asked, 'What about *Munkar* and *Nakir*?' He said, 'By Allah, they have made me sit and asked me: Who is your Lord? What is your religion? Who is your Prophet? Then I removed dust from my white beard and said, 'I am Yzid ibn Harun Al-Wasiti. I spent sixty years teaching people.' Then one said, 'You have spoken rightly. He is Yazid ibn Harun. Now rest like a pride. No fear reaches you from now on.'"

Al-Maruzi said, "In a dream, I saw Ahmad ibn Hanbal in a garden wearing two green robes and having a crown from light over his head. He walked in a way un familiar to me. Then I said, 'Ahmad, what about your walk?' He said, 'This is the walk of servants in the abode of peace (Darus -Salam).' Then I asked about his crown. He said, 'The Almighty has stationed me and accounted me lightly. Then He has adorned me and drawn me closer to Him. I behold Him. He has given me this crown saying, 'O Ahmad, this is the crown of reverence as you have said the Qur'an is not created.'"

States of the Dead since the Trumpet is Sounded until Admittance to Paradise or Hell

We have already dealt with agonies of the grave. Now we handle sounding the Trumpet, Resurrection, *Hisab*, setting the Balance, and the *Sirat*. We must believe in and contemplate over them. The majority of people do not firmly believe in the Hereafter. If man does not notice the process of procreation among animals, and he is informed about his creation from such a trivial sperm, he will never believe. In that way, man's first creation is rather more wonderful than his resurrection. How can one deny the Almighty's O mnipotence and Wisdom in this respect! If your faith in not grounded, you should enhance it by considering the first creation. Moreover, if your faith is firm, you should entertain fear from such worries and perils. You should frequently contemplate over them and be urged thereby to exert your utmost in doing good. The first sound heard by the dead is that of Israfil when he blows the Trumpet. Thus, imagine yourself being resurrected and dazzled responding to the sound. The Almighty says,

> ❴*The Trumpet shall be sounded, when behold from the sepulchres (men) will rush forth to their Lord.*❵
> (Yasin: 51)

Abu sa`id Al-Khudri (may Allah be pleased with him) reported that the Prophet (peace and blessings of Allah be upon him) said,

> *"How can I be delighted since the angel entrusted with sounding the Trumpet has prepared himself bending his forehead and listening with his ears; waiting for the command to blow the Trumpet! Muslims wondered, 'What should we say, O Messenger of Allah?' He said, 'You should repeat, for us Allah suffices and he is the best Disposer of affairs.'"*
> (Reported by At-Tirmidhi)

You should also think of people's resurrection barefooted and naked to the Land of Gathering. The Prophet (peace and blessings of Allah be upon him) said,

> *"The people will be gathered on the Day of Resurrection on reddish white land like a pure loaf of bread (made of pure fine flour)."*
> (Reported by Al-Bukhari)

Then you should consider the crowds of people and nearness of the sun to their heads, and their worries and sweat.

The Prophet (peace and blessings of Allah be upon him) also said,

> "People will be overwhelmed with sweat according to their deeds."
>
> (Reported by At-Tirmidhi)

Furthermore, meditate over your *Hisab* before your Lord. The Prophet (peace and blessings of Allah b e upon him) said,

> "No one will be dismissed unless he is questioned about four things: his life and how he has spent it; his deeds and how he has enacted them; his property and how he has earned and spent it; and his hid body and how he has exhausted it."
>
> (Reported by At-Tirmidhi)

Safwan ibn Muhriz Al-Mazini reported,

> "While I was walking with ibn `Umar (may Allah be pleased with them both) holding his hand, a man came in front of us and asked, 'What have you heard from Allah's Messenger about An-Najwa?' Ibn `Umar said, 'I heard Allah's Messenger saying, 'Allah will bring a believer near Him and shelter him with His Screen and ask him: Did you commit such-and-such sins? He will say: Yes, my Lord. Allah will keep on asking him until he will confess all his sins and will think that he is ruined. Allah will say: I did cover your sins in the world and I forgive them for you today. And then he will be given the book of his good deeds. Regarding infidels and hypocrites (their evil acts will be exposed publicly) and the witnesses will say: These are the people who lied against their Lord. Behold!

> *The Curse of Allah is upon the wrongdoers.'"*
> (Reported by Al-Bukhari)

The Prophet (peace and blessings of Allah be upon him) said,

> *"A bridge would be set over the Hell, and I and my Ummah would be the first to pass over it."*
> (Reported by Muslim)

Also, the Prophet (peace and blessings of Allah be upon him) said,

> *"The bridge would be set up over the Hell and intercession would be allowed and they will say: O Allah, keep us safe, keep us safe. It was asked: Messenger of Allah, what is this bridge? He said: The void in which one is likely to slip. There would be hooks, tongs, and spits like the thorn that is found in Najd and is known as Sa'dan. The believers would then pass over within the twinkling of an eye, like lightning, like wind, like a bird, like the finest horses and camels. Some will escape and be safe, some will be lacerated and let go, and some will be pushed into the fire of Hell until the believers will find rescue from the Fire."*
> (Reported by Muslim)

Hellfire (may Allah keep us safe from it!)

Abu Hurayrah (may Allah be pleased with him) reported,

> *"We were in the company of Allah's Messenger (peace and blessings of Allah be upon him) that we heard a terrible sound. Thereupon Allah's*

Messenger (peace and blessings of Allah be upon him) said: Do you know what (sound) is this? We said: Allah and His Messenger know best. Thereupon he said: That is a stone which was thrown seventy years before in Hell and it has been constantly slipping down and now it has reached its base."

(Reported by Muslim)

Also, Abu Hurayrah (may Allah be pleased with him) also narrated that the Prophet (peace and blessings of Allah be upon him) said,

"Your (ordinary) fire is one of seventy parts of the (Hell) Fire." Someone asked, "O Allah's Prophet, this (ordinary) fire would have been sufficient (to torture the unbelievers)." Allah's Messenger (peace and blessings of Allah be upon him) said, "The (Hell) Fire has sixty-nine parts more than the ordinary (worldly) fire, each part is as hot as this (worldly) fire."

(Reported by Al-Bukhari)

Ibn Mas`ud (may Allah be pleased with him) reported that the Prophet (peace and blessings of Allah be upon him) said,

"Hell will be brought having seventy thousand reins, each rein will held by seventy thousand angels."

(Reported by Muslim)

Abu Ad-Dardaa' (may Allah be pleased with him) said, "People of Fire will suffer hunger in a way equal to their torture. They will cry for food. Then, they will be given a bitter Dari` (a thorny bitter tree) which will neither nourish nor satisfy hunger. Then they will cry for help. They will be given food causing choking in their throats. They will remember that they used to treat it with water. Thus, they will cry for water. Hence, they will be given boiling water hung by hot metal. Approaching it, their faces will be burnt. Thence, they will ask the Keepers of Fire saying,

> ⟨*Pray to your Lord to lighten us the Penalty for a Day (at least)! They will say: Did there not come to you your Messengers with Clear Signs?' They will say, 'Yes'. They will reply, 'Then pray (as you like)! But the Prayer of those without Faith is nothing but (futile wandering) in (mazes of) error!'*⟩
> (Ghafir: 49-50)

Then, they will ask Malik (Keeper of Hell) saying

> ⟨*O Malik! Would that thy Lord put an end to us! He will say: Nay, but ye shall abide!*⟩
> (Az-Zukhruf: 77)

They will call upon Allah, saying:

> ⟨*Our Lord! Bring us out of this: if ever we return (to evil), then shall we be wrongdoers indeed! He will say: Be you driven into it (with ignominy)! And speak you not to Me!*⟩
> (Al-Mu'minun: 107-108)

Thence, they become filled with despair and suffer the torments of Fire. The Prophet (peace and blessings of Allah be upon him) said,

> "*Snakes of Fire are like necks of camels and its*

scorpions like mules."

(Reported by Ahmad)

In fact, Fire is indescribable. However, one should know some of its descriptions. Thus, being a believer, you should be aware of it and fear the Almighty. By fear, we do not mean shedding tears for a while and giving up doing good. We rather refer to such a kind of fear that holds you back from disobedience and drives you to obedience. We do not want you to entertain such a fear of the foolish people who exclaim on listening to intimidation while they insist on sinning. In that way, those fool persons suffice themselves with saying 'may Allah keep us safe', but they never enter Allah's Refuge.

Love for the Prophet (peace and blessings of Allah be upon him)

You should love the Prophet (peace and blessing s of Allah be upon him) and esteem his *Sunnah* so that he may intercede on your behalf in the Hereafter. His intercession is given priority over other Prophets on the Day of Judgment. He asks for forgiveness for the sinful among his followers. You should also have as many fellow brothers as you can. Each believer enjoys intercession. You should never be deluded by conceit thus postponing your repentance while presuming it as hope. Hoping for something incurs working for it. Dying before making up for your mischief, you get snatched on the Day of Judgment by your debtors. Abu Sa`id Al-Khudri (may Allah be pleased with him) reports that the Prophet (peace and blessings of Allah be upon him) said,

> *"When the believers pass safely over (the bridge across) Hell, they will be stopped at a bridge in between Hell and Paradise where they will retaliate upon each other for the injustices done among them*

> *in the world, and when they get purified of all their sins, they will be admitted into Paradise. By Him in Whose Hands the life of Muhammad is everybody will recognize his dwelling in Paradise better than he recognizes his dwelling in this world."*
>
> (Reported by Al-Bukhari)

Abu Hurayrah (may Allah be pleased with him) reported that the Prophet (peace and blessings of Allah be upon him) said,

> *"Do you know who is poor?" They (the Companions of the Holy Prophet) said, "A poor man amongst us is one who has neither Dirham with him nor wealth." He (the Prophet) said, "The poor of my Ummah would be he who would come on the Day of Resurrecton with Prayers and Fasts and Zakah but (he would find himself bankrupt on that day as he would have exhausted his funds of virtues since) he hurled abuses upon others, brought calumny against others and unlawfully consumed the wealth of others and shed the blood of others and beat others, and his virtues would be credited to the account of one (who suffered at his hand). And if his good deeds fall short to clear the account, then his sins would be entered in (his account) and he would be thrown in the Hell-Fire."*
>
> (Reported by Muslim)

likewise, Abu Hurayrah (may Allah be pleased with him) reported that the Prophet (peace and blessings of Allah be upon him) said,

> *"The claimants would get their claims on the Day of Judgment so much so that the hornless sheep*

would get its claim from the horned sheep."
(Reported by Muslim)

In that, you should consider the value of your good deeds to purge them from impurities such as dissemblance and backbiting. Being cleared, be careful and waste not your times. In fact, he is too poor who prefer an intermittent delight securing thereby an everlasting torture. May Allah keep us safe!

Paradise (may Allah Admit us therein!)

Abu Hurayrah (may Allah be pleased with him) said,

> *"We asked the Prophet of Allah to talk to us about Paradise and its Building. He said, 'It is built from gold and silver. Its fragrance is musk, its gravel is pearl and sapphire, and its dust is saffron. Whoever enters it, is delighted without distress. He lives forever without death. His garments are never worn out. His youth never wanes."*
> (Reported by At-Tirmidhi)

Usamah ibn Zayd (may Allah be pleased with him) narrated that the Prophet (peace and blessings of Allah be upon him) described Paradise, saying,

> *"Who is preparing himself for it? By the Almighty, it is like a dancing flower, a bright light, an affluent river, and an everlasting pleasing wife." The Companions said, "We are preparing for it." He said, "You should say if Allah so wills."*
> (Reported by Ahmad)

Also, the Prophet (peace and blessings of Allah be upon him) said,

> "The Almighty said, 'I have prepared for My righteous servants what eyes have never seen, ears have never heard, nor has it occurred to the heart of man.'"
>
> (Reported by Al-Bukhari)

He is also reported to have said,

> "The (members) of the first group to get into Paradise would have their faces as bright as full moon during the night, and the next to this group would have their faces as bright as the shining stars in the sky, and every person would have two wives and the marrow of their shanks would glimmer beneath the flesh and there would be none without a wife in Paradise."
>
> (Reported by Al-Bukhari)

Abu Musa Al-Ash`ari (may Allah be pleased with him) narrated that the Prophet (peace and blessings of Allah be upon him) said,

> "Two gardens, the utensils and the contents of which are of silver, and two other gardens, the utensils and contents of which are of gold. And nothing will prevent the people who will be in the Garden of Eden from seeing their Lord except the curtain of Majesty over His Face."
>
> (Reported by Al-Bukhari)

Abu Musa (may Allah be pleased with him) also reported that the Prophet (peace and blessings of Allah be upon him) said,

> "A tent (in Paradise) is like a hollow pearl which is

sixty miles in height and on every corner of the tent the believer will have a family that cannot be seen by the others."

(Reported by Al-Bukhari)

Likewise, the Almighty has elaborated pleasure in Paradise in the Qur'an. For example, He says,

❴*To them will be passed round, dishes and goblets of gold: there will be there all that the souls could desire, all that the eyes could delight in: and ye shall abide therein (forever).*❵

(Az-Zukhruf: 71)

❴*Wherein they shall dwell (for aye): no change will they wish for from them.*❵

(Al-Kahf: 108)

❴*Now no person knows what delights of the eye are kept hidden (in reserve) for them as a reward for their (good) Deeds.*❵

(As-Sajdah: 17)

Abu Hurayrah (may Allah be pleased with him) reported,

"Some people said, 'O Allah's Messenger! Shall we see our Lord on the Day of Resurrection?' The Prophet said, 'Yes; do you have any difficulty in seeing the sun at midday when it is bright and there is no cloud in the sky?' They replied, 'No.' He said, 'Do you have any difficulty in seeing the moon on a full moon night when it is bright and there is no cloud in the sky?' They replied, 'No.' The Prophet said, '(Similarly) you will have no difficulty in seeing Allah on the Day of Resurrection as you

have no difficulty in seeing either of them.'"
(Reported by Al-Bukhari)

The Almighty's Mercy

We conclude our book with the Almighty's Mercy, hoping for His Favors, since we have nothing else to seek His Forgiveness thereby. We hope for His Mercy and Meekness. The Almighty says,

> ❨*Say: O my Servants who have transgressed against their souls. Despair not of the Mercy of Allah: for Allah forgives all sins: for He is Oft-Forgiving, Most Merciful.*❩
> (Az-Zumar: 53)

Abu Hurayrah (may Allah be pleased with him) reported that the Prophet (peace and blessings of Allah be upon him) said,

> *"When Allah completed the creation, He wrote in His Book which is with Him on His Throne, 'My Mercy overpowers My Anger.'"*
> (Reported by Al-Bukhari)

Also, Abu Hurayrah (may Allah be pleased with him) reported that the Prophet (peace and blessings of Allah be upon him) said,

> *"The Almighty has a hundred Mercies. He has sent only one to the earth whereby all humans, Jinn, insects and animals treat in mercy among themselves. Likewise, wild animals are merciful to their infants because of it. He has withheld the remaining ninety nine to be Merciful to His servants*

on the Day of Judgment."

(Reported by Muslim)

Ibn `Abbas (may Allah be pleased with them both) narrated that the Prophet (peace and blessings of Allah be upon him) said,

"Verily, Allah is Merciful to you. If somebody intends to do a good deed and he does not do it, then Allah will write for him a full good deed (in his account with Him); and if he intends to do a good deed and actually did it, then Allah will write for him (in his account) with Him (its reward equal) from ten to seven hundred times to many more times: and if somebody intended to do a bad deed and he does not do it, then Allah will write a full good deed (in his account) with Him, and if he intended to do it (a bad deed) and actually did it, then Allah will write one bad deed (in his account)."

(Reported by Muslim)

Abu Dharr (may Allah be pleased with him) narrated that the Prophet (peace and blessings of Allah be upon him) said,

"The Almighty says, 'Whoever does good, he will have its rewards ten times or more. Whoever does a sin will be punished for it alone or forgiven...'"

(Reported by Muslim)

Abu Hurayrah (may Allah be pleased with him) reported that the Prophet (peace and blessings of Allah be upon him) said,

"A servant committed a sin and he said: O Allah,

forgive me my sins. And, Allah (the Exalted and Glorious) said: My servant committed a sin and then he came to realize that he has a Lord Who forgives the sins and takes to account (the sinner) for the sin. He then again committed a sin and said: My Lord, forgive me my sin. And, Allah, the Exalted and High, said: My servant committed a sin and then came to realize that he has a Lord Who would forgive his sin or would take (him) to account for the sin. He again committed a sin and said: My Lord, forgive me for my sin. And, Allah (the Exalted and High) said: My servant has committed a sin and then came to realize that he has a Lord Who forgives the sins or takes (him) to account for sin. O servant, do what you like. I have granted you forgiveness."

(Reported by Muslim)

`Umar ibn Al-Khattab (may Allah be pleased with him) narrated,

"Some Sabi (i.e., war prisoners) were brought before the Prophet and there was a woman amongst them who was milking her breasts to feed and whenever she found a child amongst the captives, she took it over her chest and nursed it (she had lost her child but later she found him). Then the Prophet said to us, 'Do you think that this lady can throw her son in the fire?' We replied, 'No, if she has the power not to throw it (in the fire).' The Prophet then said, 'Allah is more Merciful to His servants than this lady to her son.'"

(Reported by Al-Bukhari)

Abu Dharr (may Allah be pleased with him) narrated,

> "I came to the Prophet while he was wearing white clothes and sleeping. Then I went back to him again after he had got up from his sleep. He said, 'Nobody says: None has the right to be worshipped but Allah,' and then later on he dies while believing in that, except that he will enter Paradise.' I said, 'Even if he had committed illegal sexual intercourse and theft.' He said, 'Even If he had committed illegal sexual intercourse and theft (he said so three times adding), in spite of the Abu Dharr's abhorrence.'"

(Reported by Al-Bukhari)

`Atban ibn Malik (may Allah be pleased with him) narrated that the Prophet (peace and blessings of Allah be upon him) said,

> "The Almighty has prohibited fire to torture him who says, 'There is no god but Allah,' seeking His Face thereby.'"

(Reported by Al-Bukhari)

Anas ibn Malik (may Allah be pleased with him) reported that the Prophet (peace and blessings of Allah be upon him) said,

> "He who professed, 'There is no god but Allah,' would be brought out of the Fire even though he has in his heart virtue equal to the weight of a barley grain. Then he who professed, 'There is no god but Allah,' would come out of the Fire, even though he has in his heart virtue equal to the weight of a wheat grain. He (Allah) would then bring out from the Fire he who professed, 'There is no god but Allah,' even though he has in his heart virtue

equal to the weight of an atom."
(Reported by Al-Bukhari)

Abu Musa (may Allah be pleased with him) reported that Allah's Messenger (peace and blessings of Allah be upon him) said,

"When it will be the Day of Resurrection Allah would deliver to every Muslim a Jew or a Christian and say: That is your ransom from Hell-Fire."
(Reported by Muslim)

`Abdullah ibn `Amr (may Allah be pleased with them both) narrated that Allah's Messenger (peace and blessings of Allah be upon him) said,

"The Almighty will single out a servant from my Ummah against whom will be disclosed ninety-nine tablets each one of them is as long as one can see. Then He will ask him, 'Do you deny anything? Have My Writers wronged you?' He will answer in the negative. Then Allah will say, 'Do have any justification or a good deed?' He will get dismayed and answer in the negative. Then Allah will say, 'Nay, you have a single good deed, you will not be wronged today.' Then, a card will brought having, 'there is no god but Allah and Muhammad is His Servant and Messenger,' on it. Then he will be brought. He will wonder, 'What is this card compared to all these tablets!' Then he will be addressed, 'You will not be wronged today.' Then this card is put on the scale against his tablets. It will outweigh them all. Nothing outweighs the

Almighty's Name."

(Reported by Ahmad)

Beholding the pilgrims' praises of the Almighty and their weeping on the Day of `Arafah, Al-Fudayl ibn `Iyad remarked, "If these people were asking a person a very little sum of money, would he forsake them?" They answered in the negative. He then said, "By Allah, the Almighty's forgiveness is more tenable than this trivial money."

Ibrahim ibn Adham said, "I preferred circumambulating the Ka`bah in a very rainy night. I continued until rightly before the Dawn. Then I raised my hands towards heavens and said, 'O Lord, I ask you to protect me from all what You detest!' Then I heard a voice from above saying, 'You are asking for infallibility. All My creatures ask likewise. If your supplications are granted, who will receive My Favors!'"

All these *Ahadith* highlight the Almighty's Mercy and Meekness. We hope that the Almighty does not treat us according to our own deeds, but rather shower His favors on us according to His own Sublimity and Glory. We seek His forgiveness from our words that contradict our deeds, and from hypocrisy and dissemblance. We resort to His Generosity.

Praise be to Allah, so that He may be pleased and satisfied. Praise be to Him as the Glory of His Face and the Greatness of His Power deserve.

May peace and blessings of Allah be upon Prophet Muhammad, his family, his Companions and those who follow them with goodness until the Day of Judgment!

Amen

Glossary of Arabic Terms

Adhan: The call for the daily Praye rs are called *Adhan*. The person who calls the *Adhan* is called a *Mu'adhin* (muezzin). A *Mu'adhin* calls the *Adhan* five times a day before Muslims are to perform their daily *Salah* (Prayer). The *Adhan* is composed of specific words and phrases to be recited loud ly in the Arabic language so that the neighbors can recognize the time schedule for the prayers.

Dhikr: remembrance of Allah.

Du`a': A prayer or supplication to Allah.

Faqih (pl. *Fuqaha'*): A person who is an expert on Islamic jurisprudence (law), *Fiqh*.

Fatwa: Legal opinion concerning Islamic Law.

Fiqh: The meaning of the word *Fiqh* is understanding, comprehension, knowledge, and jurisprudence in Islam. In legal terminology, *Fiqh* refers to Islamic Jurisprudence.

Ghusl: Body-washing.

Hadith (pl. *Ahadith*): Reports on the sayings and the traditions of Prophet Muhammad (peace and blessings of Allah be upon him) or what he witnessed and approved are called *Hadith*. These are the real explanation, interpretation, and the living example of the Prophet (peace and bles sings of Allah be upon him) for teachings of the Qur'an. His sayings are found in books called the *Hadith* books.

Hajj: *Hajj* is an Arabic word which means the performance of pilgrimage to Makkah in Arabia. It is one of the five pillars of Islam. A Muslim is to perform *Hajj* at least once in his/her life, if means and health allow. There are rules and regulations and specific dress to be followed. It is to take place during the last month of the lunar calendar called the month of Dhul - Hijjah.

`Itikaf: Spiritual retreat in a mosque.

Iqamah: *Iqamah* is an Arabic word that refers to the second call for the Prayer which follows the first call (*Adhan*). *Iqamah* means that the Prayer is ready to start. It is to be recited in Arabic before every obligatory prayer. It is composed of specific words and phrases very closely related to the *Adhan*.

Jama`ah: Congregational Prayer.

Jizyah: A tax paid by non-Muslims living in a Muslim State. Since the non-Muslims are exempt from military service and *Zakah* imposed on Muslims, they must pay this tax to compensate. It guarentees them security and protection. If the State cannot protect those who paid *Jizyah*, then the amount they paid is returned to them.

Qiblah: It is the direction that Muslims face when they do their *Salah*. It is in the direction of the Ka`bah in Makkah.

Qiyam Al-Layl: Night Vigil.

Qudsi Hadith: The *Qudsi Hadith* is that in which the Prophet says that Allah says so-and-so. The meaning of the these *Ahadith* was revealed to the Prophet (peace and blessings of Allah be upon him) but he put them in his own words, unlike the Qur'an which is the word of Almighty Allah and the Prophet (peace and blessings of Allah be upon him) conveyed it exactly as it was revealed to him.

**Rak`ah** (pl. *Rak`at*): An individual unit of *Salah*.

Sadaqah: It means optional charity.

Salah: *Salah* is an Arabic word to mean a spiritual relationship and communication between the creature and his Creator. *Salah* is one of the five pillars of Islam. A special communication (*Salah*) is to take place five times a day for a Muslim: *Fajr* (Dawn), *Zuhr* (Noon), *`Asr* (Afternoon), *Magrib* (Sunset), and *`Isha'* (Night). *Salah* is to be performed with mental concentration, verbal communication, vocal recitation, and physical movement to attain the spiritual uplift, peace, harmony, and concord. There is a congregational Prayer on Friday noon (*Salatul Jumu`ah*) with a sermon (*Khutbah*) to be delivered by a religious leader (Imam) called *Khatib*. Along with the obligatory Five Daily Prayers, a Muslim c an offer many supererogatory ones.

*Shari`ah*: The root of this word is Shara`a; and some other names of it are *Shar`*, *Shir`ah* and *Tashri`*. The *Shari`ah* is the revealed and the canonical laws of the religion of Islam.

Sujud: The root of those word is *Sajada* which means that a person makes prostration to Allah in his daily Prayers. While in the position of *Sujud*, a Muslim is to praise Almighty Allah and glorify him. During the position of *Sujud*, a Muslim is to make sure that his/her forehead, nose, hands, knee s, and toes, are all touching the floor.

Surah: The Qur'an is composed of 114 chapters, each of which is called a *Surah*. The plural of *Surah* is called *Suwar*, which means chapters.

`Umrah: This is the lesser pilgrimage which is optional and can be performed at any time.

Zakah: One of the five pillars of Islam is *Zakah*, which means purification and increment of one's wealth. A Muslim who has money beyond a certain quantity is to pay the *Zakah*. It is also called the alms due or poor due.

www.ingramcontent.com/pod-product-compliance
Lightning Source LLC
LaVergne TN
LVHW010306070526
838199LV00065B/5453